SCIENCE ASTRAY

SCIENCE ASTRAY

By the Editors of Time-Life Books

TIME-LIFE BOOKS, ALEXANDRIA, VIRGINIA

CONTENTS

1
EXPLAINING THE UNIVERSE

Whys and wherefores: Humpty Earth . . . life on a cooling coal . . . return of the dinosaurs . . . wandering continents . . . fireballs from space . . . an Earth-centered universe . . . harnessing gravity . . . boxed dolls . . . a conspiracy of tails

7

2
WHEN GENIUS STUMBLES

Tangents of the great: People of the Sun . . . positively algebra . . . the wizard of od . . . big bird . . . Freudian sniffs . . . parallel evolution . . . noble Martians . . . fighting flight . . . brain snippers . . . germs from outer space

35

3
GREAT EXPECTATIONS

Believing is seeing: Moving stars . . . apocalyptic vision . . . Neptune's rings . . . dawn creature . . . ubiquitous ooze . . . predicting intelligence . . . non-rays . . . a universe of fossils . . . intimations of Pluto . . . Delphinese dialogues . . . energy in a glass

69

4
IN THE SERVICE OF BELIEF

Skewed science: Galileo's heresy . . . moving heaven and earth . . . "A Fair Chance for the Girls" . . . disorienting syndromes . . . inner spheres . . . a cosmos of ice . . . Aryans of Tibet . . . mad scientist . . . racist follies . . . postmortem IQs . . . Earth's unglobularity

101

Acknowledgments **134**

Picture Credits **134**

Bibliography **135**

Index **140**

EXPLAINING THE UNIVERSE

Confronted by a world beyond the grasp of current knowledge, human beings have invariably followed their reflex to explain what—for reasons of ignorance, orthodoxy, or some intellectual myopia—they cannot understand. Scientists of every epoch have bravely advanced hypotheses built around their observations of a steadily unfolding universe, while tethered by the knowledge of their day.

Thus, hearing that scorched rocks had fallen from the sky, naturalists forced an explanation that squared with their experience—the projectiles must be volcanic, not extraterrestrial, in origin. Noting an errant backward motion of the planets—anarchy in a perfect and spherical universe—savants diligently figured out ways in which to replicate the movement with circles and spheres. Always, the explanation accommodated observation very well—and always, often centuries later, was shown to have been dead wrong.

Only in relatively recent times have scientists come to appreciate fully that their comprehension of the universe—a still-unfolding world that tenaciously conserves much of its mystery—can be only provisional. Sooner or later, a colleague will take a piece of work in hand, turn it this way and that, add a critical new observation here and throw out a misperception there, and utterly change prevailing wisdom. Albert Einstein, who epitomized the thinking scientist, was a master at consigning the once-brilliant hypotheses of his forerunners to the wastebasket. But the process is not unfair: All the titans of science, Einstein included, have learned the hard way that human knowledge is forever incomplete.

Short Timer

When James Ussher, Anglican archbishop of Armagh, Ireland, tackled the problem of determining the age of the Earth, the records he examined were found not in stone but between the covers of the Bible. In the mid-17th century, when the science of geology was no more than a gleam in the eye of a few rock hounds, Ussher's biblical record must have seemed the best possible raw data, since it was both comprehensive and divinely inspired.

An expert in Semitic languages, Ussher examined the genealogy of patriarchs, judges, priests, and kings set forth in the "Hebrew verity," an ancient Hebrew-language text that he deemed the most reliable version of the Old Testament. The life spans noted in the genealogy began with Adam, who was said to have lived to the age of 930 years, and proceeded down through scores of succeeding generations. From these life spans, Ussher calculated that the Earth had in all likelihood been created in 4004 BC. He allowed, however, that his exegesis might err by as much as four years.

Ussher's findings, published in his 1650 volume *Annals of the Ancient and New Testaments,* were quickly accepted by other scholars and clergy as definitive. Several years later Dr. John Lightfoot, vice-chancellor of the University of Cambridge, announced his refinement of Ussher's results: Earth was created one day in October 4004 BC.

Although people quibbled over the exact age of the Earth, and James Ussher's span gradually gave way to somewhat longer lifetimes, for the next 150 years most people believed that the history of the world—of time itself, in fact—was rather short. Late in the 18th century, for example, naturalist Georges-Louis Leclerc, count of Buffon *(pages 10-11),* was attacked for going against convention and suggesting Earth might be as much as 75,000 years old. By the mid-19th century, however, a geologic reading of the Earth's rocks had transformed Bishop Ussher's theological arithmetic, and the persistent notion of a young planet, into antique curiosities. □

Archbishop James Ussher, shown at left in 17th-century clerical garb, calculated the year of Earth's creation—4004 BC—from biblical data. Striving for greater precision, Ussher's contemporary Dr. John Lightfoot *(below)* added his claim that creation had taken place in October of that year.

Planet Egg

To Thomas Burnet, the Earth was a loathsome place deserving every abusive epithet he heaped on it—a rude lump, a dirty little planet, a hideous ruin, a world lying in its rubbish. He thought the seafloor disgustingly slimy, and the Moon, which he viewed with a telescope, was rude and ragged. To a 17th-century Anglican clergyman such as Burnet, it was inconceivable that God would have created an Earth that was not beautiful and perfectly proportioned. Thus, the present ugliness and disorder must be the sequel of an earlier, lost perfection.

When and how perfection had flown was, for Burnet at least, a complicated question, and he did not approve of cutting such a scientific Gordian knot with the aid of miracles—indeed, he dismissed the notion of a miraculous intervention as irrational. He envisioned God not as a meddlesome magician but a great clockmaker whose perfectly designed invention was driven by a control system of unchanging, God-given natural laws; once the clock universe was set in motion, its creator did not fiddle with his mechanism or his laws.

When Burnet launched his analysis of the young Earth's transformations, he used his friend, the physicist and mathematician Isaac Newton, as his scientific guide—

with a certain reserve, however. Newton had described the natural laws governing celestial bodies but, to Burnet's dismay, saw no reason why God should not change the laws when it suited him.

In contrast, Burnet got all of his information about the early history of the Earth from the Bible's Old Testament, the sole reliable source, in his view. Working back through time, he first analyzed the catastrophic Flood that, according to the story recounted in Genesis, inundated the globe and destroyed all life except for the creatures aboard Noah's ark. Once he had a handle on that pivotal event, Burnet believed, he would be able to explain the far knottier problem of the pre-deluge world. A crucial unknown

quantity was the amount of water needed to submerge the world's entire surface, high mountain peaks and all. Here the scholar had little information to go on; relief maps were nonexistent, and soundings of the ocean and measurements of its extent were just as inadequate.

The oceanic estimate he finally made fell so far short of accounting for a flood of Noachian proportions that no fewer than eight additional oceans of the same capacity would have been needed. Unable to account rationally for the missing eight oceans' worth of water (in fact, the deficit was much larger; he had grossly underestimated the depth of the sea), Burnet tried a different angle. He postulated that the Earth's present topography was actually caused by the Flood; before it took place, the Earth's surface had been uniformly smooth and even—and a much smaller amount of water would have neatly covered it.

This Earth of perfect smoothness had evolved, according to Burnet, from the primordial fluid mass of jumbled elements that had emerged from chaos. The primitive materials sorted themselves out to form a hard, egg-shaped shell filled ▷

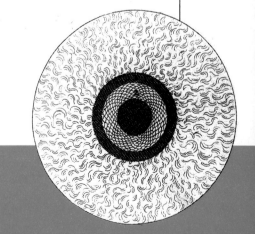

Burnet drew Earth beginning as a fluid chaos *(far left)*, compressed by gravity into a dense core surrounded by layers of water and air *(left)*. Lighter particles settling upon the young planet's fluid surface formed a soft shell that hardened into a rigid outer crust—the dark ring in the drawing above.

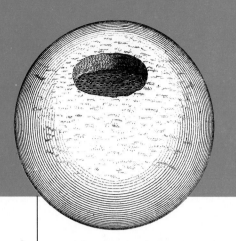

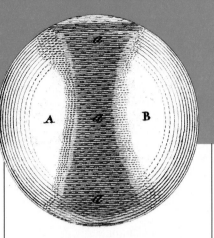

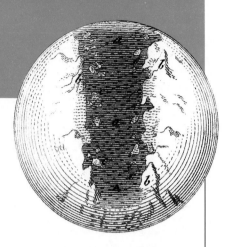

The Earth's smooth crust, which Burnet schematically opened *(far left)*, was breached when the inner waters heated and expanded, then burst across the surface *(center)*, fracturing the crust *(below)* into chaotic, post-diluvian terrain.

with water and other liquids. The Earth egg stood upright, with its axis of rotation at right angles to its orbit, and the inhabitants enjoyed a benign and unchanging climate.

But, Burnet postulated, natural processes of change were already inexorably at work. The constant heat of the Sun made the outer shell become dry and brittle; simultaneously, the water in the interior heated and vaporized, exerting continually increasing pressure on the ever more fragile shell. During the second millennium after Creation—well timed by the divine clockmaker to punish humankind for its sinfulness—the shell began to crack and give way. Portions of it collapsed into the abyss; the waters surged out and rushed in waves over the remaining surface. The force generat-

ed was so great that the entire world was shaken violently. When the tremors stopped, Earth's axis of rotation was tilted in relation to the planet's orbit. The glorious weather of Paradise was gone, replaced by the seasonal miseries of freezing winters and hot summers. The roiling waters subsided into the basins created by the shell's collapse, revealing a "broken and confus'd heap of bodies"—the rough, ugly terrain of the postdiluvian Earth.

Published in 1681, the first two parts of *The Sacred Theory of the Earth* drew fire from theorists who were more willing than Burnet to accept divine intervention or miracles in the post-Creation Earth. In a

1684 commentary on mountains, Burnet deplored this indifference to his version of scientific method. "The truth is the generality of people have not sence and curiosity enough to raise a question concerning these things or concerning the Original of them," he wrote. "You may tell them that Mountains grow out of the Earth like Fuzz-balls, or that there are Monsters under ground that throw up Mountains as Moles do Molehills; they will scarce raise one objection against your doctrine." □

Cooldown

The faculty of theology of the University of Paris could not stomach what Georges-Louis Leclerc, count of Buffon, had to say about the primordial Earth in the first volume of his *Natural History*, published in 1749. The theologians stopped a little short of insisting that he recant, demanding instead a "clarification." Apparently repentant, the count agreed to "abandon whatever in my book concerns the formation of the

earth" and declared that he had only been indulging in a little philosophical hypothesizing.

The orthodox had reason to object to Buffon's book, for his supposedly innocent speculation about the young Earth and the appearance of animal and plant life owed nothing to the biblical story of Creation. By the time he died in 1788, the count of Buffon had added thirty-five more volumes to *Natural History*, all the while managing to fend off theologians who were wounded

by his frequently heretical views.

Superintendent of the royal garden, curator of its museum, brilliant naturalist, and charming man about town, Buffon opened his laboratory to social luminaries, especially ladies; they peered through his microscope at specimens and made the experimentalist's work fashionable in the best circles. He hypothesized that the Earth had been created when a comet collided with the Sun, tearing away a blazing mass that gradually cooled and solidified into a planet. Several pretty women with soft hands played a crucial, but painful, part in Buffon's experiments to calculate how long it had taken this mass to cool. To arrive at its rate of heat loss, Buffon removed white-hot balls of a variety of metals from a furnace and, the moment they could be touched, placed them in the ladies' hands. Their job was to describe the balls' gradual cooling.

However inexact the data provided by his stoic assistants, Buffon concluded that the Earth was, instead of the conventional 6,000 years, 74,832 years old and had taken 42,964 years and 221 days to reach its present range of temperatures. Buffon secretly envisioned an Earth of infinite age—a concept that he kept to himself and unpublished writings, fearing that readers would find the idea utterly incredible or think him mad.

The polar regions, the count of

Buffon proposed, had cooled first, finally reaching a critical temperature at which nonliving matter was converted into living molecules. This had been a one-time event, he believed, triggered by a unique combination of physical and chemical conditions that would never be repeated. The quantity of organic molecules was thus forever fixed. When a plant or an animal died, its molecules were freed for another creature's growth and development; but no new life was added to Buffon's ecosystem. Buffon postulated that the control mechanism for heredity and development was what he called a *moule intérieur*—literally, an "interior mold." It performed, in his scheme, the functions that in the 20th century would be linked to each creature's genetic code.

The first plants and animals had appeared, according to Buffon, in the high latitudes. Designed for the sultry climate prevailing near the poles, the animals were forced by continually declining temperatures to migrate south in pursuit of a hospitable environment. They became extinct, and new species arose, only to succumb when the Earth became too cold for them. There were two more heat-triggered generations, the last of which spread to all the continents except South

America. Its animal species, Buffon conjectured, were unique.

In Buffon's scheme, temperature change altered a species' organic molecules and the shaping abilities of its *moules*. This evolutionary process was a negative one—instead of improving, the new characteristics were invariably degenerate. The ass, for instance, was no more than a second-rate horse. Americans were offended by the count's claim that the New World's native animals were inferior to the Asian and European ancestors from which they had evolved.

Buffon believed that similar processes had taken place on other planets. It is, he said, "permissible to believe that all of these planetary bodies are, like the terrestrial globe, covered with plants, and even peopled with creatures endowed with sensation, which are quite similar to the animals of the earth." But in modern times, Buffon speculated, it was not natural processes alone that accounted for climatic change; human activities such as felling forests and damming rivers could alter temperatures and thus change the course of evolution.

However flawed his explanation of the evolution of life, Buffon took a thoroughly modern approach for insisting that species are not forever immutable but possess an intrinsic ability to change—if only for the worse—when the environment changes. Some 70 years after Buffon died, Charles Darwin asked biologist Thomas Huxley to comment on the manuscript of *The Origin of Species.* Huxley recommended that the author read Buffon's theory of evolution. Taking his friend's advice, Darwin later wrote to him, "I have read Buffon: whole pages are laughably like mine." □

Seated in his library with animals reclining beside his chair, French naturalist Georges-Louis Leclerc, count of Buffon, appears to contemplate an exotic landscape in this 1769 painting.

On the Rocks

When Charles Lyell, wunderkind of British geology, visited Paris in 1829, Baron Georges Cuvier was kind enough to invite the foreigner to his famous soirees. An eminent anatomist, paleontologist, geologist, and walking encyclopedia reputed to have memorized the contents of his 19,000-volume library, Cuvier had been equally hospitable to Lyell six years earlier, providing him with lively scientific talk at the weekly gatherings and the added attraction of a stepdaughter. She was "of most engaging manners, and very clever," Lyell wrote in a letter to his father, "pretty, and very lively."

His enthusiastic remarks about Cuvier's stepdaughter were the closest Lyell came to saying anything nice about his host. With perhaps a twinge of envy, he sniped at the elder man for finding publishers for his books with an ease altogether suspicious. He also complained that Cuvier talked his ear off about government and politics while avoiding the subject of geology.

Perhaps Baron Cuvier thought that there was nothing to be gained by talking geology with Charles Lyell. The two held diametrically opposed views about the geologic events that shape the Earth. A catastrophist, Cuvier believed that great and sudden paroxysms, sometimes sweeping the entire globe, had created sharply delineated rock layers, cracked and displaced them, changed climate, flooded continents, wiped out species wholesale. Among his catastrophic events was the Great Flood of the Bible, which he said had occurred 5,000 to 6,000 years ago. Lyell, on the other hand, was a uniformitarian. He preached a "steady-state" Earth where wind, water, and ice produced change at a slow and uniform pace. He allowed paroxysms such as volcanic eruptions or landslides in his scheme but believed they had only local importance.

A professor of vertebrate zoology at the Museum of Natural History, Cuvier had acquired his catastrophic leanings in the early 1800s from his exploration of the Paris Basin, the rock formations in and around the city. He did not need a pick: Napoleon I had launched several public projects that kept the quarries of the Paris Basin busy. Cuvier applied his genius in anatomical classification to the fossils that he discovered in the rock layers of the basin. Sorting methodically through stray teeth, thighbones, jaws, and claws, he reconstructed an astonishing menagerie of extinct mammals never before even guessed at—the saber-toothed tiger, the cave bear, and various species of woolly rhinoceros.

Admirers may have exaggerated when they claimed that Cuvier could recognize an animal from a single bone, but not by much. His unrivaled expertise earned him the title "the pope of bones." The story is told that a prankster-student, sporting horns and wearing shoes in the shape of cloven hooves, once invaded the bedroom of the sleeping Cuvier and declared, "Wake up, thou man of catastrophes. I am the Devil. I have come to devour you!"

But the great anatomist knew a vegetarian when he saw one, and he coolly deflated the joke: "I doubt whether you can. You have horns and hooves. You only eat plants."

Cuvier did not pretend to know exactly what forces were responsible for the many revolutions he saw in the Paris Basin, but he rejected ice and wind and water as anything more than minor players. He believed that the Earth was only 75,000 or so years old—far too short a span for such forces to account for the events revealed in the rock record. Charles Lyell, on the other hand, was a good deal closer to the mark, measuring the Earth's life in millions of years.

The steady-state Earth that Lyell envisioned changed constantly in small ways, but its large features had a remarkable constancy; the proportion of ocean to continent, for instance, altered very little, because as land eroded in one place it was balanced by new sediments building up somewhere else. From this the leap to cycles in Earth history was just a short one for Lyell, and he suggested that the 19th century was in the winter phase of the "great year" of a climatic cycle. When summer returned, he wrote, the environment would again be favorable to species that had become extinct—including dinosaurs. "Then might those genera of animals return, of which the memorials are preserved in the ancient rocks of our continent," Lyell mused in 1830 in his *Principles of Geology*. "The huge iguanodon might reappear in the woods, and the ichthyosaur in the sea, while the pterodactyle might flit again through umbrageous groves of tree-ferns."

In fact, both men were both right and wrong. Threads of catastrophic and uniformitarian explanations of Earth history run through modern geology. Lyell was correct to believe in an unimaginably old Earth, and Cuvier erred to give it so short a space. Although science does not admit catastrophes so apocalyptic as the baron suggested, the ancient rock record is punctuated with the results of volcanic eruptions, hurricanes, landslides, and barrages from space. Some scientists propose that an asteroid perhaps six miles in diameter struck Earth about 60 million years ago and created such climatic havoc that the dinosaurs became extinct. But, on the whole, such cataclysmic outbursts are the exception, not the rule—brief flashes of excitement bound by eons and eons of boring Lyellian business as usual. □

The 19th century's leading uniformitarian, English geologist Charles Lyell (top), declared geologic change a slow, steady process. His dapper and brilliant opposite was the eclectic French scientist Georges Cuvier (left), leader of the catastrophist school of geologists.

Drifter

Less than a year into World War I, Reserve Lieutenant Alfred Wegener of Germany's Queen Elizabeth Grenadier Guards was put out of action by a serious neck wound. However unwelcome the wound, the ensuing convalescence gave Wegener the leisure to mull over an idea that had first popped into his head in 1910, when he was teaching meteorology at the University of Marburg, near Frankfurt. A colleague had shown him a new world atlas, and as Wegener leafed through it, his imagination had been fired by the outlines of the continents. He noted—as people had for three centuries—the curiously neat fit between the east coast of South America and the shoreline of Africa south of the continent's great westward bulge. The congruence between the submerged continental shelves of Africa and South America was even more remarkable. Perhaps, thought Wegener, these continents had once been joined, then somehow drifted apart.

As a meteorologist, Wegener was straying into foreign intellectual territory. Still, he was familiar enough with geologic dogma to know that his idea would be called improbable, if not preposterous. But the notion of drifting continents, once born, was not easily suppressed. While browsing in the university's library, Wegener happened upon a paper describing fossils of identical species of land animals discovered on Brazil's coast and also on the coast of Africa, some 2,800 miles across the Atlantic. The writer proposed that the animals had traversed a huge land bridge, long since sunk beneath the ocean. Wegener's alternative explanation: The animal populations had been separated when the continent they inhabited split and its pieces slowly diverged.

Alfred Wegener had other scientific fish to fry, however, and continental drift went on the back burner. In 1912 and 1913 he had made his second lengthy expedition to Greenland to study its climate and glaciers. Soon after his return to Germany, the war broke out.

In 1915, as the convalescent soldier once again took up the thread of continental drift, he was obliged to do his homework in geology and paleontology. The prevailing view was that the Earth had begun as a glowing molten mass. As the planet slowly cooled and shrank, its surface had crumpled to form continents and ocean basins, mountains, valleys, lakes, and seas. But if this was the case, Wegener reasoned, continents and seafloors should be formed of the same material. Yet it was already known that continents were composed of rigid, lightweight granitic rock, known as sial in Wegener's day, while oceanic floors were made of a denser, more plastic basalt rock called sima. Perhaps, the German speculated, continents moved across the Earth's surface in a slowly flowing sea of sima, much as buoyant icebergs float on the ocean's currents.

Wegener used the sima-sial dichotomy to launch a two-pronged attack on the favored land-bridge theory. A land bridge, he argued, would have been composed of sial, but no traces of that material had been found in the ocean's depths. Moreover, land-bridge backers could not plausibly explain why bridges would sink and not take the continents with them. The renegade wove in other facts, such as the mirror-image coal fields in the Appalachian Mountains and in western Europe. By the time Wegener was finished, he had organized the scattered observations of numerous scientists into a radically new picture of the Earth's evolution and structure. Declaring the ocean-spanning land bridge a scientific fiction, he envisioned a single great continent—he

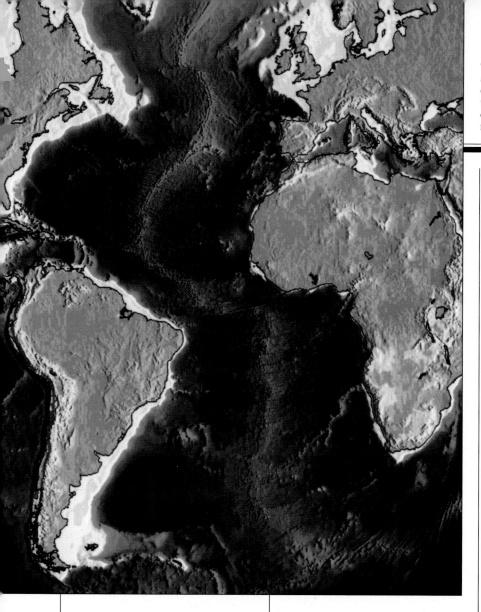

discover evidence that the huge island was, as he had predicted, drifting westward. On November 1, his 50th birthday, Alfred Wegener and a guide set out from their base camp, never to return. A search party discovered the scientist's body in a shallow grave; he had apparently died of a heart attack. The guide's fate, however, remains a mystery.

Had he not died prematurely, perhaps Alfred Wegener would have discovered how continents move, just as Isaac Newton inferred the basic laws of motion. As it was, Wegener came close. The year before his fatal expedition, Wegener had floated a hypothetical trial balloon handed him by the sympathetic Scottish geologist Arthur Holmes: Continents might be swept along by the rising and descending currents in molten rock, or magma, underlying the Earth's crust. The heat, Holmes speculated, came from decaying radioactive elements deep in the planet's interior that produced an endless cycle of melting and rising, cooling and sinking, and currents powerful enough to drive continents across the face of the Earth.

What Holmes proposed and Wegener bought into just missed the mark. Both men had correctly read the ponderously slow dance of the continents, but neither had known enough to take the final comprehending leap. In fact, the continents are rafted along on a kind of conveyor belt—a spreading seafloor constantly renewed through vast fissures by material flowing up from the interior and constantly reduced where the ocean floor dives back into the Earth. But proof of that did not come to hand until the 1960s, a generation after the despairing Wegener's frozen body was found in the Greenland snow. □

called it Pangaea, Greek for "Whole Earth"—that 200 million years ago had fractured and spawned a clutch of drifting continents.

First published in 1915, Wegener's theory drew no rave reviews from geologists. Many ignored it, while others lobbed insults at the cheeky meteorologist who had invaded their turf and attacked their cherished doctrines. Unfortunately for Wegener, the offending theory had a grave flaw that critics attached themselves to with leechlike tenacity. Feeling obliged to come up with a mechanism capable of moving continents that weigh in at some 500 million billion tons, We-

gener had postulated that one force pushed them away from the poles while a second imparted their westward drift. But the apparatus hypothesized was woefully inadequate to the task. Not even Wegener himself was convinced by the explanation. In 1929, after years spent in futile pursuit of a plausible agent, he wrote, "The Newton of the drift theory has not yet appeared."

The geologic establishment never let up on Wegener, but the meteorologist doggedly kept reinforcing his theory, although the fight pushed him toward despair. In April 1930 Wegener embarked on yet another foray to Greenland, hoping to

Balancing Act

Equilibrium, Christian Adolf Volf told anyone who would listen, has nothing to do with the ear's semi-circular canals, whatever physiologists might claim to the contrary. There is no innate sense of balance, Volf maintained; standing and walking steadily are skills acquired in infancy, as humans learn to overcome the force that the spinning Earth exerts on their bodies.

Volf, a Danish-born inventor and self-taught hearing expert, announced this radical hypothesis in 1944 in Los Angeles. In support of his theory about balance and the Earth's rotation, Volf cited examples of the way some people walk—toddlers in particular, who he said always take their first steps in an easterly direction. He discovered this tendency by watching a cousin who was just learning to walk.

Contrary to what might be expected of a young child, she apparently shunned her mother's lap and wanted to sit only in her father's. When Volf persuaded his aunt and uncle to trade chairs, the little girl happily walked to her mother. It seems that the father's chair—an inviolate and immovable seat in this strait-laced household—stood on the east side of the room, the mother's on the west. The child's apparent preference for her father's lap, Volf concluded, was in fact just an inclination to follow a path of less resistance—eastward, so that the force produced by Earth's rotation was at her back, like a fair wind.

But to Volf, if not to others, the conclusive proof of the theory came from a night of watching soldiers intoxicated by free beer on a Danish royal birthday. The men staggered giddily, but none of them lost his balance and fell when he was heading east. However, many of the soldiers wound up on their backs if they walked in a westerly direction. Volf recommended a practical application of his discovery to the police: To make it easier to herd a falling-down drunk through the paddy wagon's rear doors, park the vehicle so that it faced east.

Volf's theory flew in the face of convincing anatomical and medical research conducted since the early 19th century that demonstrated the importance of the ears' semicircular canals to equilibrium. Young people can sometimes overcome damage to these organs, as Volf had noted, by learning to rely on vision and sensory information from their muscles and joints for a sense of balance. Older people, however, often suffer severe, ongoing vertigo and disorientation that make standing and walking a continual trial.

The Dane's flair for publicity won brief public notice for his theory, despite its contrarian nature. The scientific community, however, rejected it out of hand, and police paddy wagons still park without regard to their compass headings. □

Danish balance theorist Christian Adolf Volf (right) and two onlookers monitor tuning forks used in 1955 hearing tests.

French physicist Jean-Baptiste Biot *(below)* mapped an 1803 meteorite fall near L'Aigle, France, using a dotted oval to mark the extent of the fall, which was heaviest in the dark areas.

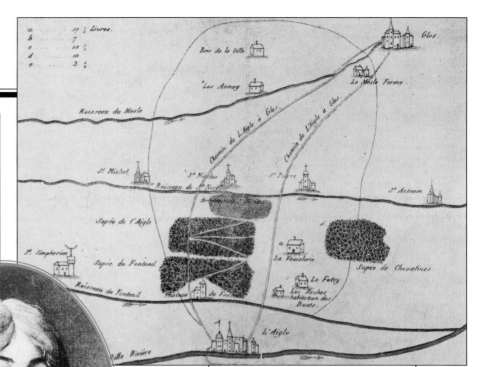

Balls of Fire

Progress in science is far from inevitable, and it sometimes happens that the most eminent savants of an age subtract from the sum of human knowledge instead of adding to it. Such was the case in 18th-century France, where meteorites suffered a century-long fall from scientific grace. For thousands of years there had been reports of rocks falling to Earth from the sky—as indeed these small bits of interplanetary rubble had. But the foremost natural philosophers of the Enlightenment, reluctant to add another mystery to a universe they had begun to comprehend, dismissed such stories as old wives' tales. The rocks, they insisted, had a terrestrial origin—as yet unknown.

So vehement was the skepticism of the scientific establishment that reports of meteorites, no matter how well attested, were dismissed out of hand. After a meteorite shower near Agen in southwestern France in 1790, for example, the mayor and 300 citizens provided a sworn account of the incident. In response, Pierre Bertholon, the editor of a leading scientific journal, condescendingly remarked, "How sad it is to see a whole municipality attempt to lend credibility, through a formal deposition, to folk tales that arouse the pity not only of physicists but of all sensible people." Swayed by a certain scorn for the laity, scientists were also thrown off the meteorite track by an article of faith—the notion that the universe was a gigantic, clocklike mechanism with no spare parts rattling around inside. The great machine included stars, the Sun, the planets and their satellites, and a few comets; these smoothly operating parts moved in a tidy void. However, this perfect machine obviously had its glitches—now and again, fireballs streaked across the sky and disappeared. It apparently did not occur to the scientists who liked their universe tidy that these incandescent visitors were actually fragments of the cosmos about to crash to Earth as meteorites.

One of the tasks that fell to scientists was to explain why these rocks looked different from their terrestrial cousins—why, for example, their exteriors showed evidence of extreme heat and partial melting. In 1769 a committee of the French Royal Academy of Sciences examined a stone said to have fallen near the village of Lucé. The team of experts, which included the great chemist Antoine-Laurent Lavoisier, concluded that the specimen was an ordinary rock that had been seared by the heat of a lightning strike. The explanation they invoked became the scientific favorite for meteorites, although a number of scientists thought that the puzzling projectiles had been hurled out of volcanoes.

But the blinders were beginning to fall. In 1794 German physicist Ernst Chladni published a treatise on meteorites showing that the rocks contained a form of iron so odd that it could not be terres- ◊

trial in origin. One of the German's specimens had come from a part of South America where there was not a trace of iron in the native rock and no stone-belching volcanoes in the neighborhood. Chladni also scrutinized eyewitness accounts and concluded that many were worthy of respectful attention. His conclusion: Meteorites came from space.

English chemist Edward Howard entered the fray in 1802 with his analysis of the composition of meteorites. The specimens he examined were very similar to one another in makeup and quite different from any known terrestrial rock. He declared that his findings, along with the body of reliable eyewitness testimony, must "remove all doubt as to the descent of these stony substances."

On July 17, 1803, French physicist Jean-Baptiste Biot delivered the final blow with a report to the National Institute of Sciences and Arts, the successor to the old Royal Academy of Sciences. In it he recounted his investigation of the meteorite shower reported by the townspeople of L'Aigle in April of that year. Biot interviewed every available witness and methodically described the incident, from the appearance of the fireball in the sky to the rock fragments recovered on the ground. He traced the dispersion pattern of the fragments and furnished a chemical analysis that tallied with Edward Howard's. The French physicist's data-packed report was convincing. As though suddenly, there seemed to be only one credible explanation for the fiery rocks from outer space. The weight of evidence at last was able to shove aside the tidy preconceptions that had blinded the enlightened for more than a century. □

Vulcanized

Urbain-Jean-Joseph Le Verrier, professor of astronomy at the University of Paris and director of the Observatory of Paris, had good reason to be confident, even proud, of his skills as a planet hunter. In 1846 he scored a remarkable triumph—deducing the existence of a previously unknown planet orbiting beyond Uranus. Astronomers had observed certain irregularities in Uranus's orbit, and Le Verrier calculated that the gravitational pull of a neighboring planet would account for them. Le Verrier determined the sector of the sky in which to look for the planet, but it was a colleague who first set eyes on the planet Neptune; he glimpsed it through his telescope within one degree of the point Le Verrier had predicted.

Thirteen years later, Le Verrier went planet hunting a second time. This search concentrated not on the outer reaches of the Solar System but on the space between Mercury and the Sun. What piqued the astronomer's interest was a minute change—a forward progression—from year to year in the planet's perihelion, the point where its orbit swings closest to the Sun. According to Le Verrier's calculations, the gravitational influence of the Sun and the known planets upon Mercury's orbit did not account entirely for the advancing perihelion—there was a seven-percent deficit in gravitational force. It raised an enticing possibility: Mercury might be feeling the tug of an undiscovered planet orbiting even closer to the Sun.

The small fraction of missing force implied that the hypothetical planet must also be small—so small, in fact, that it would be practically impossible to see it except when it crossed the face of the Sun. Nevertheless, Le Verrier was confident that other astronomers would eventually observe his conjectured planet, which he named Vulcan, for the Roman god of fire.

Not long after Le Verrier published a paper about his hypothetical planet, he received a letter in December 1859 from Edmond Lescarbault, an amateur stargazer. A physician in the small town of Orgères, Lescarbault claimed he had seen a tiny black spot pass across the Sun's face nine months earlier.

Displaying the proper skepticism, Le Verrier traveled to Orgères to examine Lescarbault—and demonstrate why the Parisian had earned the reputation of being the rudest man in France. Le Verrier later regaled his friends with an account of the salvo he aimed at the hapless country doctor: "It is then you, sir, who pretend to have observed the intramercurial planet, and who have committed the grave offense of keeping your observation secret for nine months. I warn you that I have come here with the intention of doing justice to your pretensions, and of demonstrating either that you have been dishonest or deceived. Tell me, then, unequivocally, what you have seen."

The overbearing Parisian went on to examine Lescarbault's equipment, which was decidedly amateurish. For a timekeeper, a necessity for precise astronomical observations, Lescarbault made do with an old watch without a second hand. To mark seconds, he had improvised an ivory pendulum that hung by a thread from a nail in the wall. Instead of keeping records in the ordinary way, on paper, Lescarbault, who moonlighted as the town carpenter, made notes on wooden planks in his inventory.

Whatever reservations he might have had, Le Verrier nevertheless concluded that Lescarbault's observations confirmed his own. On January 2, 1860, he announced the discovery of Vulcan. Other astronomers began scanning the sky for the planet, but their efforts were disappointing. There were only a few scattered reports that the predicted planet had been spotted, and none could be confirmed. Nonetheless, Le Verrier's faith in Vulcan's existence never wavered, for what else but a planet could explain the quirks in Mercury's orbits? Le Verrier died in 1877, still believing his figures did not lie. He could not have known that no scientist—and many others after him tried—could solve the perihelion puzzle using the concepts of 19th-century physics.

In the early years of the 20th century, Albert Einstein redefined gravity as the warping of space that occurs around massive objects. To put this new concept to the test, German astronomer Erwin Freundlich took a fresh look at the unruly Mercury, using Einstein's equations to analyze observations. The results showed that the Sun's warping effect accounted perfectly for the gravitational deficit Le Verrier had calculated. The failure had not been his—it was the failure of a science inadequate to his needs. Einstein was so overjoyed by Freundlich's results that he was speechless with excitement and he had heart palpitations. In all the excitement, planet Vulcan disappeared forever. □

Astronomer Urbain-Jean-Joseph Le Verrier *(above)* searched in vain for planet Vulcan, which his calculations indicated should orbit between the Sun and the planet Mercury, shown here in a rare closeup taken by the *Mariner 10* spacecraft in 1974.

Moonstruck

It is not recorded how many children stuck it out to the end of a 1936 radio show scripted by the U.S. Office of Education. "Have you heard that the Moon once occupied the space now filled by the Pacific Ocean?" the Friendly Guide asked the audience. "Once upon a time—a billion or so years ago, when the Earth was still young—a remarkable romance developed between the Earth and the Sun," the Guide continued. "In those days the Earth was a spirited maiden who danced about the princely Sun, was charmed by him, yielded to his attraction, and became his bride." Listeners soon learned that the romance had been fruitful: "The Sun's attraction raised great tides upon the Earth's surface; the huge crest of a bulge broke away with such momentum that it could not return to the body of mother earth. And this is the way the Moon was born!"

The astronomical explanation soaked in saccharine for the broadcast had been a widely accepted one among scientists for more than half a century. The theory was doomed, however: Colorful as it was, the notion proved totally incorrect.

George Darwin, the astronomer who had first propounded the theory, was no stranger to startling new ideas; his father was the evolutionary theorist Charles Darwin. The idea of lunar evolution came to the younger Darwin in the 1870s, when he was probing the dynamics of the young Earth. If, as astronomers had proposed, the planet had once been a rapidly spinning molten mass, solar gravity would have whipped up tides within the malleable ball and raised great bulges near its equator. If this rotation had been fast enough, Darwin speculated, one of the bulges—the neonatal Moon—might have spun off into space.

Astronomers had already discovered that, over eons, the complex gravitational tides coursing through Earth had slowed its rate of rotation, making each day infinitesimally longer. Simultaneously, these same forces had caused the Moon to move farther away from Earth. As a consequence, the satellite's orbit had expanded and the month, like the day, had lengthened. George Darwin set out to trace these two trends—the orbital periods of the Moon and the Earth and the distance separating the two bodies—back through time to the era of the Moon's birth. The journey would be purely mathematical, and Darwin was a versatile number-cruncher—his publications included two statistical papers on marriage between first cousins.

In his search for the infant Moon, Darwin calculated his way back in time for more than 54 million years before he reached the period where the two trends coincided—mathematically, at any rate—in a fascinating manner. According to Darwin's computations, days and months had shrunk to identical durations—5 hours and 36 minutes, and the Moon had orbited only 6,000 miles above the Earth's surface, moving in precise synchronization with the rotating Earth, as if rigidly fixed above a single point on the planet. To Darwin, the conclusion of his mathematical excursion was clear:

According to astronomer George Darwin (above), the Moon was cast into space by the molten, rapidly rotating young Earth. The mature planet looms above the lunar horizon in this photograph taken by *Apollo 10* astronauts in 1969.

The two bodies had once formed a single molten mass.

Astronomical theories are notoriously hard to prove or disprove, but Darwin's work was soon buttressed by what seemed to be persuasively solid terrestrial evidence. In 1882 English geologist Osmond Fisher added to Darwin's theory the idea that the Moon's separation had left a physical scar on Earth. The lunar mass split off from the Pacific Basin, Fisher said, carrying away a section of the relatively solid crust more than 30 miles deep. As the molten interior flowed into the vast rent, it set up currents that split the remainder of the floating crust into huge pieces. Fisher declared that the basin destined to become the Atlantic Ocean formed when currents pulled several pieces in opposite directions—the Americas on one side, Europe and Africa on the other. As evidence of his hypothesis, Fisher pointed out the roughly congruent contours of the Atlantic's eastern and western shores *(pages 14-15).*

Fisher's embellishment gave a tangible shape to Darwin's mathematics and his theory; by the beginning of the 20th century, it had become the preferred explanation for the Moon's origin.

The eclipse of the Earth-born Moon began around 1930. Astronomers challenged the theory because the centrifugal force required to hurl a Moon-size piece of Earth into space was too great. Still, the notion feebly endured until the late 1960s. Then, specimens brought back by Moon-walking astronauts revealed that the lunar rocks were chemically very different from Earth rocks—too different, scientists concluded, for Earth and Moon to have begun as one. □

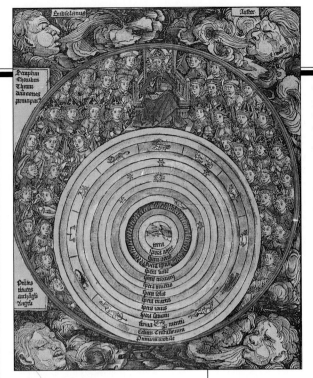

This celestial map from the 1493 encyclopedia *Chronique de Nuremberg* plots the Ptolemaic universe, bracketed by the four winds. In successively larger circular orbits, the Moon, the Sun, and the known planets orbit the Earth inside the outer, starry ring of the zodiac, watched by God and angels.

Circular Reasoning

Although the astronomers of ancient Greece were not the first to take careful measure of the stars and the planets, they were more concerned than their Mesopotamian and Egyptian predecessors with explaining the movements of celestial bodies. However, the Greeks' predictions of planetary positions—even when they correctly placed the Sun, not the Earth, at the center of their universe—frequently failed to match what they saw happening in the night sky.

Especially puzzling was a peculiarity in the tracks of Mars and Jupiter, which sometimes seemed to stop, reverse direction, and then resume their westward path across the heavens. Not until the second century AD was there a cosmic model that explained such oddities. Its creator, Ptolemy, is called the greatest of Greek astronomers, and his model prevailed for some 1,400 years for the simple reason that it worked—despite the paradoxical fact that it was founded on his basic misreading of the cosmos.

Ptolemy built on the philosophical and observational legacy of his predecessors, among whom Aristotle took pride of place. That great natural philosopher had placed Earth at the center of the cosmos, and there Ptolemy left it. In order to explain the movement of the Sun, the Moon, the stars, and the five planets then known in a geocentric universe, Ptolemy devised his ingenious geometrical system, described in a volume entitled the *Almagest.*

In Greek thinking, the most perfect of geometrical forms were the sphere and the circle. Ptolemy chose these forms for his system, declaring that the Earth was enclosed within a series of eight crystal spheres—the Moon, the Sun, and each planet had its own sphere, while the stars shared the eighth and outermost. According to Ptolemy, each of these bodies followed ◊

Moving at some 67,000 mph, Earth *(blue)* completes its 584-million-mile orbit in about 365 days; Mars *(red)*, moving at about 54,000 mph, takes some 687 days to travel its 890-million-mile course. The difference creates the illusion that Mars sometimes slows, stops, reverses its course, then suddenly resumes its eastward motion. Created by the red planet's *apparent position (pink)* on Earth's sky, the illusion is explained schematically below. Seen from position 1, for example, Mars moves steadily across the sky. But, as Earth begins to overtake it *(2, 3)*, Mars seems to slow, then pause *(4)*. As Earth speeds past *(5)*, a terrestrial observer would see Mars seem to move backward in the sky, then resume its regular trajectory *(6, 7)*.

EARTH   MARS   APPARENT POSITION OF MARS

a circular course within its crystal sphere. For some, such as the Sun and the stars, the motion could be explained with a simple circle around the Earth. But a circle could not accommodate the vastly more complicated motions of the Moon and the planets—especially the apparent backward motion seen in the tracks of Mars and Jupiter.

During their circuit of the heavens, these planets appeared at some point to halt their forward, westward motion, then negotiate a hairpin turn that sent them eastward for some distance; another sharp turn set the planets back on their original course. Astronomers now understand that this retrograde motion can be seen in the apparent tracks of all planets orbiting beyond the orbit of the Earth—and that it is an illusion produced as the Earth overtakes its more distant cousins on its faster, inside track. But for Ptolemy, with a universe centered on the Earth, the variations were misfirings of the celestial engine something to be fixed.

To account for the renegade motions, Ptolemy grafted small circles, or epicycles, onto the large ones. Other adaptations, such as placing the center of the large orbits at a slight distance from Earth, took care of other deviations. By jiggering the sizes of the circles and epicycles and selecting appropriate speeds for the planets, Ptolemy arrived at a model that allowed astronomers to predict the positions of celestial bodies with a greater accuracy than before.

From time to time, improvements in celestial measuring devices created new discrepancies between observations and predictions based on the Ptolemaic system. The problem was that Ptolemy used circles, where nature had used the flattened circles called ellipses, to shape planetary orbits. Ptolemy's solution was to add more circular epicycles. Thus when Mars's single epicycle proved inadequate, a second one was added. It traveled around the original epicycle, which in turn revolved along the circumference of the larger circle centered on the Earth.

As the epicycles multiplied, the theoretical sky became a baroque ensemble of planetary tracks requiring prodigies of predictive computations. At least some sky watchers yearned for a simpler system. The 13th-century king Alfonso of Léon and Castile reportedly remarked to his royal astronomer, "Sir, if I had been present at Creation I could have rendered profound advice."

Despite its multiple shortcomings, astrologers liked the Ptolema-

In this Renaissance miniature, Ptolemy peers into an astrolabe, surrounded by instruments made of gold.

ic system for its ability to predict the positions of stars and planets. The scheme also served the medieval Christian church, which was pleased to find scientific backing for a universe centered on humankind. But in 1543, when the Polish cleric and astronomer Nicolaus Copernicus was near death, he published a radical and ominous cosmology. It demoted Earth to the status of a mere satellite moving with the rest of the planets around the Sun. The priest had timidly delayed publication of his ideas until the end of his life, fearing criticism and charges of heresy.

Copernicus's fears were not without foundation. In the opinion of Protestant leader Martin Luther, the Copernican cosmology was an abomination since it denied Holy Writ. "The fool," Luther stormed, "will turn the whole of the science of astronomy upside down." The Roman Catholic church was slower to take umbrage, but in 1616 it banned Copernicus's book, and scholars who endorsed it opened themselves to persecution. Even the great Italian scientist Galileo was forced to mute his pro-Copernican views in 1633 *(pages 102-104)*.

The new, Sun-centered system was itself no model of simplicity—in fact, it suffered from a geometric problem that had plagued the Ptolemaic system: the circle. Sharing the Greek affection for perfect geometry, Copernicus had given the planets circular orbits. Like Ptolemy, he had to resort to epicycles to make his system work. Not until 1609 would the German astronomer Johannes Kepler produce a true description of the motion of the planets—in ellipses, around the Sun. After 15 centuries, Ptolemy's crystalline spheres finally shattered. □

Utmost Gravity

It was his friend Thomas Edison who got financial wizard Roger Babson excited about gravity technology. The famed inventor, whose own work had harnessed electricity, urged Babson to tackle a problem few scientists were willing to take on—the search for an "antigravity screen"—a mechanism for canceling gravity. Edison, who was often wrong, believed that antigravity shields existed in nature, as chemicals in the skins of some birds whose wingspan, according to his calculations, was too small to permit unaided flight. But bird skin was not the only antigravity possibility. He gave Babson a tip: "I think it's coming about from some alloy."

The idea of overcoming gravity was not new with Edison, but it had rarely fallen on more fertile ground than Babson, who was not only a millionaire stock-market analyst but a philanthropist as well. Still, it was not until 1948, 17 years after Edison's death, that Babson put some of his fortune to work on the problem and inaugurated the Gravity Research Foundation. The idea was to combine the statistical methods that had worked on Wall Street with Edisonesque experimental procedures. Babson's aim was to test thousands of substances, organic and inorganic, to see if any acted as a gravity screen.

Part of the tycoon's interest derived from his reverence for Isaac Newton, the 17th-century physicist who first eluci-

dated the law of gravitation. Babson claimed that Newton's third law of motion—for every action there is an equal and opposite reaction—was critical to predicting the stock market accurately. For instance, the financier said, Newton's third law had allowed him to predict the disastrous crash of 1929 nearly two months in advance and had saved his fortune.

To his perhaps eccentric grasp of Newton, Babson added a wealth of gravity lore gleaned from his childhood in Gloucester, Massachusetts. The tides generated by the gravitational pull of the Sun and the Moon influenced everything in the seafaring town. At high tide, the tugging of those distant bodies was presumed to dilute the powerful pull of Earth. "It was accepted knowledge," Babson once reminisced, "that when the tide was high, it was much easier to climb a mast. And doctors in Gloucester made a common practice of advising people with heart disease to wait for high tide before going upstairs."

Babson's plunge ◊

into gravitational research was finally precipitated by the drowning of a favorite grandson in 1947. In the financier's youth he had lost a beloved sister the same way, and he came to blame both of the tragedies on the inescapable clutch of gravity. It was time, Babson decided, to adapt another of Newton's laws for public benefit.

A war against gravity was, according to the greatest physicists of the day, unwinnable. Albert Einstein, in his theory of general relativity, treated gravity not as a force but as a warping of space and time and thus not susceptible to barriers. But treating gravity as a force is also fraught with difficulties. Unlike electrical force, which has mutually repellent negative and positive charges, gravity is apparently unipolar. Every scrap of evidence suggests that every mass, whatever its size or makeup, exerts a gravitational pull; as a consequence, all known masses are mutually attracted to one another.

But efforts to discover the wave or particle that *is* gravity have found nothing: Thus far, gravity seems merely to exist. Where and how to look for its opposite, antigravity, could only prompt a lot of scientific head scratching.

Such dilemmas notwithstanding, Babson's foundation announced plans to act as a clearinghouse for gravity research and offered annual prizes of $1,000 for the best essays on "some reasonable method of harnessing the power of gravity." The pick of the 1957 crop, submitted by physicist Phillip Morrison and astrophysicist Thomas Gold *(page 64)*, was suitably upbeat, suggesting the possibility "that antigravity exists and that it could be demonstrated on Earth." After Babson's death in 1967, astronomical arcana of a completely theoretical nature were added to the list of acceptable contest subjects. Four years later, the stellar British astro-

physicist Steven Hawking strayed far beyond the bounds of pragmatism and into the immense gravity of black holes, collapsed stars presumed to be the densest objects in the universe, to score a win.

The annual essay contest continues as a monument to Roger Babson's willingness to probe the improbable. There is also a 2,000-pound stone monument at Tufts University that the financier gave the school along with a $50,000 research grant in 1961. The purpose of the monument is clearly stated: "It Is To Remind Students Of The Blessings Forthcoming When A Semi-Insulator Is Discovered In Order To Harness Gravity As A Free Power And Reduce Airplane Accidents." Midnight pranksters claiming to have mastered antigravity made moving the heavy monument—nicknamed the antigravity rock—a tradition. Unfortunately, the $50,000 may run out before gravity, still as elusively pervasive as ever, can be harnessed. □

This 2,000-pound granite monument at Tufts University was erected as a reminder of Roger Babson's $50,000 gift for research designed to harness the power of gravity.

Quartet

For 2,000 years the proposition that the universe contains only four elements was firmly lodged in the science and psyche of the Western world. Air, earth, fire, and water were the essence of matter, according to Empedocles, a Greek who lived in Sicily during the fifth century BC. Given the stamp of approval by Aristotle and Plato, his theory was handed down until 18th-century chemists cast out the Empedoclean four in favor of the multiple elements of the modern universe.

In the world as explained by Empedocles, two opposite forces were responsible for every event. The attractive force of love, or harmony, caused the elements to come together and combine; the number of elements in a combination, along with their proportions, created a distinctive mix of physical properties. Conversely, everything was separated into its constituent elements by the repelling force of strife; then the combining resumed. In an endless cycle of creation and destruction, first one force and then the other held sway, but the elements survived their countless transformations with their mass and their properties unchanged. Likewise, love and strife neither diminished nor increased. In a world with scant chemistry, but filled with turmoil, Empedocles' views matched his experience.

Only a few fragments of Empedocles' works, *On Nature* and *Purifications*, remain, and the man himself is shrouded in myth. According to one account, he was exiled from Sicily for supporting democracy, and other tales credit him with ending an epidemic and raising the dead. Empedocles was so sure of his own worth that he informed his contemporaries, "I am for you as an immortal god, no longer a man; I am honored by all, as is just." If legend can be believed, his lofty self-esteem proved to be his downfall. To demonstrate that he was in fact a god, the 60-year-old philosopher-scientist jumped into the volcano of Mount Etna—and was killed by earth, fire, and something he had overlooked: gravity. □

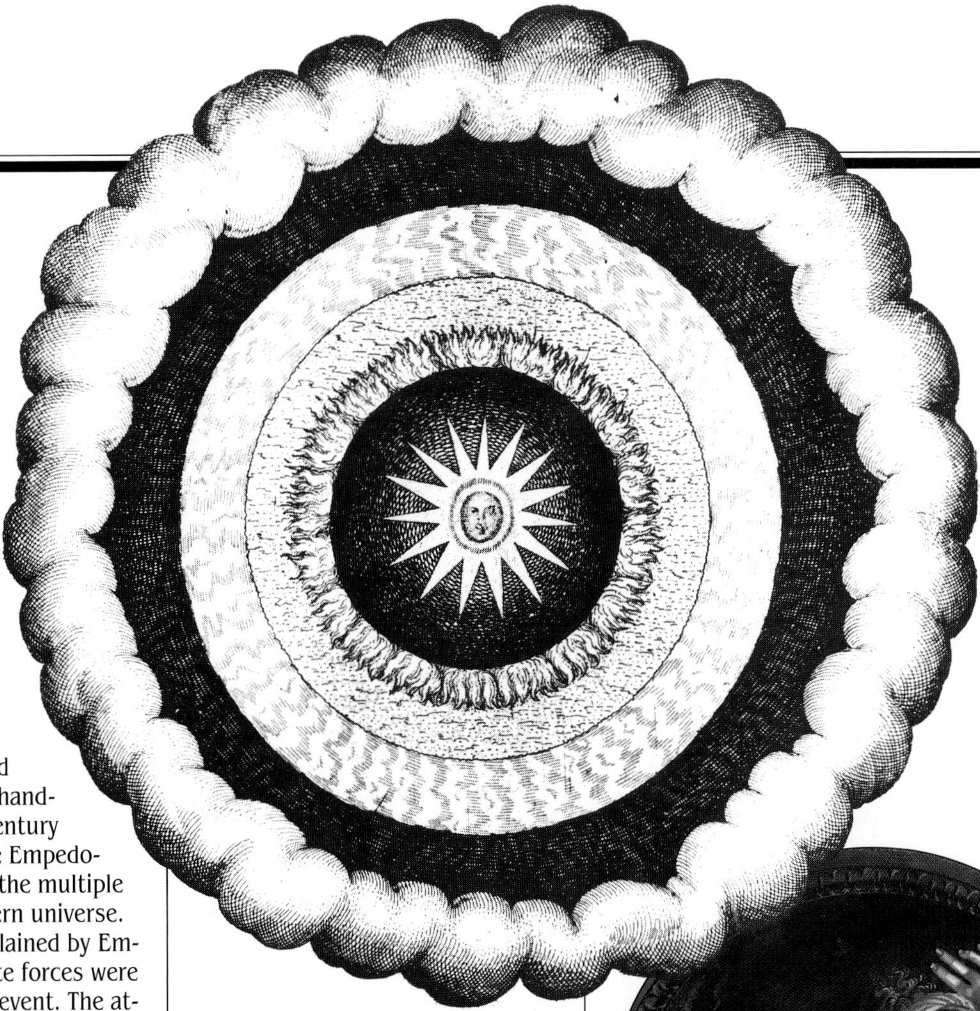

This 17th-century diagram *(top)* surrounds the Sun with rings of earth, fire, water, and air—the elements proposed by the Greek Empedocles—and two cloudy outer rings. Said to be Empedocles, the turbaned figure above appears in a 15th-century Signorelli fresco on the ceiling of Rome's Orvieto Duomo.

Eggsistentialist

What Charles Bonnet discovered about aphids in 1740 made him ponder Eve's ovaries anew—a perfectly reasonable connection for the 20-year-old Swiss biologist and his like-minded colleagues to make. In a series of experiments, Bonnet proved that a female spindle-tree aphid raised in isolation could produce perfectly normal offspring, with no help from a male. His first single parent was, moreover, no freak of nature, for he got exactly the same results with several of her daughters. In all, he tracked his aphids through nine successive generations of virgin birth.

Experimental proof that parthenogenesis—reproduction from unfertilized eggs—occurs frequently in aphids was gratifying to Bonnet. A member of the ovist faction of embryologists, he believed that every egg enclosed a minute body, preformed with all of its parts present and ready to develop. Pressing preformationist logic onward, he held that every female embryo had in her body a set of eggs, and within each of these eggs was yet another preformed embryo. Thus generation upon future generation already existed, ready to develop when its time arrived. When the preformationists took a glance backward through time, the trail led to Creation—to Eve and to every other original female creature in the Garden of Eden. Within their ovaries, germ within germ like nesting Russian dolls, had been every individual of their species that would ever exist. The preformationists called this system *emboîtement,* from *boît,* the French word for "box."

A minority preformationist faction lobbied for sperm emboîtement, but ovists and spermists presented a united front to the opposition, the epigenesists. Disdaining preformationism, the epigenesists insisted that every embryo was the product of a natural force that gave form to unorganized matter. Bonnet dismissed them as irrational and unscientific, since they could not produce any evidence for the alleged natural force.

Emboîtement seemed plausible in a time when the world was commonly believed to be only 6,000 years or so old. In that span, there might have been no more than 230 generations. Moreover, the world was not expected to go on forever. Thus, furnishing enough boxed embryos to keep a species going from the beginning to the end of time would not overtax a primordial ovary.

Despite his ovist leanings, Bonnet did not belittle the male contribution. He speculated that the little bodies swimming about in seminal fluid were tiny animals, complete with organ systems. The eggs from which they hatched had perhaps fallen into the fluid, which, he believed, exerted a powerful influence on the embryo. According to Bonnet, it made the preformed heart begin to beat, stimulated growth, and imprinted characteristics on the budding offspring, thus accounting for some of the variations among individuals. The eggs within a single ovary were not, in Bonnet's opinion, as alike as peas in a pod. Instead, embryonic Newtons and Bachs, ordinary folk, queens, and criminals could all be packed in together, tiny cheek by tiny jowl. Bon-

In an engraving from his multivolume treatise on natural history and philosophy, embryologist Charles Bonnet *(left)*, who lost much of his sight and hearing, dictates a letter to his secretary.

net also declared that the particular uterus, the climate, the geographic location, and the time of an embryo's unfolding all influenced the individual's unique makeup.

Seeing an embryo was a fuzzy and frustrating business in Bonnet's day. Two-lens microscopes could magnify up to 500 times, but the image was indistinct; a single lens produced a much sharper image but had less magnifying power. In a chicken embryo, a favorite subject for Bonnet, the lung was invisible until it was one-tenth-inch long.

An honest man, Bonnet admitted that when he could first make out the embryonic chick in its field of yolk, it looked like a worm with a large head. He ascribed its unchickenlike appearance to the fact that, although all of the embryo's parts were preformed, they changed in proportion during development and unfolded and expanded at different rates. The epigenesist opposition, he wrote, wished "to judge of the time when the parts of an organized body begin to exist by the time when they become visible to us. They do not reflect that minuteness and transparency alone can make these parts invisible to us although they really exist all the time." Like other scientists of his day, Bonnet could only guess at the lower limits of size. Hypothesizing that the smallest structures in existence must be unimaginably minute, he remarked, "Nature works as small as it wishes."

Fate was unkind to Charles Bonnet. As a boy, he was partially deaf, and by the time he was 28 years old, he had lost so much of his eyesight that he had to give up experimental work. Nature's smallest works, never quite visible to him, faded utterly in his failing light. □

The Elephant King

The letter that master surgeon Nicolas Habicot of the University of Paris received from a country surgeon could scarcely be believed: In a sand quarry near the Chateau de Chaumont, masons digging 18 feet below the surface had uncovered a coffin fit for a giant. It was 30 feet long, 12 feet wide, and 8 feet deep, with a stone lid engraved with the words *Theutobocheus Rex*—King Theutobocheus. Inside, the missive continued, were the remains of a giant no less than 25 feet tall with shoulders 10 feet across.

Habicot's correspondent, surgeon Pierre Mazuyer, had been summoned to the scene by the masons and had actually measured the skeleton. Its skull, he wrote, was 5 feet long and 10 feet around, with eye sockets as big as dinner plates. Unfortunately, most of the bones had crumbled to powder soon after they were exposed to air. All that remained were two fragments of the lower jaw, three teeth, three vertebrae, a shoulder blade, part of a thighbone, the humerus bone of one arm, and a few assorted fragments.

News of the giant Theutobocheus spread quickly, and in due time what was left of him arrived in Paris, chaperoned by Mazuyer, who had begun to make a little money from the remains. Besides submitting the remarkable bones to Habicot, Mazuyer put them on display for the curious public to view, for the price of a sou or two.

Habicot's examination indicated that there had been no fakery—the bones, he reported, were the real thing. In a pamphlet summarizing his findings, the master surgeon wrote that the shape and composition of the bones left no doubt that they had come from a human male. To naysayers who believed no mother could possibly give birth to such a huge offspring, Habicot offered the rumored examples of Marguerite, a Dutch countess reputed to have enjoyed a pregnancy that yielded 360 living infants, and a somewhat less pro- ◊

A sly artist expressed his opinion of 17th-century surgeon and self-styled paleontologist Nicolas Habicot *(right)* by depicting him mounted on a mule.

ductive Polish countess delivered of 36 babies at one fell swoop.

After boning up on his history, Habicot described King Theutobocheus as a member of a barbarian alliance that had attempted to invade the Roman Empire around 100 BC. Leading an army of some 300,000 men, Theutobocheus met the Roman general Gaius Marius in battle by the Galaure River, not far from the site of the find. Slain in combat, Theutobocheus was ordered buried in a coffin by the victorious Marius. Moreover, added Habicot, the very name of the place where the bones had been found seemed to verify the story: It was traditionally called the Giant's Field.

The idea of ancient giants was far from preposterous in 17th-century France. Many people believed that none but a race of giants could have erected the thousands of mysterious dolmens, huge stone monuments found all across France that had clearly been arranged not by na-

ture but by humans. There was also the evidence of the Bible, which states that prior to the great flood survived by Noah and his ark "there were giants in the Earth."

Jean Riolan, royal professor of anatomy, had his doubts about giants—at least about those described by Mazuyer and Habicot. It was, the professor harrumphed, "the greatest imposture," and Habicot's pamphlet was so riddled with errors that it should be "rubbed out from the beginning to the end." After a point by point attack on Habicot's anatomical descriptions, Riolan assailed the master surgeon's command of history: Theutobocheus was no king, only a chieftain. The anatomist finished with a taunting professional gibe against Mazuyer and Habicot. Surgeons, Riolan reminded the public, were scarcely more than vulgar barbers and worked under the direction of true doctors such as himself.

After another exchange of con-

tentious pamphlets, the debate died down. Its winner was not settled until the 19th century, by Baron Georges Cuvier (pages 12-13) of the Museum of Natural History in Paris. An expert in fossils, Cuvier dethroned—and dehumanized—Theutobocheus. The remains, he declared, were not those of an ancient warrior, but of an extinct elephant.

Mazuyer and Habicot's mistake had not been merely foolish, however. Like their contemporaries, they had no inkling of the long-vanished animals that once roamed the land. The best explanation for the huge but manlike bones was that they had come from an enormous human, especially as the remains were reportedly discovered buried in a crude sarcophagus. Perhaps some reverential human being had interred the giant bones that way; or perhaps, as some said, the elephant's coffin was apocryphal, and Theutobocheus had been just a king-size practical joke. □

Head for Tails

Mrs. Pinmoney, an English grande dame with a daughter of marriageable age in Thomas Love Peacock's 1817 novel *Melincourt,* at first dismisses Oran Haut-ton, the bachelor she has just met, as a possible match. Although he has fashionable friends, lovely manners, and a pleasant demeanor, he is most peculiar looking and not given to banter—in fact, he does not utter a word. However, when she discovers that he is a member of Parliament and a baronet, Mrs. Pinmoney twitters excitedly, "Well, now I look at

him again, I certainly do not think him so very plain: he has a very fashionable air. Haut-ton! French extraction, no doubt. And now I think of it, there is something very French in his physiognomy."

Sir Oran is, in fact, an orangutan. Peacock's inspiration for the hairy baronet was the theory of human evolution proposed by Lord Monboddo, a Scottish judge, amateur anthropologist, and student of Greek literature and philosophy. Born James Burnett in 1714, Monboddo asserted that the orangutan was a kind of human being, to the bemusement—or outrage—of his

contemporaries. Unlike Charles Darwin, whose 1871 work *The Descent of Man* would appear almost a century after Monboddo elevated the orangutan to its new status in *Of the Origin and Progress of Language,* the Scotsman defined humanity by its mental faculties alone. Like other intellectuals of his day, Monboddo believed in a hierarchical world that progressed from inanimate nature upward through plants and animals. Called the Great Chain of Being, this concept made man creation's crowning glory, distinguished from even the highest animals by the power of reason. More-

John Kay's 1784 cartoon satirized Lord Monboddo *(right)* and his obsession with human tails—like those on the men seen cavorting in the picture hanging behind the peer.

over, every other species remained forever fixed through all of time, but humans were destined to evolve mentally until they became the supremely endowed—but physically diminished—Intellectual Creatures.

Since mind was paramount to Monboddo, the great differences between an orangutan's body and a human being's was of no moment whatsoever—only brainpower counted. In 18th-century Europe, opportunities to see great apes in action were scant. Monboddo saw only two orangutans, both of them in London. He also paid a visit to Versailles to examine a stuffed pet "pongo," or chimpanzee; it was said to have "performed many little offices to the lady with whom he lived." But, however clever the pongo, Monboddo did not move it up the Great Chain of Being.

As evidence of orangutan IQ, Lord Monboddo cited instances of their wielding weapons and building shelters, anecdotes that he had

gleaned from the journals of travelers and explorers. He had an unfortunate propensity for taking incredible tales at face value—for example, when he read of lustful male orangutans making unwelcome overtures to women, he believed the apes were simply demonstrating their humanity.

The first creature to achieve human mental status, according to Monboddo, was a perfect physical specimen that probably lived in the benign warmth of Egypt. The judge also held the decidedly unorthodox opinion that the protohuman's ancestors had not been Adam and Eve but a zoophyte, a creature part animal and part plant. Rising from both kingdoms of life, Monboddo's perfect primitive lived in happy solitude, ran about alternately upright and on all fours, and espoused vegetarianism. Although these first humans could think, as solitaries they had no need of language. Language, Monboddo theorized, was invented only when human society became complex enough to make it a necessity. Orangutans, he claimed, were physically equipped to speak but had not yet acquired the art because of their simple lifestyle. With speech, Monboddo believed, civilization and intellect flowered, but at some cost—the perfect body began to degenerate into its present, puny form. He calculated that the ancient Greek hero Achilles and the builders of Stonehenge

had measured a magnificent 14 feet or more in height.

Monboddo was himself perhaps an instance of the physically diminished Intellectual Creature—not even five feet tall, he gobbled up facts and fancies and spun off 12 volumes' worth of ideas and speculation between 1773 and 1799, the year of his death. In Lord Monboddo's day, Edinburgh was reckoned the Athens of the north, and he counted the city's great philosophers, scholars, and scientists among his friends and entertained them at fortnightly "learned suppers," strewing the table with roses in emulation of the Roman poet Horace's soirees.

The judge had equally eminent associates in London. Introduced to King George III, he so charmed the monarch that the two often met when Monboddo paid visits to the city. The 400-mile journey between Edinburgh and London took more than a week because Monboddo, perhaps in imitation of the more physical ancient Greeks, eschewed carriages as effeminate modern conveniences. He traveled on horseback, like the virile ancients had, even when he was in his 80s. On at least one occasion, however, he ignored his scruples and hired a carriage during a downpour to spare his wig a soaking. The wig traveled without its owner, who retrieved it at its destination.

Although Monboddo was greatly esteemed as a scholar and a man of the law, his placing the orangutan on man's level in the Great Chain of Being was considered preposterous. People were not ready to admit kinship with apes; the very concept of evolution, not just of humans but of the Earth itself, was too radical to have won over many adherents. ◊

But the snickers and snide remarks were directed not at Monboddo's evolutionary ideas so much as at a single odd fixation of his: Every human baby, he declared, was born with a tail, but a vast conspiracy of midwives had kept the appendage secret by cutting it off at birth.

The too-credulous Monboddo had swallowed whole a Swedish sailor's book claiming that he and his mates had experienced an unpleasant brush with natives of the Nicobar Islands west of Malaysia—a tribe of cannibals, wrote the Swede, that sported catlike tails. And, because humans *are* occasionally born with tails, Monboddo's further research turned up more purported cases, one of them a deceased Scotsman with a six-inch caudal appendage. A witness to the birth of his own children, Monboddo attributed his failure to see their tails to midwifely sleight of hand.

Multiple barbs were aimed at the evolutionist. Accusing Lord Monboddo of being as jealous of his tail as a squirrel, lexicographer Samuel Johnson quipped, "Other people have strange notions, but they conceal them. If they have tails, they hide them." Once Lord Kames, an eminent Edinburgh acquaintance of Monboddo's, insisted that the judge precede him: "You must walk first that I may see your tail." And Horace Walpole—like Sir Oran Haut-ton a titled member of Parliament—wrote to the countess of Upper Os-sory, "Does your Ladyship know that Lord Monboddo has twice proposed to Mrs. Garrick? She refused him; I don't know whether because he says in his book that men were born with tails, or because they have lost them."

Nineteenth-century evolutionists paid little heed to Monboddo. But he may have done Charles Darwin a great favor: He drew the fire of antievolutionary jokesters, and by Darwin's day the taunts about tails and apish cousins were stale. Thus a bishop's wife kept her composure when she learned of Darwin's theory. "Descended from the apes? Dear me, let us hope it is not true. But if it is true, let us hope it does not become widely known." □

Fly Papers

The world is full of unexplained phenomena, large and small, and honor is due researchers such as John Blackwall of Llanrwst, North Wales, who take on the seemingly insignificant and leave more glamorous subjects to others. In 1864 Blackwall, a retiree from the linen trade, had more than 35 years of studying spiders under his belt and had recently completed *A History of the Spiders of Great Britain and Ireland,* when, perhaps wishing for a little diversion, he had a go at a different topic: the mechanism that enables flies to walk up walls and across ceilings. What prompted Blackwall's interest is unrecorded, but it may have been a painstaking researcher's irritation with the sloppy speculation that thus far had been the only scientific contribution to the subject.

The offhand consensus was that flies owed their pedestrian agility to a suction mechanism on their feet. To test this proposition, Blackwall put flies in a glass jar and expelled all the air with a pump, a move that should have equalized air pressure on both sides of the flies' suction devices, rendering them inoperative. The partial vacuum may have made the subjects short of breath, but Blackwall's insects climbed walls as usual.

When Blackwall put flies under his microscope, he discovered that a sticky substance was exuded by tiny

hairs on the bottom of the insects' feet. Blackwall's conclusion: Flies literally glued themselves, one step at a time, to surfaces made difficult by gravity.

It may be that the Linnean Society, to which Blackwall described his results, applauded his meticulous exposition. But his research had not killed the suction canard outside Great Britain. Nearly two decades later, German books on entomology gave Blackwall and his air-pump experiment a curt nod, if they acknowledged him at all.

Perhaps belatedly, entomologist Hermann Dewitz of the Zoological Museum in Berlin became John Blackwall's advocate in Germany. On January 17, 1882, eight months after the Briton's death, Hermann Dewitz delivered a paper on fly feet to the members of Berlin's Society of Friends for the Research of Natural History. Dewitz, like his late colleague, was outside of his ordinary territory—his specialty was *schmetterlingen,* or "butterflies." Nevertheless, he devised a clever experiment that reinforced Blackwall's findings. With a strip of paper and glue he tethered a fly to a pane of glass feet down and with enough slack to take a few steps. Dewitz then turned the glass over and positioned it under his microscope in order to scrutinize the feet upside down. As the obliging insect took several steps, Dewitz saw for himself the gluey substance Blackwall had described.

Neither man was equipped to go the last explanatory mile and grapple with fly-glue production and composition. Such complex questions were left for others as determined as Blackwall and Dewitz to know what happens when a fly goes for a gravity-defying crawl. □

Hermann Dewitz *(opposite),* a German entomologist with an interest in the climbing apparatus of flies, sat for this photograph around 1880.

This worried-looking "mine fish" *(right)* was embedded in a discourse on fossils in Athanasius Kircher's 1665 encyclopedia, which also featured such oddities as the mythical creatures shown below.

Not Quite Right

Athanasius Kircher had a thing or two to say about fossils—as he did on almost every other phenomenon, to judge by the contents of his hefty 1665 encyclopedia *Mundus Subterraneus.* There the Jesuit scholar held forth on the weather, celestial bodies, ocean currents, the remains of giants, minerals, metallurgy, poisons, herbs, fireworks, hydraulics, astrological medicine, and, of course, the subterranean world—its waters and fires, and the dragons and demons lurking there.

Kircher entertained some fantastic medieval notions, including the idea that a force called the *spiritus plasticus* created wondrous images in rocks of trees, animals, human beings, and castles; it even inscribed the letters of the Greek and Latin alphabets. But not all images in rock were the work of the plastic spirit, according to Kircher. The remains of a handful of living things including leaves, mussels, and fish had also left their marks in stone.

Sounding remarkably modern, Kircher explained how a "mine fish," as he called a fossilized fish, was created. When a fish was trapped in mud, Kircher wrote, its flesh wasted away or turned to a fine dust; but the bones remained and turned into stone, along with the mud in which they were embedded. He declared that rock images of snakes and other animals were sometimes created by the same process—one that roughly matched the modern geologic definition of fossils.

Kircher could not stay modern for very long, however. In the next paragraph, he declared that a "saltstone force" could petrify an entire body, flesh and bones alike. This radiant force was said to draw salty particles from the animal and the mud. They flowed together to preserve in "miraculous uniformity" all parts of the animal. Suddenly, Kircher was back in the Middle Ages. In a sense, his was the eternal pace of science: two steps forward, one step back. □

Honey from Heaven

Around 343 BC, the Greek philosopher Aristotle began an inquiry into the life and works of the honeybee. He picked the brains of beekeepers about the care and feeding of the young and distinguished among the various species of bees while mangling the facts about a hive's social organization. Flying in the face of beekeeping lore, he erred in insisting that hives are ruled by kings rather than queens. He was tripped up by his overriding conviction that nature arms none but males—thus a queen bee equipped with a sting, although a fact, was to Aristotle's way of thinking a logical impossibility.

As to the origin of the honey that sustains a hive, Aristotle knew that bees made a beeline for flowers with sweet juices, extracted them with a tonguelike organ, and carried their booty back to the hive. But the philosopher also pointed out in his *History of Animals* that bees harvest honeydew, a confection that appears on leaves as a sweet and gleaming coat. Aristotle believed that this other kind of honey came from the atmosphere, usually when there was a rainbow in the sky. Aristotle's fancy was charming, but he needed to look somewhere besides a rainbow-spangled sky for the source of honeydew. It is a thoroughly earthy present bestowed by common insects, the most generous being aphids. As they feed on plant juices, the tiny creatures discharge copious amounts of a sugar-laden liquid—that is, honeydew. What misled Aristotle is uncertain, but he may have supposed that aphids, like bees, gathered on leaves to feed on the ethereal condensation.

The misconception about honeydew had a long life. In *The Feminine Monarchie*, his 1609 treatise on bees, Charles Butler corrected Aristotle's error about who ruled the hive but still rhapsodized about "the very quintessence of all the sweetness of the earth" that is drawn up into the air as vapors and condensed into a honey rain. Even after aphids were discovered by 19th-century researchers to be the source of honeydew, many resisted the idea that the sweet substance found its way into the world—and ultimately onto their toast—by way of the aphids' anal passages. Until further research forced them to face the aphids' actual plumbing, the fastidious believed that honeydew issued from invisibly minute tubes on the insects' backs. □

In this composite, the stony gaze of Aristotle, Greek philosopher and student of honey, rests upon a branch where German bark aphids have deposited their honeydew.

Eelusive Truth

In ancient Rome, according to legend at least, a noblewoman once took a fancy to an eel, made it her pet, and adorned it with earrings—history is silent on how she attached them to the lobeless fish. Her slippery companion was very much the exception, however. Then as now, the usual fate of eels falling into human hands was to be eaten. From the Mediterranean northward through Europe, people eagerly anticipated the springtime arrival of tender young eels; first making their appearance near the mouths of rivers, they swam upstream and into the stewpot. In fall large adults headed downstream to disappear in the sea. Where they went, no one knew. As to the returning young, they seemed to materialize out of nowhere, for no one had seen a female lay eggs and an obliging male release its fertilizing milt, or seminal fluid, as other fish did. It was as if young eels were made, not born—from mud.

Scientists began to demystify the elusive eel only in the late 18th century. Dissections demonstrated that the creatures possessed sexual organs very like those of other fish whose reproductive behavior was not so private an affair. And in 1856 German naturalist Johann ◊

Danish biologist Johannes Schmidt *(left)* was the first to discover the larvae of the young European eels *(background)* that once seemed to come out of nowhere.

Kaup plucked from Italy's Strait of Messina a wiggly clue to the eels' still-secret breeding grounds. As transparent as glass and shaped like a willow leaf, Kaup's three-inch fish was so unlike anything he had ever seen before that he supposed he had discovered a new species. Inexplicably, Kaup did not test his proposition, which seemed fishy to Italian naturalists Giovanni Battista Grassi and Salvador Calandruccio. The skeptics put several of Kaup's "species" in a saltwater aquarium—and were rewarded to see them grow into adult eels. What Kaup had found was an eel larva. Therefore, eels must breed in the ocean—somewhere.

From Grassi and Calandruccio the baton passed to Danish marine biologist Johannes Schmidt in 1904. His tactic was simple: He searched the Atlantic Ocean for concentrations of ever-smaller eel larvae. He struck pay dirt in the Sargasso Sea, an area of the middle Atlantic some 3,000 miles from the nearest of Europe's coastal streams. Schmidt found none of the adult eels, which die soon after spawning. But the area's thick masses of sargassum seaweed teemed with the tiniest larvae he had yet seen. This was the missing nursery—and a very inconvenient one at that. Even with a boost from friendly currents, it took the larvae some two and a half years to get to Europe.

Schmidt's discovery was illuminating, but it put scientists at "Go" on a different and more complicated game board. What, they have wondered ever since then, compels eels to swim such distances in order to breed, and what innate mechanism guides them on their 6,000-mile round trip? Some researchers speculate that when eels first evolved, about 140 million years ago, their breeding migrations were not the marathons they are today. The North Atlantic would have been much smaller then, perhaps no more than a few hundred miles in width. The primordial supercontinent of Pangaea had broken up some 60 million years earlier, and North America and Europe were creeping apart (pages 14-15). As the continents diverged, the nuptial journey to the Sargasso Sea lengthened imperceptibly over eons, until what had been a comparatively short splash for the eels became an extraordinary pilgrimage.

But this is no more than an educated guess. For every scientist who thinks continental drift a plausible explanation, there is another to dispute it. Eels have always been a tough case. □

WHEN GENIUS STUMBLES

Even Homer nods. This cautionary phrase, handed down from the days of the great Greek poet, warns that even the most talented individuals may lose their bearings. But among scientists, for whom the single-minded pursuit of understanding is everything, the admonition carries special force—their history is populated with towering figures who, for one reason or another, wandered off toward failure.

Some of them were lured by a powerful, but wrongheaded, distraction—a sudden spurious intuition, perhaps, that disguised the knowable false in the raiment of truth. Some were decoyed beyond the safety of their disciplines into a veritable wilderness of unfamiliar science: Physicists blundered through the thickets of biology, biologists embraced ridiculous mathematical schemes, astronomers hallucinated extraterrestrial creatures. Frequently, the deviation was mere stubbornness. Men and women of great stature, having revolutionized the way in which their world was perceived, rejected the very comprehension that flowed from their discoveries—the scientist who discovered energy in the atom, for example, scoffed at its eventual release.

The consequences of such straying have varied widely. The greatest luminaries usually have been forgiven if their lapse was momentary—distraction and absent-mindedness are seen as accessories to intelligence, after all. But an enduring scientific belief in the unbelievable has caused reputations to dim—or die. No one is safe: Even Homer nods.

Extraterrestrials Everywhere

In the field of astronomy, few names are more lustrous than that of William Herschel, reaper of a huge harvest of heavenly knowledge during the late 18th and early 19th centuries. In one respect, however, Herschel's reach for observational facts far exceeded his grasp: He was inclined to see signs of life practically everywhere he looked.

Celestial studies were a late calling for Herschel. Born in Hanover, Germany, in 1738, he chose a career as a military musician in the Hanoverian Guards. When he was 18, his regiment was ordered to England by George II, who was both Hanover's ruling prince and the British king. Herschel learned the language and found England to be so appealing that he settled there the following year. For a time, he earned his living as an organist and oboist; but in 1766 another sort of instrument came into his hands: He borrowed a small telescope and was so fascinated by what it revealed that his astronomical dabbling quickly coalesced into an obsession.

To study the skies more closely, he constructed his own reflecting telescopes, regarded as the finest of the day. Their power enabled him to catalog new stars by the thousands and determine that some of the mysterious luminous patches called nebulae were not celestial clouds but congregations of stars. Fame arrived in 1781, when Herschel spotted a previously unknown planet, subse-

quently named Uranus, that occupied an orbit beyond Saturn. For this feat, he was awarded the title of king's astronomer, along with a handsome pension.

Now able to devote all his energies to the heavens, Herschel built bigger telescopes, gathered additional shoals of stars into his observational net, determined the approximate shape of the Milky Way galaxy, found new moons around Saturn, and, in a momentous contribution to physics, discovered the existence of invisible radiation beyond the red end of the visible spectrum—the region now called infrared. But even as his scientific reputation grew, some colleagues were troubled by a persistent inter-

est that had surfaced early in the great astronomer's sky-watching career. Herschel, it seems, had been much impressed by the works of James Ferguson, a Scottish shepherd turned instrument maker who declared in his astronomical treatises that God had spread the gift of life throughout the universe. The pious Herschel hoped to find proof of this dispersion.

On many occasions, Herschel thought he had succeeded. In his observations of the Moon, for example, he believed that he saw slight changes taking place on the lunar surface and attributed them to the growth of forests. Later he wondered whether the alterations might not be towns under construction by the Lunarians. "Now if we could discover any new erection," Herschel wrote in his journal, "it is evident an exact list of those Towns that are already built will be necessary."

Herschel was persuaded not only of "the high probability of the moon's being inhabited like the earth"; he also felt that living creatures resided on all other moons

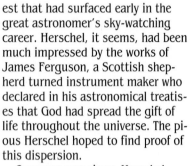

Clothed in a rich fur gown in this 1794 sketch, William Herschel holds a diagram of Uranus and two of its moons. Measurements of extreme heat on the Sun's surface *(right)* later disproved his belief that life could exist there.

and planets of the solar family, and he surmised that some of these worlds—Mars, for example—might well rival Earth in attractiveness. But his most daring proposals dealt with the Sun—in particular, with the dark areas called sunspots, now known to represent relatively cool areas on the hot, magnetically tortured exterior of the Sun. Some scholars had suggested that sunspots were smoke from solar volcanoes. Not so, said Herschel. According to his scenario, what looked like spots were in all likelihood glimpses of a layer of dense, opaque clouds seen through breaks in an overlying, luminous stratum. Within this double envelope, he believed, was a solid sphere that surely supported living creatures. Herschel ventured that these Solarians were not burned up by the blazing heat produced by the Sun's outer layer because the dense inner clouds were highly reflective. He also found a happy universal corollary to a populated Sun. "If stars are suns," he argued, "and suns are inhabitable, we see at once what an extensive field for animation opens itself to our view." Otherwise, Herschel inferred, the stars would be "mere useless brilliant points."

Herschel had his share of critics; some even called his solar ideas preposterous. English physicist Thomas Young, for instance, argued that a cloud layer could not reflect enough heat for creatures to survive on the solar surface. Nevertheless, such was Herschel's eminence that his theory was taken seriously in some quarters until the 1850s, when astronomers began to get a glimmer of how unbearably inhospitable the Sun, whose surface temperature runs to millions of degrees, really is. □

Eliminate the Negative

In the late 18th century, a British mathematician and scholar named William Frend *(below)* did his best to destroy algebra; had he succeeded, generations of equation-shy students would have owed him a debt of gratitude. But Frend was no enemy of mathematics. He mastered algebra at Cambridge University during the 1770s and, when he became a fellow and tutor at the university, taught the subject that he would later revile.

What turned Frend against algebra was its use of negative numbers, which have values of less than zero. Such quantities, he came to believe, did not really exist; they were chimeras, and the results of algebraic equations employing them were delusions.

Frend was prompted to take up his numerical cudgel by experiences in a seemingly unrelated area—religion. He was ordained a priest in the Church of England in 1783 and added the care of a flock attending a church near Cambridge to his teaching responsibilities. But in 1787 he turned his back on the Christian doctrine of the Trinity and became a Unitarian,

publishing such tracts as "An Address to the Inhabitants of Cambridge and Its Neighborhood to Turn from the False Worship of Three Persons to the Worship of the One True God." In response to Frend's heresies, Cambridge banished him, and undergraduates outraged by their tutor's exit chalked "Frend for ever!" on the venerable walls. Unrepentant, Frend resolved never again to accept anything simply because it had the backing of authority—and that included not just religious precepts but the rules of algebra. He would vigorously oppose all the false doctrines he had been duped into believing.

In the 18th century, mathematics was defined not as a symbolic system but as a science of quantities. Therefore, a negative number was simply a quantity whose value was less than nothing—pure nonsense, in the opinion of the reconstructed William Frend. Although the mathematician allowed that such numbers might be useful in calculations, he believed that they had rendered algebra obscure and difficult, even disgusting to anyone committed to logic and reason. He called for complete abandonment of the false negatives and urged mathematicians to practice subtraction only in cases where the number subtracted was equal to or less than the number from which it was ◊

subtracted. The result would never fall below zero and produce the repulsively negative quantities.

Seeking to salvage tools that seemed to be functioning perfectly well, British mathematicians struggled to answer Frend's blast. One algebraist seeking a way out of the difficulty seemed to compound it when he declared that a negative number was not only a quantity but also a "quality"—that is, susceptible to interpretation. "It is not the quantity which is less than zero; it is the quality which is inferior to nullity," the algebraist wrote. "For example, if my debts exceed my assets, I am poorer than if I had neither assets nor debts."

Such analogies were unacceptably fuzzy to Frend and his allies—for he was not algebra's only enemy. Francis Maseres, Frend's friend and an antinegative Cantabrigian, was said to be an avid, even excessive, calculator of decimal places. "The Science of Algebra, or Universal Arithmetick," he fulminated, "has been disgraced and rendered obscure and difficult, and disgust-

ing to men of a just taste for accurate reasoning."

But algebraic science stuck to the course that Frend decried, and it was destined, even before his death in 1841, to become still less a business of clear and distinct ideas. In 1830 Cambridge mathematician George Peacock observed that algebra could be a symbolic science with its own independent principles, including the use of negative numbers and subtraction of larger numbers from smaller ones.

"In symbolical algebra," said Peacock, "the rules determine the meaning of the operations, or more properly speaking, they furnish the means of interpreting them."

For those who understood him, Peacock had described the wave of the future—but Frend was not one to recant. In 1836, in a letter to an algebraist who embraced such nonsensical calculations as negative square roots, Frend declared, "I am very much inclined to believe that your figment √-1 will keep its hold among mathematicians not much longer than the Trinity does among theologians." In that, at least, he was dead right. □

Iowa State mathematics professor Alexander Abian proposes a lunar solution to Earth's weather problems. Abian's half-playful idea assumes that the Moon's gravity tips the Earth 23 degrees off the vertical. Destroying the Moon would remove the tilt, eliminating the uneven distribution of sunlight that produces extreme weather. But going vertical has a significant downside: The resulting earthquakes would wipe out civilization.

Bad Chemistry

France in the second half of the 18th century was in disarray, its social hierarchy unraveling and its institutions of governance so detested that they would be smashed in a revolution that shook all of Europe. In science, too, old and new contended, and the result would be another sort of revolution. Two of the leading scientific antagonists were Jean-Baptiste Lamarck and Antoine-Laurent Lavoisier, who had utterly different ideas about the chemical construction of nature.

Lavoisier believed in experiment, measurement, and the careful gathering of small facts to get at the root of such phenomena as combustion—still widely held to result when a flammable material gave off its store of phlogiston, a hypothetical substance said to have no weight, color, odor, or taste. Lavoisier's experiments demonstrated that phlogiston, a nonexistent substance, was merely a convenient chemical myth. Combustion, he showed, was a chemical reaction in which combining elements produced heat and light.

Lamarck worked in an opposite way, hunting for a simple logic in nature without bothering much about the particulars. He endorsed the venerable idea that just four elements—fire, earth, air, and water—gave rise to every form of matter. In spite of his disdain for fact gathering and experimentation, Lamarck was a man of wide-ranging interests who made valuable contributions to science. For years he worked in the field of botany, inventing a system for the identification of plants, among other achievements. While his theory of evolution erred in stating that individuals could pass acquired traits to their offspring, it correctly dwelled on the crucial impact environment has on characteristics. On the matter of weather, however, Lamarck betrayed his fondness for sweeping and unsubstantiated ideas: He attributed all weather to the gravitational effects of the Moon on the Earth's atmosphere, without any shred of documentation.

His chemistry suffered from his penchant for streamlining and simplicity. Chemical compounds, said Lamarck, were combinations of the four basic elements in different amounts and with bonds of differing strength. Whatever its composition, every compound had a tendency to decompose and return the elements to their natural state. Of the four elements, fire was by far the most important and came in several guises, one of which was the energy of life itself.

It was all very tidy—a marked contrast to the proliferation of elements and reactions that seemed to be indicated by Lavoisier's methods. In Lavoisier's hands, complained Lamarck, the principles of chemistry were "daily becoming more complicated, less clear, and far less general." Perhaps so, but modern chemistry would be built on his rival's foundation of facts, not Lamarck's scaffolding of speculations. Ironically, their fates were the reverse of what their science merited: Lamarck's career flourished as France went through revolution; Lavoisier, a member of the nobility and a tax collector, was guillotined. □

Aided by his wife, Antoine-Laurent Lavoisier uses a pneumatic trough to study the behavior of gases in the bas relief above, part of a Paris monument destroyed in World War II. Rival Jean-Baptiste Lamarck, shown at left in an 1802 portrait by Charles Thevenin, shunned experimentation in favor of intuition.

Od Man Out

In the scientific struggle to comprehend nature's inner workings, imagination can be a liability as well as an asset, sometimes leading an overeager investigator into a world of illusion. Such was the case with Karl von Reichenbach, a talented German chemist and industrialist who spent much of his career pursuing a mysterious force that he thought pervaded the universe.

Born in Stuttgart, Germany, in 1788, Reichenbach showed a bent for offbeat ideas early on. At the age of 16, he formed a secret society that was dedicated to establishing a German Reich in the South Pacific—a scheme that earned him a few months in prison as a political agitator. After that chastening experience, he turned to a career in industrial chemistry. The highly efficient charcoal oven Reichenbach developed produced fuel at a low cost for his ironworks and made him a wealthy man. He also isolated two valuable chemical compounds, paraffin and creosote, from wood tar. He purchased several estates, was knighted, and retired to a castle in Austria. And there, in the mid-1840s, Reichenbach began to perform experiments designed to penetrate a strange force he had discovered—something he called od.

Od, Reichenbach decided, was as ubiquitous and fundamental as electromagnetism, but it could not be perceived by everyone—a special sensitivity to od was required. Over the years he identified more than a hundred sensitives, most of them excitable young women, who supposedly employed od for such feats as detecting water underground or making a pendulum move without touching it. From his studies of sensitives, he concluded that negative od manifested itself as a blue light and positive od as a red light. To a sensitive, negative od was cool and pleasant, positive od warm and unpleasant. Reichenbach worked out an exhaustive list of other od facts: its strong directionality; its bipolar nature, which caused objects embued with like od to repel one another; its differing strength in various susbtances; and so on. The interplay of od, Reichenbach asserted, explained much in human affairs. Seating honored guests on the host's right, for example, automatically stimulated a favorable od flow and made for a pleasant party. Not even the dead escaped the reach of od: The ghosts sometimes seen in graveyards were simply odic light given off by decaying corpses.

The father of od published many books and pamphlets explaining his universal force, but when he presented the results of his odic experiments to professors at the University of Berlin, they were not just unappreciative—they were downright hostile. Nor, as time passed, did his odic knowledge serve him well in nonscientific matters. Reichenbach lost his fortune to bad luck and some unwise investments and gradually withdrew into seclusion in his castle. But his interest in the strange power he had been the first to describe evidently never waned. Neighbors said that Reichenbach often visited the local graveyard wrapped in a long white mantle to watch for emanations of odic light. □

Chemist Karl von Reichenbach's calm smile in this 1832 lithograph conceals a budding lifelong obsession with a supposedly fundamental force he called "od."

For the Birds

During the first half of the 19th century geologists accumulated evidence of a venerable Earth many millions of years old. Moreover, they knew it had once been inhabited by creatures unlike any in the world today, as indicated by fossils and prints found in ancient rocks. But the nature of these creatures—inferred from a bone fragment or faint impression in stone—was not always clear, and many a surmise went wide of the mark.

Such was the case with some indentations found in rocks of the Connecticut River valley. In 1835 these markings came to the attention of Edward Hitchcock, a professor of geology, chemistry, natural history, and natural theology at Amherst College and later its president. They were certainly footprints, most of them three toed and, although very big, birdlike; natives of that area said that the fossil tracks had been made by "Noah's raven." For the rest of his life, Hitchcock spent his summers searching for additional evidence of these mysterious creatures and a way of classifying them—a tricky task, since there were no skeletal remains to suggest an anatomical shape. Although the size of many prints was extraordinary—18 inches long, with a six-foot stride—Hitchcock con-

curred with the folk assumption of an avian origin. The tracks had been made, he finally concluded, by apterous, or wingless, ostrichlike birds on a sandy shore that later hardened into sandstone. "I have seen, in scientific vision," he wrote, "an apterous bird, some twelve or fifteen feet high,—nay, large flocks of them,—walking over the muddy surface, followed by many others of analogous character, but of a smaller size." Within this imaginary tableau, he identified 32 species of erect, three- and four-toed wading birds, along with a motley collection of lizards, amphibians, and other nonavian animals.

Edward Hitchcock's scheme was dealt a serious jolt in 1861, when the fossil remains of a creature that was dubbed *Archaeopteryx* was discovered in a limestone deposit in Germany. The impressions of feathers in the fine-grained limestone left no doubt that this creature was a bird. Unfortunately for Hitchcock, the rock stratum of *Archaeopteryx* was millions of years younger than the sandstone of the Connecticut River valley. This implied that Hitchcock's species were substantially older—and, presumably, less advanced—than *Archaeopteryx* and suggested that Hitchcock's fossil footprints had not been made by birds at all.

Despite the troublesome intru- ◊

sion of the German fossil, Hitchcock clung to his vision of huge birds striding along the Connecticut strand, a view he held until his death in 1864. He was wrong, but understandably so: Birds and reptiles have a common ancestry that is reflected in their feet, among other features, and the scholar had confused them. In fact, Hitchcock's animals had not been birds, but dinosaurs, earthbound and featherless. The Amherst professor, while wrong, had nonetheless performed a considerable scientific service: His tracks were the first convincing evidence that dinosaurs had once roamed North America. □

Nasal Passage

On any list of major intellectual contributors to modernity, the name of Sigmund Freud, the father of psychoanalysis, is likely to enjoy a prominent place. The name of Wilhelm Fliess is equally certain to be absent. Yet these two men were kindred thinkers in the last decade of the 19th century, convinced that they possessed a key not only to the workings of human nature but perhaps to the entire cosmos.

They first met in 1887 when Wilhelm Fliess interrupted his practice as an ear, nose, and throat specialist in Berlin to visit Vienna for postgraduate studies. Freud, a Viennese native and 31 years old at the time, was an obscure psychiatrist and lecturer in neurology. The two became friends, and their relationship deepened over a period of years—difficult years for Freud. He was prey to depression and much derided for his efforts to trace the emotional problems of his patients to sexual conflicts in early childhood. Fliess alone encouraged the psychiatrist

during this dark period, and in 1894 a grateful Freud wrote to him, "Your praise is nectar and ambrosia to me." Nor did Freud limit himself to gratitude—he enthusiastically endorsed his friend's increasingly eccentric ideas.

Intelligent, ambitious, and vain, Fliess sought what he called the "foundations of an exact biology." After much pondering, he decided that all things in nature were controlled by two underlying cycles: a male cycle of 23 days and a female cycle of 28 days. In living creatures, he claimed, these cycles began at birth and regulated all mental and bodily states by their interplay. Fliess even determined a person's supposed date of death by performing various arithmetical operations with 23 and 28. The cycles, in Fliess's judgment, very likely determined all sorts of nonbiological phenomena, such as the movements of celestial bodies. He engaged in elaborate numerical games

With matching beards and jackets, Sigmund Freud (left) and his eccentric friend Wilhelm Fliess (right) pose for an 1890 photograph. Obsessed with numbers, Fliess also believed that the nose was linked to sexual activity.

with 23 and 28 to adapt them to the operations of the universe, adding or subtracting them, applying exponents, multiplying them together, introducing constants, and so on. Eventually, the manipulations always produced the desired numerical result. Freud believed that Fliess's obsessive numerology could explain almost everything that had happened in his own life—in fact, he was convinced that he would die at 51, the sum of 23 and 28.

But numbers formed only part of the ear, nose, and throat doctor's "exact biology." Fliess also believed that all humans were bisexual and that the nose was the source of various disorders elsewhere in the body, many of them remediable by nasal anesthesia with cocaine. There was, according to Fliess, a direct physiological link between the nose and the sexual organs: Inside the nose, he said, were "genital spots" associated with many sexual and reproductive matters, including menstrual problems and difficulties during pregnancy.

Fliess operated twice on the enthralled Freud's nose. In 1895 the admiring analyst sent Fliess a patient, a woman whose neurosis Freud ascribed to sex-based anxieties—which could, of course, be eased by treating the nose. Fliess operated—and inadvertently left a wad of gauze in her nasal cavity. She experi-enced a near-fatal series of hemorrhages, which Freud attributed to hysteria and to her longing to gain his affection. He absolved Wilhelm Fliess of any professional failure, declaring that "as far as the blood is concerned, you are completely without blame."

Eventually Freud began to have doubts about his Berlin friend, and by the end of the century, the two had ceased trading scientific ideas. Fliess continued to explore his theories, however, publishing lengthy explanations of how numbers ruled the cosmos. His ideas suffered a blow when it was shown that 23 and 28 were not, as Fliess had erroneously believed, mathematically unique—and that a desired result could be easily derived from any two positive numbers that lack a common divisor. Resolutely wrong, Fliess pursued his numerical fantasy until his death in 1928.

Despite Fliess's errors, some popular versions of his predictive system live on in schemes built around the notion of so-called biorhythms. Proponents of biorhythms claim to forecast the performance of body and mind on the basis of the two Fliessian cycles plus an additional 33-day cycle advanced in the 1920s by an Austrian teacher and engineer named Arthur Teltscher. Known as the intellectual cycle, this third oscillation supposedly governs such mental powers as concentration and memory.

Freud died in 1939—far past the time that he had once believed was allotted to him and not quite by Fliessian numbers after all. He was 83 years old—23 plus 28 plus 32, one year short of a full intellectual cycle. □

+
0
-

November 5   November 16

Above, a weary Clark Gable flashes his trademark grin in 1960, the year that he died from the second of two heart attacks. Supposedly, both of the attacks could have been predicted by biorhythms, which are modern descendants of Fliess's cycles. In the chart shown above, Gable's first attack appears on November 5, and the second, fatal one 11 days later. Biorhythm enthusiasts warn of danger when cycles intersect the centerline; in the actor's case, the male cycle of aggression and strength (blue) and the female cycle of creativity and intuition (red) crossed the centerline near his heart attacks, with only the intellectual cycle (yellow) at a propitious level.

Ill Repute

The scientific camp that decried Charles Darwin's theory of evolution had no member more prestigious than Sir Richard Owen, Britain's reigning authority on comparative anatomy. But, while highly respected as a scientist, Owen had a curiously quarrelsome, meanspirited side that finally lost the argument to Darwin and Owen's reputation with it.

Trained as a physician in Edinburgh in the 1820s, Owen had established himself as a masterful dissector. But a stint as an assistant in the huge natural-history collection of the Royal College of Surgeons prompted Owen to desert medicine for biology. He went on to break new anatomical ground all across the animal kingdom, describing and cataloging creatures ranging from lowly parasites to whales. Long interested in paleontology, Owen became an authority on Australia's extinct marsupial mammals and on dinosaurs—it was he who coined their generic name from the Greek words *deinos* (terrible) and *sauros* (lizard).

In 1836 Owen had the good fortune to be introduced to Charles Darwin, who had just returned from a five-year-long voyage that had taken him around the world. The huge collection of specimens he had acquired in South America included a large number of fossils, which Darwin now turned over to his new acquaintance. To a paleontologist of Owen's expertise the message of this fossil record was starkly clear: Countless species had come and gone over an enormously long period of time. He had, however, no clear-cut view of what might have caused this changing parade of species, although he ascribed it to a divine plan. As to a possible mechanism, he offered the vague suggestion that animals had "an innate tendency to deviate from parental type." Further than this Owen was not prepared to go.

Darwin's 1859 *Origin of Species*, on the other hand, proposed the evolutionary mechanism of natural selection and backed it up with masses of evidence suggesting that random variations within members of a species made some better adapted than others to survive adverse environmental conditions. Ignoring Darwin's generosity with his South American fossils and their long acquaintance, Owen quickly took the offensive with an anonymous attack in the April 1860 issue of the prominent *Edinburgh Review*. Hardly bothering with analysis, Owen brushed aside the evolutionary mechanism Darwin argued for so well. The assault was couched in tones so hateful that no one was fooled as to the author of the review. Darwin wrote a friend that it was "without doubt by Owen," adding that it was "extremely malignant" and perhaps very damaging to Darwin's theory.

No doubt encouraged by the effect of his initial volley, Owen went public and took on the role of leader

Leaning against a mound of assorted animal bones in the photographic portrait above, British zoologist Richard Owen forfeited his considerable scientific reputation when he fought Darwinism with false claims about the anatomy of ape brains.

of the anti-Darwinist faction in Britain, only to suffer a series of stinging defeats in open debates with pro-natural-selection scientists. It was a bitter pill for an envious, arrogant man to choke down.

Since the weight of his prestige could not silence the Darwinists, Owen turned to anatomical ammunition he could aim at the most sensitive point in Darwin's scheme: the implication that humans were closely related to apes. Owen said his studies showed that the cerebral lobes of an ape's brain were arranged differently from those of a human. Moreover, he claimed, humans were unique because they alone possessed a lobe called the hippocampus minor.

Coming from Owen, the man at the apex of anatomical science, the allegation was astonishing—but not for its devastating effect on Darwin. In his intemperate desire to destroy the enemy, Owen had gone too far: His anatomical evidence was simply false, as zoologists in the Darwinian camp hastened to point out. Few of Owen's colleagues believed that a man of his experience could have blundered so badly; some even called him a liar. One, the brilliant and aggressive Thomas Henry Huxley, swore to a friend, "Before I have done with that mendacious humbug I will nail him out, like a kite to a barn door, an example to all evil-doers."

It was not necessary—Owen had already nailed himself out, squandering his reputation in vituperative assaults and what appeared to be fabricated evidence. After his death in 1892 he would be remembered, but not for his many solid achievements—Owen became eternally the man who had gone after Darwin, lied, and lost. □

Survival of the Fitter

The history of science offers many examples of great minds thinking alike, but one of the most notable instances of convergent genius— the independent discovery of the prime mechanism of evolution by British naturalists Charles Darwin and Alfred Russel Wallace—was followed by a parting of the ways.

In Victorian England, the subject of evolution was a scientific puzzle, but not a new one. From the latter half of the 18th century on, there had been many advocates of the idea that the characteristics of plants and animals changed over time—Erasmus Darwin, Charles's naturalist grandfather, was a stout evolutionist. What was missing was a mechanism for such change. In the search for that mechanism, Charles Darwin, being older, had a sizable head start on Alfred Wallace. Yet the two men, working separately, hit upon the same solution almost at the same time.

Darwin spent 5 years in the 1830s as a naturalist aboard HMS *Beagle*, a British ship that had carried out surveys from Tahiti to South Africa to South America and the Galápagos Islands. He came home in 1836 with a huge store of information gleaned from ▷

The simultaneous discoverers of natural selection, Charles Darwin *(above)* and Alfred Russel Wallace, at right in a portrait painted over a photograph, differed on one key point: Wallace exempted humans from the otherwise universal process of species evolution.

observing animals, but not until 8 years later did he first commit to paper a scheme summarizing an evolutionary mechanism. Individuals of the same species, Darwin proposed, differed in their ability to cope with environmental conditions because of differences in their physical makeup. The better-adapted individuals flourished, the less-adapted failed, and the species as a whole evolved accordingly. Not one to rush the mechanism that he called natural selection into print, the methodical Darwin spent another 15 years marshaling his facts and strengthening the logic of his theory, eventually made public in 1859 in *The Origin of Species.*

Wallace, 14 years younger, also took to the field, exploring the Amazon Basin from 1848 to 1852, then moving on to the Malaya Archipelago to become an authority on its flora and fauna. In 1858 Wallace, laid up with malaria, feverishly mulled over checks on human population such as war and famine. His thoughts strayed to similar pressures on animals, and as he later wrote, "there suddenly flashed upon me the idea of *the survival of the fittest*—that the individuals removed by these checks must be, on the whole, *inferior* to those that survived." Within two hours Wallace had sketched out the main points of his evolutionary theory.

Wallace fired off a letter outlining his idea to kindred spirit Charles Darwin. The two had exchanged a few letters previously—Darwin had initiated the correspondence with an admiring letter after reading a book and several articles Wallace had written. Stunned by Wallace's bombshell, Darwin momentarily considered dropping his book project and letting Wallace reap the glory. But his friends took matters into their own hands, arranged a presentation of both men's work that credited Wallace as a codiscoverer of natural selection but made it clear that Darwin had arrived at the idea first by a comfortable margin. Wallace was entirely gracious in the affair. In later years he referred to the theory of natural selection as "Darwinism."

But on the issue of human evolution the two men soon found themselves at odds. Wallace, whose standards of scientific proof were elastic enough to accommodate a belief in telepathy and communication with the dead, insisted that the usual laws of evolution did not apply to creatures possessing human intellect. "A superior intelligence has guided the development of man," he wrote. He even suggested that not just one but an unknown number of "higher intelligent beings" directly influenced human intellect and some physical traits as well. Thus, according to Wallace, the evolution of the human mind had been largely free of the rigors of natural selection.

Unlike many of his colleagues, Wallace believed that the mental capacity of all peoples was essentially equal, whatever their race or culture. But in contemporary primitive societies, Wallace felt, and probably in early humans as well, a significant portion of brain power had lain dormant because it provided no survival advantage whatsoever. By Wallace's logic, the development of superior intelligence—or any other attribute that did not contribute to survival—simply could not be explained by Darwinism.

Wallace argued that another peculiar human trait—relative hairlessness—was actually harmful because it reduced one's protection from the elements. He also saw no reason to think nature would favor "the wonderful power, range, flexibility, and sweetness, of the musical sounds producible by the human larynx, especially in the female sex." Savages, he argued, chose mates for health, strength, and beauty—a coloratura soprano would have no sexual edge over a tone-deaf alto.

Darwin was appalled. On a copy of a paper setting forth Wallace's views, he scribbled "No!!" and he chided his cotheorist, "I hope you have not murdered too completely your own and my child." In spite of their differences, however, the two remained on friendly terms until Darwin's death in 1882, and Wallace enjoyed a productive career well into the next century. But his scientific reputation never quite recovered from exempting humans from the struggle he and Darwin had so clearly perceived. □

Cheerleader

When Charles Darwin published his path-breaking ideas on evolution in 1859, a young German zoologist was so impressed that he foresaw a complete overhaul of biology—and given Darwin's reticent nature, the zoologist thought he might be the man to lead the way. Ernst Haeckel became a fervent proselytizer for the new theory, preaching the word at scientific meetings and writing a flood of articles and books over four decades. His goal was grand: to transform Darwinism into an all-embracing theory of life.

The two men first became ac-

quainted in the 1860s through the letters they exchanged, and Haeckel subsequently visited Darwin in England. Haeckel was a boisterous, talkative person, and after one visit Mrs. Darwin wrote to her son Leonard, "Haeckel came on Tuesday. He was very nice and hearty and affectionate, but he bellowed out his bad English in such a voice that he nearly deafened us."

Although he apparently preferred theorizing and speechifying to fact gathering, Haeckel nevertheless was a many-sided scientist. He pioneered in plankton; became an expert in invertebrates such as sea sponges and jellyfish; wrote the

first history of evolutionary theories; and, at a time when heredity was still a grand puzzle, suggested that cell nuclei are critical to the transmission of traits.

Although a scientist, Haeckel had the instincts of an artist. He had once considered taking up painting as a career, and he always felt a deep attraction to such aesthetic qualities as unity and symmetry. Darwinian evolution evoked in his mind the ultimate vision of unity—there was, Haeckel concluded, no essential difference between life and inorganic matter. The notion of continuity between them, which he labeled monism, did not come to him

Surrounded by papers, drawings, and specimens of sea creatures, German zoologist and avid Darwin enthusiast Ernst Haeckel works in his study in Jena, Germany, in 1903.

out of nowhere. Its germ had been generated early in his career, when he had studied one-celled creatures called radiolarians and noticed how strikingly similar their form was to crystals common in minerals and other lifeless matter.

In Haeckel's monistic universe, the primary distinction between lifeless and living matter was movement—and the cause of movement was rooted in the peculiar proper- ◊

ties of carbon. According to Haeckel, life had arisen spontaneously when carbon, along with oxygen, sulfur, nitrogen, and hydrogen, had formed complex molecules that clumped into structureless blobs of protoplasm. From this first living creature, or monera, had come the animal and the vegetable kingdoms, and a third borderland between them that he called the Protista.

But, in Haeckel's view, the continuity between the inorganic and the organic realms was not strictly chemical. Every creature, from humans to protozoa, possessed a soul—and so did every atom. As Haeckel himself put it, "No matter can be conceived without spirit, and no spirit without matter."

Pressing Darwinian evolution to extremes its author had never dreamed of, Haeckel traced the descent of all higher, multicellular animals from an ancestral globe of cells that he called the gastraea. A species' descent, according to Haeckel, was recorded in the successive changes of each individual embryo. In its earliest days, the embryo's form displayed the characteristics of its earliest ancestors, from the gastraea onward. As the embryo developed, its sequential transformations represented, in chronological order, more recent forebears. Thus, in the gestation of every species, millions of years of evolution were compressed into a span of days or weeks or months.

The notion that ontogeny, the development of the individual, recapitulated phylogeny, the development of the species, was not entirely Haeckel's invention. However, he vastly inflated its importance, conferring on it the status of "fundamental biogenetic law." Besides revealing the history of a species, he believed, comparing embryos of different animals would indicate how closely related they were.

Numerous skeptics among Haeckel's con-

temporaries complained that he regularly ignored contravening evidence, and they also denounced the manner in which he used his artistic skills to bend the facts about embryos. Some biologists even went so far as to call his illustrations forgeries. But the wrongness of Haeckel's biogenetic law scarcely lessened its impact. The cosmic sweep of his evolutionary world view won him a huge following among nonscientists. In 1899 he published *The Riddle of the Universe*, a rambling discourse on biology, cosmology, psychology, and theology. In it he elaborated on his "monistic religion," which embraced what the biologist-philosopher described as the three "cult ideals of the True, the Good, and the Beautiful." Germans snapped up over 100,000 copies. The book was also a big seller in England and was even used in Japanese schools.

Haeckel's scientific religion eventually lost its adherents, and his biogenetic law in time lost the last shreds of plausibility. Still, long after experimental embryologists had repealed Haeckel's "fundamental" law, mid-20th-century biology teachers were still drilling the handy mnemonic "ontogeny recapitulates phylogeny" into their students.

Perhaps the greatest contribution made by Haeckel, however, was the service he inadvertently did Charles Darwin. In Germany the pulpit-banging Haeckel drew to himself "all the hatred and bitterness which Evolution excited in certain quarters," according to one observer, with the result that "in a surprisingly short time it became the fashion in Germany that Haeckel alone should be abused, while Darwin was held up as the ideal of forethought and moderation." □

At left, an 1866 illustration of Ernst Haeckel's proposed evolutionary tree depicts a trunk of inanimate protoplasm, or "monera," branching into the kingdoms of plants *(left)*, minute organisms that the zoologist called protists *(center)*, and animals *(right)*.

Blue-green vegetation, tan desert, brown soil, and interlinked canals fill circular sketches of the planet Mars *(insets)* published by Percival Lowell in 1906. Seven decades later, a NASA Viking orbiter photographed ancient riverbeds on Mars *(background)* but found no artificial structures.

Lowell of Mars

No sooner were the first crude telescopes trained on the heavens in the 17th century than astronomers began to see similarities between Earth and Mars. The fourth planet rotated in a 24-hour, 40-minute day; it had white polar caps that advanced and retreated in response to the Martian seasons; and it displayed periodic changes of color suggestive of clouds and weather. In 1877 the Italian astronomer Giovanni Schiaparelli studied Mars during a period of orbital proximity to Earth. Although his telescope was small, Schiaparelli felt sure he saw a network of fine, crisscrossing lines on the Martian surface. He called them *canali*, meaning "channels" or "grooves."

When news of Schiaparelli's canali was published in English, however, what he described was translated as "canals," inspiring a rash of speculations about Martian master builders. One excited soul recommended that a Europe-size inscription of the Pythagorean theorem be traced in the Sahara Desert to show watching Martians proof of Earthly intelligence.

Of all the believers in Martian life by far the most influential one was Percival Lowell, who fashioned a career as a kind of celestial Columbus. Born into a family of wealthy and distinguished Bostonians, Lowell earned honors in mathematics at Harvard, devoted himself to business for a few years, gave it up to travel the world, and finally, in ◊

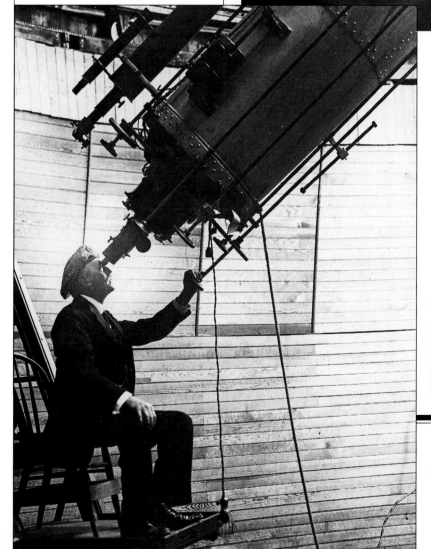

Photographed at his private Arizona observatory on Mars Hill, gentleman astronomer Percival Lowell *(left)* turns a powerful refractor telescope toward Venus, one of the heavenly bodies he studied between his surveys of imagined structures on Mars.

1893, at age 39, plunged headlong into astronomy. Sky watching had long been a hobby for him, and he was especially fascinated by Giovanni Schiaparelli's writings about the "canals" of Mars. A favorable period for viewing that planet was approaching, and Lowell reached into his deep pockets to build an observatory in the high, clear air near Flagstaff, Arizona.

What Lowell observed in two months of staring through his 18-inch Flagstaff telescope in the summer of 1894 allowed him to map out a system of canals far more extensive and regular than Schiaparelli's. Lowell became the world's most indefatigable Mars booster, triumphantly publicizing his network of some 180 canals in lectures, books, and articles that enthralled the public almost as much as they irritated other astronomers.

Lowell often criticized scientists for a lack of imagination and took pride in his own, but he sensed no possible element of fancy in this matter. The canals had "the clear cut character of a steel engraving." They were remarkably straight, sometimes thousands of miles long, and were connected to large circular "oases," more than 100 miles in diameter. Given the apparent aridity of Mars and what Lowell took to be Earth-type icecaps at the poles, he concluded that the canals constituted a gigantic irrigation system built to convey water across the dry landscape and make the oases verdant when seasonal warmth melted the polar coverings.

The construction of an irrigation system on such a vast scale implied that the Martians were highly intelligent. But in other ways they were, in Lowell's estimation, unlike Earthlings. They had, he said, a "non-bellicose character" that enabled them to "work together for the common good." Lowell's Martians were a heroic people, as well, fated to lose their contest with the steady desiccation of their planet, which, Lowell wrote, "will roll a dead world in space, its evolutionary career forever ended."

Lowell was undeterred by the failure of other astronomers to see what he saw or by proof that Mars seemed utterly devoid of water. He paid no attention to one critic's experimental demonstration that, in a scene full of fine detail, the eye tends to perceive illusory geometrical connections. He clung to his belief in an endangered Martian civilization to the end of his life.

But the notion of Martian canals was a long time dying even after its champion's death in 1916. It was finally put to rest only during the 1960s by the unmanned Mariner space probes to Mars. The images they transmitted showed a lifeless desert swept by dust storms and pockmarked with craters. In all of the bleak terrain there was no canal—or any other sign of Lowell's noble race of doomed engineers. □

Atom Smashers

The idea that invisibly small particles of matter called atoms make up the universe is an old one, first proposed by the ancient Greeks and subsequently endorsed by such intellectual giants as Isaac Newton. Yet as late as the dawn of the 20th century, the existence of atoms was still unproven—indeed, it was strongly denied in some quarters. Leading the debate were three European luminaries: Austrian physicist Ludwig Boltzmann, squared off against his fellow physicist and countryman Ernest Mach and German chemist Wilhelm Ostwald. Boltzmann believed that atoms, which to this day cannot be observed directly, could be seen indirectly in the generation of heat. As a proponent of the kinetic theory of heat, he declared that heat was a mechanical phenomenon, caused by friction between moving atoms. When atoms by the billions randomly jostled against one another, Boltzmann theorized, they simultaneously created and transmitted heat. During the 1870s he used his great math-

One of the few published images of Austrian physicist Ludwig Boltzmann (left) was printed in 1898, just eight years before his suicide ended a lifetime of scientific controversy over his belief in the existence of atoms.

...ematical gifts to describe this mechanical view of heat in statistical terms.

But Ernest Mach would have none of his compatriot's mathematical argument for atoms. An expert on optics and acoustics whose research is memorialized in the Mach number—a representation of speed in terms of the local speed of sound waves—he had, like many other 19th-century scientists, a strong philosophical bias in favor of observation. Theorizing about heat, atoms, and statistics proved absolutely nothing, in his opinion. What Mach valued was the evidence of the senses, and to anyone who spoke of atoms as a fact, he would angrily counter, "Have you ever seen one?"

Wilhelm Ostwald, a physical chemist later honored with a Nobel Prize, had an even more extreme aversion to Boltzmann's hypothesis: He asserted that matter, the supposed stuff of atoms, was merely a convenient abstraction—the mind's way of expressing the interplay of energy. The true constituents of physical reality, Ostwald said, were not matter, space, and time, but energy, space, and time. He was not alone in preferring this view, called energetics, to a mechanistic scheme based on atoms. Boltzmann

found himself very much in the minority among scientists. The embattled physicist fought hard for his ideas, but the acrimonious arguments with his opponents took a toll. Boltzmann worried about his failing eyesight and his intellectual powers, which seemed to him to be fading. The bouts of depression that had plagued him for several years became more severe, and in 1906 he committed suicide.

Ironically, support for Ludwig Boltzmann's hypothesis was building when he died.

The year before, Albert Einstein had shown that Brownian motion, the random vibrations of very small particles, is, as Boltzmann had inferred, the product of atomic activity. And Ernest Rutherford of Cambridge University was using the odd property of radioactivity in certain elements to explore the hitherto hidden architecture of atomic nuclei *(pages 56-57)*. If Boltzmann had stayed his hand those few more years, he might have discovered hope, rather than despair, in his tiny statistical universe. □

Lacking observational evidence of the existence of atoms, such eminent turn-of-the-20th-century scientists as Austrian physicist Ernest Mach *(above, left)* and German chemist Wilhelm Ostwald *(above)* scoffed at the idea that such particles might be real.

Simon Says

When the eminent American astronomer Simon Newcomb pronounced his verdict on the likelihood of powered flight in a speech in 1901, most of the world had already made up its mind. Experimental flying machines had been flailing at the air like fledgling birds for decades, and small, unmanned craft had already flown. Such famous inventors as Thomas Edison and Alexander Graham Bell were optimistic. Given the amount of effort and intelligence being applied to the problem, it had to be just a matter of time before the age-old dream of human flight was finally realized.

Simon Newcomb disagreed. It was quite impossible, he said.

Newcomb, then 66, was a man of stature—an expert in the mathematically demanding field of celestial mechanics, a member of many scientific societies, and a prolific writer on technical subjects. On the particular issue of heavier-than-air flying machines, however, he was relentlessly negative. His most fundamental objection involved size: The weight of a flying machine, he noted, would tend to increase cubically with an increase in size, whereas the area of the surfaces designed to support the craft in the air and propel it would tend to increase only by the square. In other words, the larger such a machine became, the less capable of flight it would be. His idea also explained, to him at least, why in nature "the most numerous fliers are little insects, and the rising series stops with the condor, which, though having much less weight than a man, is said to fly with difficulty when gorged with food."

Even if the weight problem could be overcome, powered flight made no sense, in Newcomb's judgment. Unlike a ship or a train, he argued, a flying machine could not stop safely in midpassage but "could remain in the air only by the action of its machinery, and would fall to the ground like a wounded bird the moment any accident stopped it." Surely it was obvious, he went on, that if a ship sank to the bottom of the sea whenever it stopped, the dream of steam navigation would have come to naught.

Two years after Newcomb advised flight enthusiasts to put aside their dreams, Orville Wright wobbled over the sands of Kitty Hawk in a self-propelled craft, and, before the decade was out, he and his brother were building aircraft that could fly more than 100 miles at a stretch. Given these surprising facts, Newcomb had to admit that he had erred on some points, but he regretted that such pioneering achievements "had led to a widespread impression that aerial flight is soon to play an important part as an agency in commerce." That, of course, could never be. Not only was there the disastrous problem of an aircraft's falling to the ground if it stopped in midflight—navigation promised to be extremely difficult on a windy day. Moreover, Newcomb's conclusions about size suggested that, while machines might fly, they would never be able to carry more than one person safely.

And, he wondered, what was the point of flying,

anyway? After all, "every part of the earth's surface on which men now live in large numbers, and in which important industries are prosecuted, can now be reached by railways." With that statement, Simon Newcomb rested his case, determinedly wrong to the end. □

Until his death in 1909, astronomer and naval officer Simon Newcomb *(above)* stood by his claim that human flight would never be practical, despite such evidence to the contrary as the Wright brothers' 20-mile flight in 1905 in the *Flyer III (background, left).*

Heated Argument

In 1902 two young scientists at Montreal's McGill University, Ernest Rutherford and Frederick Soddy, announced that they had discovered the mechanism that made radium, uranium, and other radioactive elements feel warm to the touch. The heat was generated, they said, when atoms spontaneously broke down and emitted a variety of particles. Moreover, losing particles changed the disintegrating atom so radically that it was sometimes transmuted into a different element.

At the time, even the existence of atoms was not universally accepted *(pages 50-51)*, and virtually all scientists assumed that if there were such things as atoms they must be permanent and indestructible; they could interact, but they could not change. As the two researchers prepared to publish their findings, they worried about the reaction of the scientific community. "They'll have our heads off as alchemists," Ernest Rutherford remarked, referring to the age-old alchemical quest to transmute base metals into gold.

For the most part, their colleagues' response proved to be one of great excitement and admiration. But there were loud protests, some of them from

chemists who felt that the behavior of atoms was their bailiwick, not that of the physicists. The most serious challenge, however, came from a physicist, Lord Kelvin of Britain, a 79-year-old living legend.

Born William Thomson in Belfast, Ireland, in 1824, Kelvin had ranged the dominion of physics like some warrior of old, wielding the sharp lance of his mathematics to elucidate the workings of electricity, magnetism, heat, fluids, and much more. In one particularly famous bit of work, he had used his expertise on thermodynamics to assess the age of the Earth. He believed—correctly—that the planet had been formed from an assemblage of material that heated to a molten state as it collapsed under the influence of its own gravity, then cooled and hardened. By analyzing the heat conductivity of rocks, the temperatures in deep mines, and the rate at which heat would radiate into space, Kelvin concluded that the Earth has existed for no more than 400 million years and possibly as little as 25 million years. By 1897 he had settled on the low end of this range. His conclusions caused great distress for geologists whose studies seemed to indicate that the Earth's age was far greater than Lord Kelvin allowed. There was even more skepticism among Darwinian evolutionists because the ◊

The picture of authority in academic robe and long white beard, British physicist William Thomson, Lord Kelvin *(above),* was so intimidating that few colleagues dared contradict his firm but irrational opposition to the idea of radioactive decay.

span seemed much too brief to accommodate the slow process of change in plants and animals. But Kelvin's limits, based on his closely reckoned cooling rate for the Earth, seemed unassailable—at least until Rutherford and Soddy came along. Their discovery renewed the age debate: The disintegration of radioactive elements within the Earth would have resulted in substantial heating, throwing the orderly cooling that was envisioned by Kelvin far wide of the mark.

At the annual meeting of the British Association for the Advancement of Science in 1903, Rutherford gave a report on the radioactivity studies, then listened gloomily as another physicist, Sir Oliver Lodge, presented a paper by the absent Lord Kelvin. Linking atomic disintegration and radioactivity was nonsense, Kelvin declared through his surrogate, because radioactivity was the result of energy derived from the "ether," a hypothetical medium widely believed to pervade all of space *(pages 81-83)*. He did not venture to describe this energy, instead saying that "it exists in a form which we have not yet found a means of detecting." In effect, Lord Kelvin was denying that Rutherford and Soddy had discovered a new heat source in radioactivity.

A few months later Rutherford and Lord Kelvin met at a social gathering. "Lord Kelvin has talked radium most of the day," Rutherford later wrote to his wife, "and I admire his confidence in talking about a subject of which he had taken the trouble to learn so little."

Although increasingly isolated in his position, Kelvin never gave up the fight. He died in 1907, still certain that the heating of the Earth was entirely due to gravitational collapse. But even before Lord Kelvin's death, an American chemist named Bernard Boltwood worked out the rates at which uranium would decay into a succession of lighter elements until it was transmuted into lead, its stable and final form. He used this timetable and measurements of the proportion of the relevant elements in rocks to show that Earth is more than a billion years old. Radioactive dating would later yield an age of 4.6 billion years—a figure that, like Kelvin's 25 million, is also subject to change. □

In 1896, smudged exposures on a photographic plate *(left)* stored near uranium ore led to the discovery of radioactivity by French physicist Antoine Henri Becquerel. The breakthrough inspired a host of eager experimenters that included Ernest Rutherford, pictured below in a McGill University laboratory in 1905.

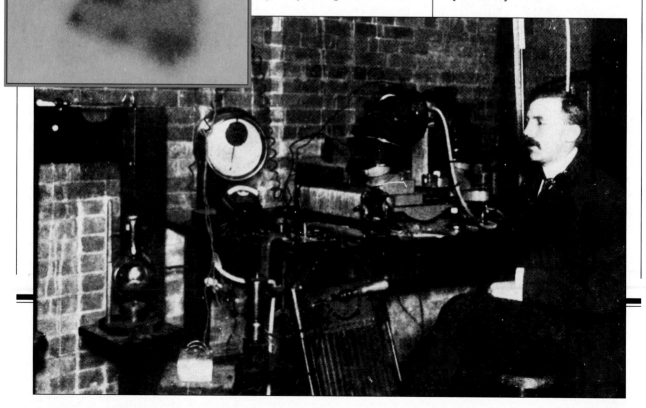

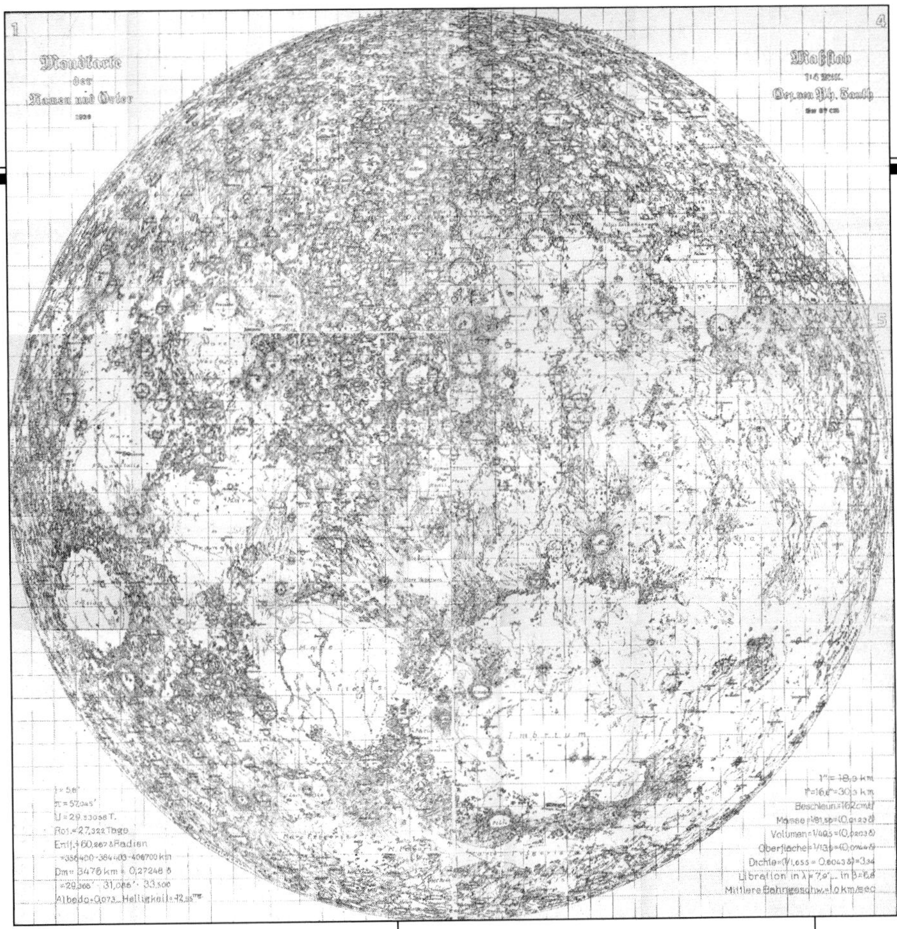

Despite his erroneous belief that the Moon was wrapped in ice, German astronomy enthusiast Philipp Fauth compiled such meticulously detailed maps of lunar terrain as the 1936 composite shown at left.

Fauth claimed that, early in lunar history, huge lakes had formed in the crust and then frozen, and a cosmic hailstorm had built up a surface layer of ice more than 100 miles thick. The frozen shell did not melt, said Fauth, because the Moon lacked an atmosphere that could store heat.

More objective astronomers pointed out that the surface of the Moon in fact absorbs more than enough heat from sunlight to melt ice and that, in any event, any lumpy ice features would have flattened out over time from their own weight. Philipp Fauth was undissuaded, however, stubbornly clinging to the theory of an icy Moon until his death in 1941. □

Lunar Rime

Among the most diligent students of the Moon was Philipp Fauth, a German schoolteacher and self-taught astronomer. Between 1890 and 1930 he built several observatories where he spent countless hours at the telescope, spotting previously unrecorded small craters and clefts and recording a mountain of lunar detail. The maps that he published won him recognition as an authority on the Moon's topography. When the satellite was not in the night sky, he mapped the planets Jupiter and Mars.

But Fauth's explanation for what he saw on the Moon differed from that of most other observers—a difference that proved fatal for his scientific reputation. Unlike many other selenologists, he rejected the proposition that ancient volcanic action might account for many lunar features and was unwilling to attribute craters to meteorite bombardment. In his judgment, Earth's companion was covered with a thick layer of ice, which had produced the features that he observed through the telescope.

Fauth came to this conclusion as a disciple of Austrian mechanical engineer Hans Hörbiger, who had promulgated the cosmic ice theory *(pages 115-116)* of an icy universe—in which the Milky Way, for instance, was composed not of stars but of blocks of ice. Applying Hörbiger's hypothesis to the Moon,

A man with an abiding passion for examining the lunar surface, amateur astronomer Philipp Fauth looks out from a telescope dome near Munich—his fourth and last observatory—in 1939, two years before his death.

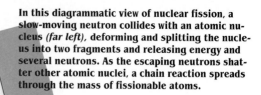

Atomic Vision

The challenge of harnessing the energy of the atom occupied many of the world's best scientific minds for decades. But one of the quest's great pivotal moments occurred in 1933, when the dismissive pessimism of one great physicist, Ernest Rutherford of Cambridge University, stimulated a crucial theoretical breakthrough by another genius, Hungarian-born Leo Szilard.

Rutherford was a titan. In the first decade of the century, he and his coworker Frederick Soddy had shown that radioactivity was the outward sign of atomic disintegration in certain elements, as they gradually transmuted from one element into another—from uranium, for example, into lead *(pages 53-54)*. The discovery, along with his other contributions to physics, won Rutherford a Nobel Prize in 1908. He went on to discern the essential structure of the atom and, in 1919, became the first human being to initiate a nuclear transmutation. His experiment left no doubt that atoms could change. Moreover, the laboratory transmutation yielded a small amount of energy—the first physical hint that the process might be turned to practical advantage.

In 1932 Sir James Chadwick, a physicist working under Rutherford, discovered the neutron, an electrically neutral particle that together with the positively charged proton makes up an atomic nucleus. In the laboratory at least, the uncharged neutron promised to be the perfect nucleus-splitting missile, since it would not be repelled by the positive charge of its target. Although the neutron appeared to be a key to forcing nuclear reactions, most physicists were nonetheless skeptical that useful amounts of energy could be extracted from atoms divided one at a time. At a conference held in Leicester, England, early in September of 1933, the now-elderly Rutherford deemed talk of drawing power from the transformation of atoms nothing but "moonshine."

That opinion was read in a London newspaper by 35-year-old physicist Leo Szilard, who had recently left Nazi Germany and come to England in search of work. He was known as an exceptionally original trailblazer in the field of thermodynamics, but he often wondered if his future lay outside physics. Always restless, he had at times turned his talents toward commerce—among other projects, he

had once designed a refrigerator with Albert Einstein—and he was fascinated by biology. Still, nuclear physics and the vast potential he saw for atomic energy stirred his imagination deeply.

A few days after the Leicester conference, Szilard was walking through London, pondering Rutherford's moonshine jibe. He came to an intersection, waited for the light to change, and began crossing the street. At that instant he saw the atomic future. "It suddenly occurred to me," he later recounted, "that if we could find an element which is split by neutrons and which would emit two neutrons when it absorbed one neutron, such an element, if assembled in sufficiently large mass, could sustain a nuclear chain reaction." He had glimpsed the possibility of the wholesale splitting of atoms. Less than six months later, Szilard secretly patented his insight and later turned the patent over to the British navy.

Szilard's greatest fear was that the Germans would hit upon the idea of fission, or atom splitting, and use it for purposes of conquest. His worries were justified: By the end of the decade, Germany had begun to explore fission, as had the Soviet Union, Japan, France, Britain, and the United States. The top-secret American Manhattan Project won the desperate competition. On August 6, 1945, the United States effectively ended the Second World War by detonating an atomic bomb over the Japanese city of Hiroshima. The project owed much of its success to a refugee from Europe, Leo Szilard—and, indirectly, to the closed-minded old man who had inspired the Hungarian with contemptuous talk of moonshine. □

Energy Glut

If the greatest ideas are those with most explanatory breadth then Wilhelm Reich's should have won him boundless scientific glory. No other serious researcher ever explained the world more sweepingly—or ignored more contrary scientific evidence in the process.

Born in Austria in 1897, Reich graduated from the University of Vienna Medical School in 1922, joined the psychoanalytic community associated with Sigmund Freud, and over the next few years, earned a solid reputation as a psychiatrist, a writer, and a teacher. Politics interested him as well. His sympathies were Marxist—but with a distinctive angle summed up in his 1927 book, *The Function of Orgasm.* It argued

that the problems of the working class were due to incomplete sexual release—unadulterated "un-Marxist rubbish," according to Reich's leftist critics. In subsequent works, he proclaimed that society was thoroughly crippled—"armored," as he put it—by enforced monogamy, premarital chastity, and other attitudes that he considered antisexual. In 1934 he was expelled from the International Psychoanalytic Association, and shortly thereafter the ascendant Nazis, whom Reich had called repressed neurotics, forced him to flee to Scandinavia.

Reich was just beginning to find his pace, however. In Norway he announced the discovery of a fundamental form of life called "bions," said to appear spontaneously out of nonliving matter. The self-taught biologist ignored the fact that in 1862 French chemist Louis Pasteur's experiments had proven conclusively that such spontaneous generation was a myth. The unstoppable Reich then discovered something even more basic than bions— a discovery that, in his opinion, ranked with the Copernican revolution. He called his find "orgone energy," a pervasive natural force that, as its name suggests, derived from sex. For the rest of his life, Reich would obsessively explore and exploit its mysteries. ◊

Aging radioactivity pioneer Ernest Rutherford *(inset, left)* mocked the notion of splitting atoms to obtain large amounts of energy, but his skepticism inspired Hungarian emigré Leo Szilard, seen here near Oxford in 1936, to hit upon the idea of producing a chain reaction.

An open door beckons patients into the Orgone Energy Accumulator *(above),* designed by Wilhelm Reich to draw on an alleged energy he called orgone.

Deemed by its discoverer to be nothing less than the fundamental power source of the universe, orgone energy could be found everywhere—in plants, soil, and animals, in the air and in the stars, and in anything that was blue. As a sexual force, it could melt the armor of inhibition and anxiety. The weather, according to Reich, was a result of changing concentrations of atmospheric orgone, and streams of orgone energy drew celestial bodies together—a phenomenon usually attributed to gravity. Reich explained that the sky was blue because of orgone energy, not because of the scattering of blue wavelengths of sunlight. Oceans and lakes, being bluish, were obviously full of orgone energy. Protoplasm, said Reich, had a blue tinge until it died, when its orgone energy drained away. He called the applied study of all this orgonomy.

Reich put his insight to practical use after he immigrated to the United States in 1939, inventing an apparatus that he called the Orgone Energy Accumulator. Miraculously simple, the standard model was a little smaller than a telephone booth and was constructed of layers of an organic material such as wood alternating with metal. Orgone energy, he explained, was attracted by the organic surface and transmitted through the other layers, accumulating in the central space. A person who sat in such a box would be charged with the energy, which would restore tissues and counter such repression-induced ailments as cancer, ulcers, obesity, alcoholism, and the common cold.

The originator of orgonomy did a brisk business selling and renting orgone boxes—both the large units and smaller, ottoman-size ones that could be placed on the chest to focus ambient orgone. But the claims made for his devices—and perhaps the sexual vector of his research—was attracting more than orgone: The U.S. Food and Drug Administration began to take an interest. In 1954 the agency ruled that the device was ineffective and fraudulent and ordered Reich to stop selling it.

In the meantime Reich had become convinced that he was not dealing merely with a government agency; his enemies were not bureaucrats, but hostile aliens. In order to thwart their conspiracy against him, he adopted an earlier design called the Cloudbuster—basically a set of hollow pipes—to draw off the orgone energy he surmised must power his foe's flying saucers. But the forces mounted against him were too great to be defeated by Reich's space gun. In 1956 he was sent to prison for ignoring the FDA's ruling. He died there a year later, a pathetic and broken figure—but a martyr to those who shared his views.

Reich's following remains strong. Several journals are devoted to his philosophy, and therapists are schooled at the American College of Orgonomy in Princeton, New Jersey, in techniques of analysis that, they believe, root out neuroses. Orgone accumulators are still in use, as is another unique device invented by Reich to help achieve this goal. Called the medical DOR-buster (for Deadly Orgone Radiation), it comprises hollow tubes linked through an "accumulator device" to a source of running water. The DOR-buster is said to reduce tensions and free blocked emotions by improving the purity and circulation through the body of orgone energy, the resilient Reichian candidate for a single, universal force. □

Brainstorming

In many primitive societies, healers opened up the skulls of patients to release evil spirits thought to cause severe headaches or mental disorders—a practice called trepanning. Only a few decades ago, an even more drastic treatment was devised by doctors who were dealing with mental illness: They sliced apart supposedly faulty brain-lobe circuits. Known as a lobotomy, the operation was all the rage for more than a decade—then came to be regarded with revulsion.

The genesis of the psychosurgical movement can be traced to an international convention of neurologists held in 1935 in London. A primate specialist reported that after he removed the frontal lobes of two highly trained chimpanzees, he noticed that they displayed much less tension and frustration during their training sessions, yet seemed to have suffered no intellectual impairment. The report prompted the renowned Portuguese neurologist Antonio de Egas Moniz to wonder aloud, "Would it not be feasible to relieve anxiety states in man by surgical means?"

Moniz was emboldened by his own question to have a go at such brain surgery. Back in Portugal, the neurologist quietly began experimenting on mental patients suffering from delusions, severe depression, or extreme agitation. With a rotating device that resembled an apple corer, he extracted a section of tissue connecting the frontal lobes, which are associated with thinking, to the underlying thalamus, which is associated with the emotions. Moniz claimed that, of the first 20 patients to undergo this procedure, 7 regained their mental health, 7 showed improvement, and 6 experienced no apparent change for good or ill. He pronounced his brand of psychosurgery "a simple operation, always safe."

The most enthusiastic American proselytizer of pyschosurgery was Walter Freeman, who had gained a reputation as a brilliant neurologist at the George Washington University Hospital in Washington, D.C. Instead of using Moniz's apple corer, Freeman perfected a technique in 1948 that earned the name "ice-pick surgery." His tool was a gold-plated ice pick that he carried around in a velvet-lined case. After applying a local anaesthetic, Freeman would thrust the instrument through the thin bone at the top of one of the patient's eye sockets and, by scraping the point back and forth, blindly sever the nerve connections beyond. The neurologist often performed the operation in his office or in patients' homes, typically charging $1,000 for his pick work, although he sometimes took on mass-production jobs in mental institutions at the rate of only $25 per patient. ◊

The specially made "ice pick" leucotome used by neurologist Walter Freeman in thousands of prefrontal lobotomies glistens below, a relic of an awful 20th-century surgical fad.

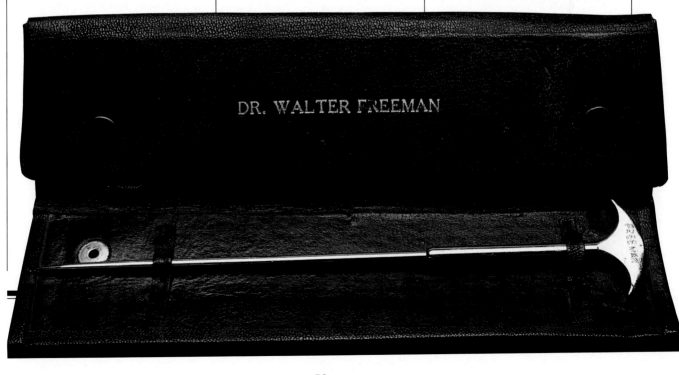

DR. WALTER FREEMAN

Freeman claimed dramatically positive results. He described lobotomies as a kind of miracle treatment, insisting that even the most disturbed mental patients were sometimes able to resume normal lives. Between 1942 and 1960 he performed at least 3,500 ice-pick lobotomies. Other enthusiasts in the United States—using a variety of nerve-severing procedures—may have carried out another 40,000 operations or so, and thousands more were performed elsewhere in the world.

Over the years it became clear that such surgical picking at the brain carried a heavy price. Many patients lapsed into a postoperative state of deep apathy and intellectual impairment that came to be known as frontal-lobe syndrome. Although many physicians began to view psychosurgery as a dangerous treatment only of last resort, Walter Freeman clung to ice-pick surgery and gave short shrift to electro-

shock therapy and other less drastic measures. Despite concerns about its efficacy, such corrective surgery continued to be applied by Freeman and other doctors until a revolutionary alternative came along in the 1950s—powerful tranquilizers that could control the symptoms of extreme derangement.

Psychosurgery has since largely faded from the scene. The career of the pioneering Moniz could almost symbolize psychosurgery's course through medical history. In 1949 the Portuguese neurologist won a Nobel Prize, in part for his pioneering lobotomizing experiments. In 1955 he was beaten to death in his office by one of his patients. □

Portuguese neurologist Antonio de Egas Moniz *(below, left)* **won a Nobel Prize for developing the prefrontal lobotomy, a now-discredited surgical technique popularized in the 1940s and 1950s by American neurologist Walter Freeman** *(below).*

Fear and Terror

In the late 1950s Ukrainian astrophysicist Iosif Shmuelovich Shklovskii advanced a startling doubleheader theory of life in the solar neighborhood: An advanced civilization might have flourished on Mars billions of years ago. Moreover, ancient Martians had left a sign of both their presence and high technology. The two small companions of Mars, Phobos and Deimos—in Greek myth, Fear and Terror, offspring of the god of war—might not be moons at all, but artificial satellites launched by the red planet's vanished inhabitants.

Shklovskii was treading a time-honored path of bold scientific speculation about Mars, which astronomer Percival Lowell *(pages 49-50)* had believed was watered by huge irrigation projects that were constructed by a noble, but disappearing, Martian race. The canals had been shown to be mere optical illusions long before Shklovskii's 1959 pronouncements about the planet's moons, however, and another man might have been laughed out of astronomy.

But Shklovskii was no ordinary researcher. He had demystified odd periodic x-ray emissions, for instance, by explaining that their sources were pairs of superdense stars circling each other. He also described a form of radiation—synchrotron radiation—that electrons emit when they are set spinning by a galaxy's magnetic field. Despite the international reputation he had earned among fellow astronomers, Shklovskii also had a nonconformist side—he argued strongly, for example, for the existence

Soviet astronomer Iosif Shmue-lovich Shklovskii, shown at Cornell University in 1968, believed the satellites of Mars might be alien artifacts, but NASA images of Phobos *(left)* and Deimos *(above)* revealed natural moons.

of extraterrestrial intelligence.

Focusing his maverick attention closer to home, Shklovskii hazarded that Mars could now support only the simplest forms of life because of its sparse atmosphere, coldness, and aridity. But long ago, he suspected, it might have had an environment hospitable to inhabitants superior even to human beings. He based his roundabout case on what he described as peculiarities in the motion of the Martian moons, particularly Phobos. When Shklovskii factored in the drag of Mars's thin upper atmosphere, the result suggested that the satellites had an extraordinarily low density—so low, in fact, that Phobos, and Deimos too, could only be hollow. Phobos, he guessed, had a solid outer shell only a foot or so thick weighing billions of tons.

Because no natural satellite is hollow, "only one possibility remains," wrote Shklovskii. "We are led to the possibility that Phobos—and possibly Deimos as well—may be artificial satellites of Mars." Shklovskii wondered whether the odd moons had been launched as way stations when the Martians were forced into the wider reaches of the galaxy by a dwindling oxygen supply on their native planet. "The idea that the moons of Mars are artificial satellites may seem fantastic, at first glance," Shklovskii concluded. "In my opinion, however, it merits serious consideration."

But fabricated orbiters, like Martian canals, turned out to be illusions. In 1971 the unmanned American space probe *Mariner 9* took a close look at Phobos and sent pictures back to Earth proving that the little moon is a natural, heavily cratered, solid object. Faced with this deflating evidence, Shklovskii coolly, but not very convincingly, confessed: His proposal had been only a practical joke. □

Meteoric Career

One of the biggest and most protracted cases of mistaken identity in the annals of science began to take shape in the summer of 1891. In terms of size, the subject was hard to overlook—an immense circular crater, more than 4,000 feet wide and 570 feet deep, that had somehow been blasted out of the sandstone and limestone terrain near Winslow in northeast Arizona. A few years earlier a shepherd had discovered lumps of metal in the area. He thought they were silver, but a professional mineralogist determined that they were actually a nickel-iron alloy commonly found in meteorites. The possibility of a stupendous impact sometime in the past stirred intense interest among scientists and in 1891 brought the nation's top geologist, Grove Gilbert, to the scene.

Justly honored for a career that ranged from glaciology to the Moon to the origin of landforms in the American West, Gilbert was then chief geologist of the United States Geological Survey and the very model of scientific acumen. Gilbert arrived in Arizona with two possible causes in mind: A meteorite was one, and the second was an underground steam explosion, possibly caused by volcanic heat.

Reasoning his way through the problem, Gilbert decided that if the genesis of the crater was by impact, the circular shape of the great scar indicated that the projectile had come straight down—an oblique impact, he believed, would have blasted an elliptical crater. That being the case, the main corpus of the supposed meteorite would still be somewhere in the ground at the bottom of the crater, where its large mass of metal could be detected magnetically.

But when the compasses that he used for his metal survey did not react, Gilbert's ordinarily impeccable logic took a curiously illogical turn. Because he had not detected metal in the ground, he quickly accepted his alternative hypothesis of a volcanic origin for the crater. Gilbert did this, however, despite the absence of lava or any other ge-

Dwarfed by a California outcrop of chert and shale in this 1906 image, geologist Grove Gilbert said the Arizona crater at right was volcanic—despite a lack of lava.

ologic evidence of volcanism. The remarkable fact that fragments of meteoric iron lay scattered on the plain surrounding the crater, Gilbert concluded, must be simple coincidence. Such was his prestige in geologic matters that his judgment was accepted.

A mining engineer named Daniel Barringer was disgusted. "It does not seem possible that any experienced geologist could have arrived at such a conclusion," he fumed. Barringer was so convinced that a great lode of metal lay in the huge crater that he secured the mining rights to the area in 1903. When he drilled test holes, he did not find a mass of metal. There were, however, small bits and pieces of nickel-rich meteoric iron. Barringer also found that some of the iron samples contained the elements platinum and iridium, both known to occur in meteorites.

In 1908 a U.S. government geologist proved that sandstone at the site had been metamorphosed by a blast of extremely high heat. Some of it had been smashed to a fine powder, or rock flour, that was mixed in with chunks of limestone and sandstone. He proposed that a "sharp and tremendously powerful blow," as of a meteorite, had pulverized the rock and sent it surging out of the crater along with larger fragments. In the face of all this evidence, Grove Gilbert maintained a prim silence. Evidently he knew full well that his theory had been wrong but let his conclusion stand rather than acknowledge his monumental error of judgment.

Over the years Barringer mined the crater off and on, finding a growing heap of evidence that pointed to a meteoric impact and hoping someday to encounter the main mass of the meteorite. But it was a vain hope. The missile, measuring somewhere between 80 to 100 feet in diameter, was traveling an estimated 43,000 miles per hour when it crashed into Arizona approximately 50,000 years ago, and most of the multimillion-ton projectile, scientists later determined, had been vaporized in the impact. Today, the scar it left is variously known as Barringer Crater or Meteor Crater—both names a quiet rebuke to Grove Gilbert. □

Shown here inspecting a meteorite around 1929, mining engineer Daniel Barringer corrected Gilbert's error by drilling for meteoritic iron in the disputed crater.

Gold Dust

Thomas Gold, one of the world's leading astrophysicists, likes nothing better than going against the scientific grain. Often he has proved dazzlingly correct—as when he surmised that the radio-emitting celestial objects called pulsars are the neutron-packed relics of exploding stars, or supernovas. Other offbeat ideas of Gold's, such as his claim that natural gas is an inorganic substance existing in huge amounts hundreds of miles down in the earth's mantle, have been strenuously disputed. As tenacious as he is imaginative, Gold is not quick to back down. For example, he still clings to a widely debunked idea he advanced in the mid-1950s—that much of the Moon's surface is covered with a veritable ocean of dust.

At the time, most lunar scientists believed that rocky particles, both coarse and fine, made up much of the moon's surface; some said that the particles were the result of eons of meteorite bombardment, others that they were the ash of extinct volcanoes. Whatever their opinion on the surface particles, most selenologists agreed that the smooth, dark areas known as maria, or lunar seas, were the rocky remains of ancient lava flows.

Gold rejected the lava hypothesis, proposing instead that the maria are oceans of very fine dust. In his view, lunar rock had been broken down by countless meteorites and constant exposure to solar radiation. Radiation would also give the dust particles an electric charge, and, according to Gold, the combination of electrostatic repulsion and gravity would cause powder to migrate gradually from the lunar highlands to lower-lying areas—the maria. The seas are darker than the highlands, Gold says, because the dust in the lowlands is older and thus has been exposed for a longer period to radiation, which tends to make things darken.

This vision alarmed NASA officials, who were planning to send probes to the lunar surface. A Moon lander, Gold warned, "would simply sink into the dust with all its gear." Plans for exploration proceeded, however, since so much evidence supported the conventional view of maria as lava seas. For example, numerous clefts and faults could be seen in the maria; such fissures would have been completely obscured by a thickness of dust as great as Gold proposed.

As far as most lunar scientists were concerned, the matter was settled in 1966, when the unmanned Soviet craft *Luna 9* landed in a mare, followed four months later by the U.S. probe *Surveyor 1*. Neither sank into Goldian drifts of dust. Subsequent examination of lunar rocks left virtually no doubt that many were of volcanic origin. His dusty seas proven as insubstantial, finally, as the canals of Mars *(pages 49-50)*, Gold continues to insist the Moon never experienced volcanism. The presumed lava flows, he says, are simply "boundaries between different masses of powder." Today few but Gold believe it. □

Feet firmly planted on the Moon, the *Apollo 11* lander *(above)* did not sink in a sea of dust, as foreseen by astrophysicist Thomas Gold, who also denied the existence of lunar volcanism—despite such compelling proofs as the volcanic Moonrock at right.

Ricochet

The long-running dispute about the cause of the Moon's craters pitted the provolcano faction against the scientists who attributed the features to meteoric impacts. In 1952 Harvey Nininger, an expert on terrestrial meteorites, came up with a radical proposition after studying two closely spaced lunar craters and the peculiarly patterned debris nearby: A single meteorite had created both of them, in the process blasting out a tunnel between them.

Self-taught in his chosen specialty, Nininger by that time had been studying meteorites and craters for three decades. He had investigated terrestrial impact sites such as Arizona's Meteor Crater *(pages 62-63)* and had amassed one of the worlds largest meteorite collections. The lunar craters he scrutinized, Messier and Pickering (now Messier and Messier A), lie in a region called the Sea of Fertility. They are respectively about eight and seven miles in diameter and, to Nininger's eye, appeared to lie on either side of a high ridge. Rays of debris are usually visible around relatively young craters such as Nininger's pair, but Pickering's debris forms two long, parallel streaks stretching away from one side of the crater.

Determined that these observations could be assembled to produce the natural tunnel he envisioned, Nininger composed an elaborate scenario. A large meteorite traveling at 20 to 30 miles per second had hit the Moon at a very shallow angle and plunged through the Moon's loose surface material ◊

Pictured searching for meteorites in the American Southwest, Harvey Nininger *(inset)* argued that a meteorite had drilled a tunnel between lunar craters Messier and Messier A, nestled cheek by jowl in the image above.

to dig Messier. Carried along by its momentum, the projectile had burrowed through the ridge until it struck a hard rock stratum below, which had caused it to ricochet upward through the far side of the ridge. Exploding into the open, the meteorite had created a large exit wound: Pickering. Then, still moving, the missile shed debris along its course, producing the curious double ray. Nininger speculated that the tunnel walls had been melted by the heat of the meteorite's passage, then hardened again. He wrapped up his hypothesis with a forward-looking thought: "If and when the first explorers to the moon have succeeded in landing there, perhaps they will find already prepared for them a shelter from small meteorites and, more important, from flying lunite slivers."

This comforting notion was dismissed with skepticism by the scientific community, for Nininger's hypothesis had a fatal flaw: Even if the meteorite had managed to bore into and out of the lunar surface, the roof of the tunnel would have instantly collapsed under its own weight. Nininger's "ridge" also crumbled: According to later lunar observers, it was an illusion. Instead of lying on two sides of a ridge, the craters ride on a gentle swell in the Sea of Fertility. As to Pickering's double streak of debris, selenologists now ascribe its odd form to the extremely low angle at which the meteorite smashed into the Moon. What one sees is not always what one gets. □

Andromeda Strain

Originality is a virtue in science, but British astrophysicist Fred Hoyle may on occasion be more virtuous than necessary. To be sure, his triumphs are numerous. Working with various collaborators over the past four decades, he has explained such knotty problems as the evolution of the Sunlike stars into bloated monsters called red giants and the thermonuclear fusion processes that turn stellar hydrogen and helium into heavier elements, liberating vast amounts of energy in the process. A practiced iconoclast, Hoyle went so far as to reject the centerpiece of orthodox cosmology, the big bang

theory that describes the birth of the universe from a primordial fireball. With two other leading astrophysicists, Hermann Bondi and Thomas Gold *(page 64)*, Hoyle proposed a steady state universe that, like the big bang universe, is constantly expanding, but also constantly replenished.

Hoyle's sweepingly grand iconoclasm also has its homely side. Since the 1970s, with the aid of an Indian colleague, Chandra Wickramasinghe, Hoyle has urged fellow scientists to look skyward for the source of the first living creatures—and of the occasional epidemics that have afflicted human life through its history.

Spectrographic studies, which identify chemical elements from ◊

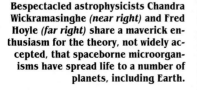

Bespectacled astrophysicists Chandra Wickramasinghe *(near right)* and Fred Hoyle *(far right)* share a maverick enthusiasm for the theory, not widely accepted, that spaceborne microorganisms have spread life to a number of planets, including Earth.

On October 28, 1965, Comet Ikeya-Seki streaks across the sky over Flagstaff, Arizona. Hoyle and Wickramasinghe believe that such fiery visitors could bring with them living matter that may include deadly germs.

wavelengths of light, have indicated the presence of dozens of carbon-based, or organic, substances in clouds of interstellar dust and gas. As the billions of comets that orbit the Sun coalesced from such clouds, Hoyle maintains, they would have soaked up these organic building blocks of life as well. The astronomer believes that conditions within the comets would have fostered the transformation of those compounds into the simplest forms of life—viruses and bacteria. Because the young Earth was so much less hospitable to life, Hoyle argues, terrestrial life was probably an import, transferred to the planet billions of years ago in a rain of cometary material.

But, according to Hoyle, comets imported death as well: During their passage through the inner Solar System, the celestial visitors fed germs into the upper atmosphere that eventually percolated down to the surface. During periods of intense sunspot activity, the scientist says, an unusually large flow of high-energy particles from the Sun entered the atmosphere and drove cometary germs earthward with a greater than normal force—and a greater than normal effect.

Hoyle has linked pandemics of influenza to the sunspot cycle, which peaks roughly every 11 years. Citing statistical and historical information about such outbreaks over the past 200 years, he insists that person-to-person infection cannot account for the rapid spread of wildfire flu epidemics. He believes that he and his colleague have also demonstrated a correlation between influenza outbreaks and the return of Halley's comet every 76 years.

Almost no one else accepts Hoyle's shower of comet-borne germs as a source of either life or death. Critics assert that high-energy solar radiation would in all likelihood destroy any unshielded microorganisms in space. Naysayers also claim that the correlation between influenza epidemics and sunspots is weak—indeed, they point out that the oscillations of solar activity have been made to correlate with almost everything, from vintage years to the performance of the stock market.

Hoyle has stuck to his guns, however. He is, he says, "99.9 per cent sure" that American scientists have found cometary germs but are keeping the discovery secret. Their motive: The pathogens from outer space, says Hoyle, are clandestine candidates for biological warfare. □

GREAT EXPECTATIONS

S cientists will go to great lengths to insulate experiments from unwanted influences that might skew the objectivity of their results. But the central apparatus of scientific inquiry—the human mind—must be used as is, unshielded, subject to a battery of influential intrusions. Unlike a machine, the mind is propelled by hosts of motives, not the least of which is the wish to find what one is looking for—a new energy source, a secret planet, or the answer to some stony riddle from the distant past. Often, believing is seeing.

There are, of course, communal checks to detect science that has been steered by expectation. But even the cool, detached scrutiny of colleagues often cannot deflect collective wrongheadedness, when whole gangs of men and women who should know better jump on a scientific bandwagon—and later express surprise when their vehicle of exploration sputters and breaks down. Although it may take years, the community of scientists eventually discovers and corrects such error and patches the resulting rifts in understanding.

Individuals are less adaptable, however. Despite logic, compelling evidence to the contrary, and the pain of a plummeting reputation, many scholars resolutely cling to what they think they found and go to their graves still fiercely cherishing the illusion of discovery.

New Angle

Copernicus dismantled the traditional Earth-centered universe in the 16th century, placing the Sun at the center of his system and the Earth in orbit around the Sun. But well over a century after the Polish astronomer's theory began to circulate—and gain many adherents—no one had been able to prove its validity. Pro-Copernican scientists looked to the stars for proof: Because the stars appear to be fixed in space, the movement of the Earth around the Sun, the savants reasoned, would make stars seem to shift minutely over the course of the year. Measuring such a tiny displacement, called a stellar parallax, was no easy matter with the instruments that were available in the 17th century. If, however, one believed that the Earth was moving, the elusive parallax became—or seemed to become—easier to detect.

It fell to Robert Hooke, master of mechanics and scientific jack-of-all-trades, to try his hand at pinning down the parallax. Hooke was the paid curator of experiments at London's Royal Society, an organization whose well-educated and well-to-do members were on the genteel cutting edge of the scientific revolution in Great Britain. In return for a modest salary, they required their curator to perform three or four experiments each week for the members, and beginning in 1666 Hooke's attempts to measure star locations were, off and on, the subject of Royal Society discussions.

Proving the Copernican theory was high on the agenda, and Hooke was under pressure, however mannerly, to perform.

Hooke's technique was to observe the stars through a perpendicular telescope, which was housed in a long tube protruding through the roof of his lodgings. He focused on the stars' passage across the zenith at different times of the year. If a star was closer to the zenith than it had been a month earlier, the difference in position would suggest that the viewing platform—that is, the Earth—had moved to a different location in space. Although Hooke had no way of reckoning the vast distances to the stars, he knew that only those nearest the Earth would be good subjects; at great distances, the parallax produced by the movement of the Earth would become immeasurably small.

Hooke diligently made his observations, settling on Gamma Draconis, a bright star in the constellation Draco, as his principal subject. The obligatory progress reports he made to the Royal Society were light on numerical specifics until at last, in 1669, he believed he had succeeded: Gamma Draconis, Hooke advised, had shifted 24 seconds of arc—a second is $1/3600$ of a degree—from July to August. Perhaps his data were too skimpy to be convincing, for his report was given little credence. Hooke's parallax stock fell even further when French astronomer Jean Picard made similar observations on another prominent star and failed to find Hooke's stellar shift. The Englishman might have been less ready to claim success had he heeded his own complaints about the problems that had been inflicted on his telescope and its housing by rain, wind, sudden temperature changes, or extremes of heat and cold. In any case, the parallax he thought he had seen was seen no more.

But Hooke was not the last for whom the stars were moved by the demand for positive results, it seems. Twenty-five years after his blooper, another pair of English and French astronomers had a remarkably similar contretemps. John Flamsteed, the first astronomer royal at Greenwich, was widely respected for the precision of his measurements. In 1699 he reported that he had been able to detect stellar par-allax in the polestar, which moves slightly with respect to the north celestial pole—an imaginary point projected upward from the Earth's North Pole. Seven years' measurements, he said, showed that Polaris was closest to the pole in December and farthest from it in July; the shift in apparent position Flamsteed put at 40 seconds of arc.

Within weeks the director of the Paris Observatory, Jacques Cassini, attacked with a devastatingly accurate critique. Flamsteed could not have seen what he claimed to have seen—at least not in the months of July and December. The polestar was farthest from the celestial pole in late March or early April and made its closest approach six months later. Flamsteed never replied to the criticism publicly, but in private he conceded that the Frenchman might have a point—the right times to look for the polestar's parallax were "perhaps not much different from the times on which Mr. Cassini places them." The best explanation he could muster for his nonexistent polar parallax was some flaw or inadequacy in the instruments he used.

It was not until 1838, when much more refined telescopes were available, that astronomers were at last able to measure the parallax and prove that the Earth did indeed circle the Sun. Their results made it clear why the achievement had been so long delayed: The apparent position shifts were minuscule and very difficult to find, the largest being no more than 0.76 second of arc—more than 50 times smaller than Flamsteed's estimate. The instruments used by Hooke and Flamsteed, unlike the expectations of the astronomers themselves, were simply not up to the task. □

Hard Times

A rosy glow of utopianism enveloped England in the late 18th century. Theologians, intellectuals, and scientists put their faith in reason and natural law to improve humankind gradually until, in the distant future, a virtual heaven on earth would come into being. War and crime would vanish, along with extremes of wealth and poverty, and harmony would be so complete that government could be dispensed with. The advocates of this optimistic new faith believed that a large and growing population was a national asset: the more hands available to work, the more wealth generated for everyone to share.

But even a cursory look at the reality of British life circa 1800 was enough to convince a more pessimistic observer that, in fact, the only true inevitabilities were those of rising population, grinding poverty, plague, war, and famine. Thomas Robert Malthus, the man whose bleak prophecies forever marked economics as the Dismal Science, was the great pessimist of his age. The son of a wealthy country gentlemen, he was ordained an Anglican minister soon after graduating from Cambridge University's Jesus College with honors in mathematics in 1788. In his parish in Surrey, south of London, the good-hearted young minister saw too much suffering and despair among the poor to make utopia seem at all plausible. Arguing this point with his eccentric, upbeat father, Daniel Malthus, the brilliant Robert (he was never called Thomas) was so effective that his parent urged him to publish his dour but compelling views.

Thus encouraged, the younger Malthus turned demographer. In ◊

1798 he published anonymously a novel-length pamphlet that presented a strenuous argument against even-tempered optimism for the future. Entitled *An Essay on the Principle of Population as It Affects the Future Improvement of Society*, it asserted that much of humanity was destined to live in poverty because human procreative powers would always far exceed the Earth's ability to sustain new mouths—population would explode, but the planet's land area would remain the same. Poverty was ineradicable, according to Malthus, because population would always increase geometrically while the food supply would increase arithmetically. "Taking the whole earth," he wrote, "and supposing the present population to be equal to a thousand millions, the human species would increase as the numbers 1, 2, 4, 8, 16, 32, 64, 128, 256 and subsistence as 1, 2, 3, 4, 5, 6, 7, 8, 9. In two centuries the population would be to the means of subsistence as 256 to 9; in three centuries as 4096 to 13, and in two thousand years the difference would be incalculable." The mathematician in Malthus had discovered doubling—the process that turns one penny into well over

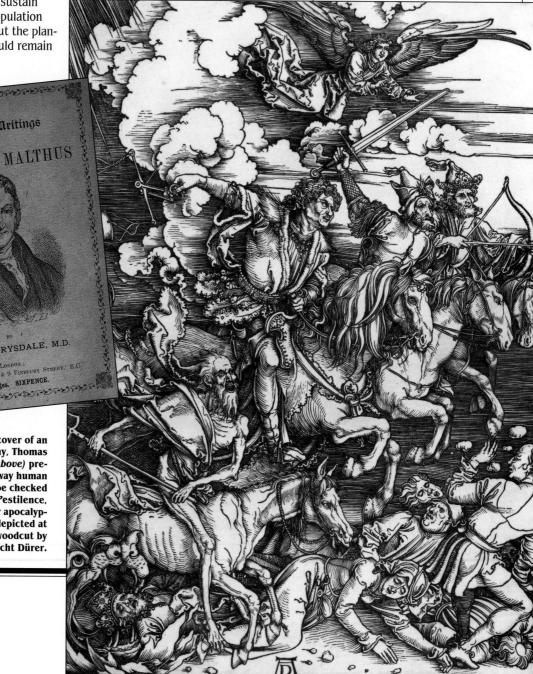

Pictured on the cover of an 1892 biography, Thomas Robert Malthus *(above)* predicted that runaway human population would be checked by Death, Famine, Pestilence, and War—the four apocalyptic horsemen depicted at right in a 1498 woodcut by Albrecht Dürer.

a million dollars in only 27 steps.

Humanity, the minister wrote, was caught up in an entirely natural cycle, perpetually oscillating between times of plenty and periods of utter poverty. Good economic times led to high wages, which in turn encouraged men and women to marry young and have large families. Their numerous children brought about poverty by straining the food supply and creating a labor surplus when they entered the work force, causing wages to drop—the market's way of warning sensible people to refrain from sex and marriage. But sexual impulses frequently won out over common sense. When they did, in Malthus's view, nature was waiting in the wings, ready to impose what he called "positive checks" to cut population and shorten human life: "unwholesome occupations, severe labour and exposure to the seasons, bad and insufficient food and clothing arising from poverty, bad nursing of children, excesses of all kind, great towns and manufactures, the whole train of common diseases and epidemics, wars, infanticide, plague, and famine."

The poor, he noted, were most vulnerable to the inevitable cycle of good and bad times; the rich could support families of almost any size and therefore did not have to pinch pennies, go hungry, or restrain themselves sexually. Thus, in Malthus's opinion, the aid the government gave to the needy was counterproductive because it encouraged people to marry and reproduce even in lean times, and merely deepened their plight.

Paradoxically, Malthus was a vehement opponent of birth control. He urged his countrymen to practice abstinence before marriage and to marry late. Even for married couples, however, contraception was out of the question. "I should always particularly reprobate any artificial or unnatural modes of checking population," he wrote, "both on account of their immorality and their tendency to remove a necessary stimulus to industry. If it were possible for each married couple to limit by a wish the number of their children, there is certainly reason to fear that the indolence of the human race would be very greatly increased."

Clergymen denounced Malthus for seeming to call divine beneficence into question with his harsh view of the human condition, while the general public vilified him as a cold-hearted fiend. Cooler and more clinical critics attacking his essay pointed out that although Great Britain made provisions for the poor, its birth and marriage rates were comparable to that of nations that did not have such charitable policies—that is, it was not destructive to help the needy. Despite such criticisms, his work had a powerful impact on British policy. In 1834—the year of Malthus's death at 58—the government revised its laws to make able-bodied persons ineligible for public relief. To do otherwise, according to the lawmakers, waxing Malthusian, would be tantamount to paying "a bounty on indolence and vice." It was their duty to make poverty as disgraceful and disagreeable as it was inevitable.

History has tested Malthus's gloomy expectations—and found them wanting in more ways than one. His prediction that the human population will rise until it triggers the grim "positive checks" he once described may apply today to some primitive cultures, but the industrialized nations seem to have escaped it. In many countries, population has been on the decline. Keenly aware of human failures everywhere about him, Malthus had underestimated the ability of his species to survive. Correct about land area being fixed, he could not anticipate that technology would geometrically increase the agricultural yield of existing land. He dismissed the power of industrialization to create wealth, admitting that it could provide "conveniences and luxuries" but doubting that agriculture would ever become mechanized enough to keep pace with his nation's expanding population. Perhaps most important, Malthus failed to foresee the spread of birth control, which has dampened the population booms and busts that he considered inexorable.

Still, his was a timely caution: If things continued as they were, humanity would expand until it crashed down upon itself. The argument he began two centuries ago continues today. The world described by Robert Malthus has not happened, say the optimists. Pessimists add: Not yet. □

In 1970 Georges Ungar, a pharmacology professor at Houston's Baylor College of Medicine, announced that he had isolated the chemical stuff of memory in the brains of laboratory rats and had been able to transmit an acquired affinity for light by injecting the substance, which he called "scotophobin," into untrained rats. When other scientists failed to reproduce his results, however, Georges Ungar and scotophobin faded from memory.

British physician-hypnotist John Elliotson plays a client like a piano in this 1843 caricature from the magazine *Punch*.

Entranced

Physician John Elliotson stood at the forefront of contemporary medicine in London during the 1830s. He was an eminent member of the faculty of University College, an eloquent speaker, and an innovator known for his brilliance. He also held some views that were well ahead of his time. For example, he criticized the common practice of blood-letting, then used to treat almost every known ailment. Bleeding, he rightly observed, did patients no good at best; at worst, it weakened and killed them. Elliotson also tried to persuade his colleagues to use a relatively new device, the stethoscope, as a tool for diagnosing heart and lung ailments. Many of his peers thought this laughable.

But Elliotson was not always so wise. He became infatuated with mesmerism, a school of treatment named for its originator, Franz Anton Mesmer, an Austrian physician who had practiced in Paris near the end of the 18th century. At its simplest, mesmerism amounted to no more than using a hypnotic trance for therapeutic purposes. But to explain the workings of the trance, Mesmer constructed a tortuous theory that included the presence of an invisible fluid that traveled from his body to the patient—a process Mesmer attributed to what he described as animal magnetism.

In fact, Mesmer had merely organized a widely held presumption that two of the era's most intri-

guing entities—electricity and magnetism—must have some biological application. As later experience established and modern research has confirmed, Mesmer had joined his misunderstanding of magnetic forces to the practice of hypnotism, now known to be a valuable therapeutic tool. In 1784 a blue-ribbon commission in Paris—its members included Benjamin Franklin—concluded that mesmerism had no value: The "fluid" of animal magnetism did not exist and the reported healing effects were the products of "mere imagination." Nevertheless, mesmerism and its supporting theories lived on, even after the charismatic Austrian's death in 1815.

Elliotson first encountered these ideas in 1829, and again in 1837, when the French practitioner Jean Dupotet de Sennevoy, a self-styled baron, demonstrated the techniques in London. Soon Elliotson himself became a practitioner, using mesmeric trances to treat nervous disorders and—most dramati-

cally, in a time that lacked safe and effective anesthetics—to perform major surgery without inflicting pain. Like others before him, Elliotson accepted Mesmer's explanation for the magnetic underpinnings of his techniques but also added some theory of his own. For example, he noted that the magnetic fluid seemed to flow more easily through such metals as nickel and gold and less efficiently through such inert metals as lead.

As Elliotson evolved from mere practitioner to paraclete, he began to spread the word of this marvelous practice with dramatic demonstrations that drew large crowds to the university lecture hall. But Elliotson's colleagues scorned his new interest, calling it quackery. Even Thomas Wakley, editor of the influential medical journal *Lancet* and a former ally of Elliotson's, began to have his suspicions.

Often, Elliotson's demonstration subjects were two sisters named Elizabeth and Jane Okey, both patients whom he had successfully treated for a variety of ailments, using all the techniques of his modified brand of mesmerism, including the use of a nickel disk to help induce a healing trance. As later practitioners have learned, there are several ways—a swinging pendulum, a spot on the wall, controlled breathing—to help focus a subject's attention and ease the transition into a hypnotic trance; but Elliotson clung to the belief that something magnetic also occurred.

In August 1838, Wakley asked Elliotson to demonstrate his hypnotic techniques at the editor's house. As the experiment unfolded, Wakley, unseen by the doctor, replaced Elliotson's mesmerizing nickel disk with one of lead, an inert substance that made a poor conductor for the magnetic fluid that supposedly produced the spell. Nevertheless, Elizabeth Okey immediately fell into a trance upon touching the lead. One metal seemed to work as well as another; or, put another way, neither metal had the slightest effect. Wakley concluded that Elliotson, the Okey sisters, and mesmerism were frauds and denounced them in the *Lancet.*

The effect was devastating. The university banned the practice of mesmerism in its hospital, and proud John Elliotson resigned. But his influence endured: A Mesmeric Infirmary was established in London and Mesmeric Institutions opened in Edinburgh, Dublin, and other cities. With his supporters Elliotson launched a quarterly journal called the *Zoist* for the new profession in 1843. Although born in the zeal for mesmerism, the *Zoist* was filled with case studies covering other aspects of medicine; even today its articles ring with the clear voice of Elliotson, the acute observer and diagnostician, rising from the chorus of magnetic expectation.

During the 1840s, Scottish physician James Braid coined the word *hypnotism* to describe the induced trances Mesmer and Elliotson espoused. The term distanced the phenomenon from spurious theories about magnetism, a distinction that might have salvaged some of Elliotson's reputation. But the old doctor would have none of it. Until his death at 77, in 1868, he clung to his belief that magnetic forces, not suggestion, produced his healing trances. □

Readers of the Lost Arc

William Lassell *(below)* clipped an exciting announcement from the October 1, 1846, edition of the *Times* of London: Two scientists working at the Berlin Observatory had discovered the eighth planet of the solar system, Neptune. A beer brewer by profession and a highly respected amateur astronomer, Lassell would later be credited with discovering one of Saturn's moons and two moons orbiting Uranus. On the day that the item appeared in the London newspaper, John Herschel, whose father William had discovered Uranus 75 years earlier *(pages 36-37),* wrote a letter urging Lassell to search for satellites around the eighth planet "with all possible expedition!!"

The summons could not have come at a better time. Only months before, Lassell had completed a 24-inch reflector telescope that was reputed to be the most powerful in all of England. Lassell himself said the instrument was faultless, although as he learned too late, it was not. The talented amateur immediately set to work and on the night of October 2 spotted Neptune and something else as well—what appeared to be a ring around the planet similar to those of Saturn. Eight days later, after another night of observation, Lassell wrote in his diary that he had detected "a suspicious looking star"—by which he meant a moon—in addition to the ringlike phenomenon.

Although Lassell had his doubts about the ring, he sent a letter to the *Times* staking his claim: "With respect to the existence of the ring, I am not able absolutely to declare it, but I received so many impressions of it, always in the same form and direction, and with all the different magnifying powers, that I feel a very strong persuasion that nothing but a finer state of atmosphere is necessary to enable me to verify the discovery. Of the existence of the star, having every aspect of a satellite, there is not the shadow of a doubt." Lassell was right about the moon, which was named Triton after the fish-tailed son of the god Neptune.

Lassell was gratified when other astronomers, sent to their telescopes by the excitement, also reported seeing what might have been a ring. John Russell Hind, director of a private observatory in London, had been among the first to see Neptune, using a refractor telescope capable of ◊

The suspected existence of rings around Neptune was finally verified by this 1989 image from the *Voyager 2* spacecraft, which masked the planet's glare so that the extremely faint rings could be seen.

producing very sharp images. In December, hearing of Lassell's tentative discovery, Hind took another look at Neptune and saw what he described as an oblong form—an indication that the new planet was circled by a ring. Director James Challis of the Cambridge Observatory soon followed suit, describing a symmetrical, bright form at an angle oblique to the planet: an inclined ring. In 1847 the prestigious Royal Astronomical Society pronounced the ring's existence "almost certain."

But Neptune's ring was less obvious to others. The Reverend William R. Dawes, a respected astronomical observer and a close friend of Lassell, noted that the angle of the ring differed in the accounts of Lassell and Challis. When Dawes questioned his friend about this discrepancy, Lassell responded that the apparent conflict arose from differences in orientation of the sketches made from the telescope image. Lassell also wondered whether the ring's capricious appearances

and disappearances could be attributed to poor viewing conditions, a chronic hazard in the moist English climate.

In 1852 Lassell took his telescope to the Mediterranean island of Malta in search of clearer night skies. Writing in his diary, he again reported seeing something around Neptune—and noted his growing suspicion that it was not real but an artifact created by his "flawless" instrument. By the end of the year, Lassell had abandoned his cherished discovery as an illusion. He was forced to this mournful conclusion by the fact that the angle of the apparition changed when he rotated the telescope tube—the real thing would have kept the same orientation.

In fact, Lassell had been doubly deceived, first by his own inclination to believe that Neptune, like Saturn, must have a ring, and again by the hidden imperfections of his telescope mirror. The supposedly state-of-the-art telescope had fooled not only its builder but other

competent astronomers, who initially had no reason to doubt observations that were made with such an instrument.

For more than a century after Lassell gave up on his spurious sighting, Neptune remained apparently ringless—even observations with the largest modern telescopes turned up no evidence at all of a ring. But in 1984, when the planet eclipsed a star, astronomers noted a fleeting but definite reduction of the star's light shortly before it was occluded by Neptune. The momentary dimming strongly suggested that a ring, perhaps an incomplete one, had briefly blocked the starlight; observations during subsequent eclipses hinted that Neptune might have three partial arc rings. Such intimations, however, were the best that ground-based telescopes could do. Then, in 1989, the American spacecraft *Voyager 2* swept past Neptune and took a series of closeup photographs. The images revealed faint full rings—four of them in all. □

Dead Ringer

The fossil record as it existed in the mid-19th century made Darwinian evolutionists fret. A huge variety of plants and animals such as crustaceans, jellyfish, and the primitive crablike creatures called trilobites crowded the rock layers of the Cambrian era, which, according to modern estimates, began about 570 million years ago. But there were virtually no fossils from earlier periods. To the opponents of evolution, the stark contrast was taken as proof of the divine creation that is described in the Bible's Book of Genesis. Darwinists rejected the notion of life's sudden appearance on Earth, but they needed the evidence of more ancient forms—the ancestors of the Cambrian creatures—to demonstrate that complex animals and plants had evolved from simpler beings.

Thus in 1864 evolutionists were primed to welcome the news that Canada's illustrious paleon-

tologist John William Dawson had identified a pre-Cambrian fossil embedded in limestone from North America's oldest rock formation. Modern oceans swarm with tiny shell-encased invertebrates called foraminifers, and Dawson's fossil was declared an ancient ancestor—but, with a diameter of several inches, an ancestor many times larger than any of its living descendants. Like them, the creature appeared to have had a concentric spiral shell composed of separate chambers with a system of tubes linking them. Dawson christened the stony image *Eozoon canadense*—"dawn animal of Canada."

Dawson himself was no evolutionist. Indeed, he believed that the persistence of similarities between *Eozoon* and modern foraminifers for hundreds of millions of years undercut the Darwinian notion that natural selection gradually altered the form of animals. Nevertheless, he was glad to be the man who had discovered the first sign of pre-Cambrian life and did not reject endorsements for *Eozoon* from the opposing camp. Paleontologist and ardent evolutionist Thomas Henry Huxley, for example, declared that the case for *Eozoon* was "fairly proved," and Charles Darwin himself blessed

the discovery by including *Eozoon* as a type of primitive foraminifer in a revised edition of *The Origin of Species*. Naturalists went on hunts for local specimens of *Eozoon*. In 1866 a German announced finding a close cousin in Bavaria—*Eozoon bavaricum*—and other spots as scattered as Ireland, Massachusetts, and the Isle of Skye yielded fossils of the presumed dawn creatures as well. Once scientists knew what to look for, evidence of pre-Cambrian foraminifers seemed to be everywhere.

The enthusiastic chorus did not drown out the negative note first sounded in 1865 by mineralogists William King and Thomas H. Rowney at the Queen's College in Galway, on Ireland's west coast. When they learned about Dawson's purported foraminifer, they set about examining rock formations in Galway similar to those in Canada—and at first thought that they had found a Gaelic *Eozoon*. But analysis forced them to conclude that the skeleton-like structures were actually rock crystals in a spiral arrangement—and that *Eozoon* was as well.

When King and Rowney's first salvo appeared in print, Dawson's principal cheerleader in Great Britain, microscopist and paleontologist William B. Carpenter, published a nasty letter that belittled Thomas ◊

Seen in Wyatt Eaton's 1891 portrait, paleontologist John William Dawson *(above)* insisted that dark and light bands in rocks *(right)* were fossil remains. In fact, the distinctive striations were caused by mineral crystallization.

Rowney's professional competence and implied that King enjoyed damaging the scientific reputation of his betters. Not one to turn the other cheek, King responded by assailing Carpenter's "undignified and intemperate style" and, loftily claiming the high moral ground, declared that he and his collaborator deemed it "more honourable to be employed in educing truth, than in vanquishing Dr. Carpenter."

The battle stretched on for almost two decades, with King and Rowney slowly winning defectors to their side. In 1894 evidence that proved fatal to *Eozoon* literally surfaced in Italy. Some of the rocks spewed out of Mount Vesuvius, one of Europe's great active volcanoes, had been partially melted, then solidified—a metamorphic beating that would have eliminated all traces of Dawson's *Eozoon*, but not the crystalline spirals discovered by King and Rowney. Yet in the supposedly fossil-free rocks from Mount Vesuvius, scientists found the distinctive crystal whorls of *Eozoon*. The conclusion was inevitable: The supposed ancient foraminifer remains were not ossified skeletons at all, but artifacts of mineral metamorphosis.

The evidence convinced everyone but John William Dawson. Until his death in November 1899, he clung to his dawn creature of Canada, unwilling to admit that *Eozoon* had been mere scientific wishful thinking. The broader expectation that pre-Cambrian rocks would finally yield some sign of early life was met that same year, when American paleontologist Charles Doolittle Walcott *(pages 87-88)* reported finding an 850-million-year-old fossil algae called *Chuaria* in Grand Canyon rock formations. □

The Slime of His Life

On its 1857 voyage across the Atlantic Ocean to take soundings for a telegraph cable between England and Newfoundland, HMS *Cyclops* also fulfilled a special request made by biologist Thomas Henry Huxley for samples of the seafloor. Following Huxley's directions, the crew dredged up specimens of submarine mud and put them in a strong alcohol mixture to preserve the soft tissues of any creatures that might be present in the sediments. Previous samplings of the ocean floor, Huxley knew, had contained large numbers of tiny, one-celled animals with limy shells. Whether the creatures, called foraminifers, were bottom dwellers or whether their remains drifted down from a higher level after death was a puzzle that Huxley hoped to solve with the *Cyclops*'s gleanings.

Duly delivered to Huxley, the jars contained a fine brown sediment, large quantities of foraminifer skeletons and curious rounded particles that he dubbed coccoliths. But the haul was disappointing. He could not determine what the odd globules were and was unable to resolve the matter of the foraminifers' habitat. Huxley set the material aside and, for the moment at least, lost interest—with evolution looming on the horizon, the mysterious particles must have seemed trivial.

In the years following, another researcher, London physician and amateur marine researcher George Charles Wallich, discovered in other seafloor samples what he called coccospheres. The tiny globes contained gelatinous blobs, according to Wallich, who speculated that the coccosphere might be a foraminifer in a larval stage. And there the matter rested until Huxley's interest was revived.

It may have been the much more powerful microscope he had recently acquired that prompted Huxley to haul out his dusty collection of *Cyclops* jars and take another look at their contents in 1868. When he resuscitated the long-neglected samples, he examined them in a different scientific light than in 1857. For one thing he had become the most ardent defender of Charles Darwin's theory of evolution, published in 1859. For another he had read the books in which German zoologist Ernst Haeckel *(pages 46-48)* proposed that all higher forms of life had evolved from homogeneous, unstructured blobs called monera. So extremely primitive were these lowly beings, Haeckel thought, that they were scarcely distinguishable from nonliving matter. He had, unfortunately, no captive monera to point to, nor a fossilized one, but he proposed the ocean floor as the most likely place to find some trace of them. Lured by the German's assumptions, Huxley set out to discover whether his coccoliths were, in fact, something like Haeckel's monera.

With his fine new instrument, Huxley could see many more details of the coccoliths, and he also picked out Wallich's coccospheres. But there was something more—something that he had not seen in 1857: a blobby, protoplasm-like matter that had neither the nuclei nor the outer membranes of a mass of ordinary cells. Announcing his findings at a meeting of the British Association for the Advancement of Science, Huxley declared that this primitive slime from the deep ◊

Victorian biologist Thomas Henry Huxley concluded that coccoliths—the round shells in the scanning electron micrograph at right—were the skeletal remains of the ubiquitous *Bathybius haeckelii,* an "organism" that was only a chemical reaction.

Seen in an 1891 portrait by John Collier, Thomas Henry Huxley graciously conceded that *Bathybius*, the coccolith-strewn ooze sketched below by German Darwinist Ernst Haeckel, was a chemical illusion.

sea "must, I think, be regarded as a new form of those simple animated beings which have recently been so well described by Haeckel." In honor of the German scientist, Huxley named the slime *Bathybius haeckelii*—literally, "Haeckel's life of the deep." Huxley dashed off a letter to Haeckel, who responded, "I am, of course, most especially delighted by Bathybius Haeckelii and am very proud to be the godfather at its christening." He concluded his letter with a stirring "Vive Monera!" (Monera lives!)

Other British naturalists quickly embraced *Bathybius* as a form of life—whether plant or animal Huxley did not hazard to guess. Within months of Huxley's lecture, *Bathybius* appeared in a seafloor dredging operation off the coast of Scotland. Attested to by other scientists, samples from points as distant as the South Atlantic and the Indian Ocean prompted Huxley to suggest that the primal slime was a global phenomenon, stretching in a continuous film from sea to sea. Watching from the sidelines, Haeckel was so bold as to wonder, "Is protoplasm perhaps originating continually through spontaneous generation? Here we stand before a series of dark questions, the answers to which can only be hoped for from subsequent researches."

In 1872 an American expedition to the North Pole dredged up an astonishing find off Greenland—even simpler than *Bathybius*, this slime had no coccoliths to disturb its primeval simplicity. Assuming its extreme antiquity, the slime's discoverer, Emil Bessels, named it *Protobathybius*—the first deep-dwelling life. It was also the last; after *Bathybius*'s Greenland cousin, no other members of the family turned up.

That same year, HMS *Challenger* set off from England on a globe-circling oceanographic mission. Its scientists scrutinized samples of water from the bottom of the ocean for fresh *Bathybius* in its natural state—but after three years had found not a sign of it. His curiosity aroused by the bewildering dearth of the presumably global slime, *Challenger* chemist John Young Buchanan tested the water samples to see whether they contained any carbon, an element found in all plant and animal tissues. Failing to find any carbon, he then examined bottom samples that his shipmate, geologist John Murray, had preserved in alcohol. Sure enough, some of Murray's bottles contained a gelatinous, *Bathybius*-like stuff. Buchanan's analysis proved the substance to be calcium sulfate that had precipitated out of seawater when it was mixed with alcohol. *Bathybius*, it appeared, was no more than an accident of inorganic chemistry.

It fell to the chief scientific officer of the *Challenger*, Sir Charles Wyville Thomson, to deliver the bad news of *Bathybius*'s sadly altered condition to Thomas Huxley. The letter was virtually a death notice, although Thomson offered a faint ray of hope that the primordial slime might somehow survive the blow. He need not have hemmed and hawed so, for Huxley gracefully acknowledged his error and without delay published passages from Thomson's letter in the widely read journal *Nature*. In an address to the same British scientific association where he had first revealed his find, Huxley told his audience, "I thought my young friend *Bathybius* would turn out a credit to me. But I am sorry to say, as time has gone on, he has not altogether verified the promise of his youth."

Huxley not only proved himself a scientist of exemplary integrity but a man willing to follow his own advice. "Sit down before fact as a little child," he once counseled a friend, "be prepared to give up every preconceived notion, follow humbly wherever and to whatever abysses nature leads, or you shall learn nothing." And, he might have added, you may be slimed. □

Spirit Medium

In the second half of the 19th century, most physicists were persuaded that light traveled in waves through a medium called the ether, thought to be a colorless, gelatin-like substance that filled the universe. The assumption of this universal medium—a medium, it became obvious in the 1930s, that does not really exist—raised an interesting question: How, scientists were curious to know, was the ether affected by the Earth and other celestial bodies moving through it? Some scholars held that the Earth must drag ether along with it. Others believed that the Earth exerted only a partial drag on the medium, a hypothesis that might be proved if the difference between the movement of the Earth and the ether—a quantity known as ether drift—could be measured.

This possibility led two Cleveland physicists to set up an experiment in a campus basement in 1887. The better known of the pair was Albert A. Michelson of the Case School of Applied Science, who had made a name for himself in the field of optics and was destined to win a Nobel Prize for his distinguished work. His partner, Edward W. Morley of Western Reserve University, was a chemist noted for the precision of his measurements. The two scientists thought they could verify the partial-drag hypothesis by measuring the effect of moving ether on the speed of light waves. If changes in the speed of light were detected, they reasoned, it would mean that ether and Earth did not move entirely in concert. Perhaps more important, such measurements would verify the existence of the invisible medium itself. The centerpiece of the basement experiment was an interferometer, a device of Michelson's invention capable of detecting extremely minute changes in the speed of light.

Michelson's first instrument had been completed in 1881 and tested at Germany's University of Berlin, where he was pursuing postgraduate studies. This interferometer had two straight arms, four feet long, set at right angles to one another, with a mirror where they joined. The mirror was half-silvered to split the ray of light; part of the beam went through the mirror along one arm, and part was deflected up the other arm. At the end of each arm, a mirror reflected the beams back to their source, where they combined at a focal point. If the two combining beams had traveled at exactly the same speed, the peaks and valleys of the light waves would coincide perfectly, producing a charac- ◊

teristic "fringe pattern" that could be observed through a small telescope. But if one beam moved more slowly—if it were altered by the movement of ether, for example—the combining waves would not coincide, and the experimenters would see a shift in the fringe pattern.

Michelson had returned to the United States in 1882 and had begun working with Morley in 1885. In 1887, applying the lessons learned with the German prototype, the pair completed a second, more complex instrument for a new series of experiments. This interferometer was installed on a slab of granite, which in turn floated on a pool of mercury. Because the subtle differences in fringe pattern became more detectable when the light traveled farther, the light path was increased by reflecting the beams back and forth with a series of mirrors.

Michelson and Morley assumed that if one arm pointed into the hypothetical onrushing stream of ether, the light beam traveling in that direction would have to beat its way against the current; thus it would take longer to reach the focal point than the beam traveling along the second arm, set at an angle to the hypothetical current. After being tested in this position, the interferometer was rotated, and the test was run again. Proceeding in this manner, Michelson and Morley rotated the arms of the interferometer through a full circle. But to their amazement, they found that the orientation of the arms made no difference whatsoever. Wherever they pointed, the two beams of light took exactly the same time to make their round trips—and the fringe pattern was consequently unchanging. The ether, if it was there at all, seemed to have no effect

whatsoever on the speed of light.

Physicists were stunned to learn that the most favored ether hypothesis had been tested and found very seriously wanting. Another physicist at Case, named Dayton C. Miller, who believed passionately in ether, thought the pair must have somehow gone wrong in their experimental procedures. This was a bold, even audacious assumption, in view of Michelson's expertise in optics and Morley's measurement skills. But Miller was no secondrater. A leading expert in the behavior of acoustical waves, he was a man other scientists listened to.

At the International Congress of Physics held in Paris in 1900, Lord Kelvin, the pro-ether giant of British science, urged Miller and Morley to repeat the experiment with a more sensitive apparatus. Morley agreed to team up with Miller to put the interferometer through its paces once again, presumably with greater care. When they ran their tests, however, the results were the same: They detected no sign of moving ether's presumed effect.

This puzzled Miller, as he and Morley had modified the instrument considerably. Instead of using a pair of joined arms, they had used a cross-shaped device and had again increased the length of the light path with mirrors. Pondering their results, the pair decided that the experiments might have failed because they had been carried out in a basement sheltered from the ether current. Miller and Morley set up an interferometer in an exposed spot on the summit of a low hill overlooking Lake Erie and carried out a painstaking series of experiments during the summer and fall of 1905. Again the results were utter disappointments.

Morley retired in 1905, aged 67, but Dayton Miller continued his energetic advocacy of ether and his resistance to Albert Einstein's newly coined ideas about special relativity—which held that the speed of light is changeless and hinted that ether, whether real or imagined, could simply be ignored. Experimental evidence supporting the relativist's theories steadily mounted, and in 1919 Miller decided to have another experimental go at partial drag. This time he chose a location still more elevated and exposed to ether drift—the 6000-foot heights of Mount Wilson in California, site of a famous astronomical observatory. In 1921 Miller installed his interferometer in a tar-and-canvas hut—and for the first time got what seemed to be significant signs of ether-induced changes in the speed of light. He realized, however, that factors such as sharp fluctuations in temperature or magnetic distortions of his interferometer's steel base could have produced misleading readings.

To counteract such influences, Miller took his detector back to his Cleveland laboratory and carefully refined it. Returning to a new site on Mount Wilson in 1924, he finally obtained the result he had pursued for years—apparently trustworthy interferometer readings demonstrating ether drift. The speed of the Earth with respect to the ether was measured at approximately 2,232 miles per hour—a good deal slower than Miller had expected, but nevertheless a most satisfactory result. As far as he was concerned, he had corroborated the partial-drag hypothesis, proved the existence of ether, and refuted Einstein.

The anti-relativity contingent among physicists acclaimed Miller's work, which in 1925 was honored with a $1,000 prize from the American Association for the Advancement of Science. Miller's reputation had also won him election to the National Academy of Sciences and the presidency of the American Physical Society. But this noisy round of plaudits, now heard mainly on only one side of the hall, soon began to die away.

At Miller's Mount Wilson haunt, Roy Kennedy of the California Institute of Technology set up his own interferometer, sealing it in a gas-filled metal case to isolate the device from changes in temperature and pressure that could skew the measurements. In 1926 Kennedy reported his results: no ether wind. He was not alone. On the heights of the Alps, even suspended from high-flying balloons, in winter cold and summer heat, interferometers searching for ether found not a single sign of its existence.

Shrugging off the accumulating anti-ether data, Miller doggedly clung to his belief—he was right and every other experimentalist was dead wrong. But the position he occupied became increasingly lonely. As the 1920s and 1930s wore on, most of the remaining holdouts among American physicists were bidding ether farewell. Even the aging Albert Michelson, now a Nobel laureate, reentered the fray. In a move suggesting an admirable modesty about his experimental achievements, he built an enormous interferometer with a light path of about 83 feet—an instrument of unrivaled accuracy for measuring the speed of light. Albert Michelson's data, published in 1930, was enough to convert anyone—except Dayton Miller, who died in 1941, an etherist to the end. □

Headmaster

In the late 19th century, scientists thought they could calculate a person's brain power by measuring the size of the skull. The practice was known as "craniometry," and its basic tenets were simple: Among humans, at least, the bigger the skull, the larger the brain; and the larger the brain, the more intelligent the person. At the time, the logic of matching skull size with mental ability was so compelling that craniometry attracted a host of respected adherents, who saw an opportunity to add precision to the inexact business of assessing mental performance.

One of those drawn to craniometry was the great French psychologist Alfred Binet (below), director of the Sorbonne University's Laboratory of Physiological Psychology in Paris. He embraced the technique with enthusiasm. "The relationship between the intelligence of subjects and the volume of their head," he wrote confidently in 1898, "is very real and has been confirmed by all methodical investigators without exception." Over the next three years, Binet published no fewer than nine scientific papers about using craniometry as a guide to intelligence.

But as he measured and studied the heads of hundreds of French children, Binet felt his belief in the technique begin to crumble. The reason, he discovered, was what he later called auto-suggestion—an unconscious tendency to weight observations in favor of a preconceived outcome. "I feared," he wrote with notable candor in 1900, "that in making measurements on heads with the intention of finding a difference in volume between an intelligent and a less intelligent head, I would be led to increase, unconsciously and in good faith, the cephalic volume of intelligent heads and to decrease that of unintelligent heads."

Evidence of this error had come from a study done by Binet and his assistant Théodore Simon that compared the skull sizes of children identified by teachers as their best and worst pupils. Binet and Simon discovered to their dismay that they each had obtained different skull measurements for the same set of 10 children. Simon's data were consistently smaller.

Binet went back to the school ◊

and remeasured the pupils. This time, Binet's own measurements seemed to shrink the childrens' heads, resulting in smaller skulls for 8 out of 10 of them. Not only that, but the average difference between Binet's first batch of measurements and the second—three millimeters—was quite significant. It was far more than the average difference—only one millimeter—Binet had found between the brightest and dullest children. To him, the potential for self-deception was all too clear, and he turned away from craniometry.

While Binet continued to believe that head size and intelligence were related, he decided that the physical differences between bright and dull children were "vague and uncertain." In 1904, commissioned by the French government to search for ways of identifying children who needed special educational help, he began to develop another kind of measuring scheme. Beginning in 1905, he tested several variations of an examination designed to detect low intelligence among children. He asked students to complete a series of tasks indexed to age, then subtracted their chronological age from the mental age yielded by the tests. This, he believed, provided an indication of which students needed special help. Beyond that, Binet was reluctant to go. "The scale," he wrote, "does not permit the measure of the intelligence, because intellectual qualities are not superposable, and therefore cannot be measured as linear surfaces are measured."

Despite his clarity of vision, however, Alfred Binet had loosed a kind of monster into the ranks of educational psychology. Within seven years, the German psychologist L. William Stern had adapted Binet's tests, dividing by chronological age rather than subtracting to obtain a number, which he then multiplied by 100 to eliminate the decimal. The result: The intelligence quotient, or IQ, used for nearly a century now to predict—and, against Binet's intentions, to rank—the mental abilities of the young. □

N, As in Not

Fashions come and go in scientific research, and around the turn of the 20th century studying—with an eye to discovering—new forms of radiation was all the rage. The trendsetter was German physicist Wilhelm Röntgen, who in 1895 discovered a previously unsuspected form of energy that penetrated solid objects as readily as sunlight passed through a windowpane. After these x-rays, as Röntgen called them, came still more discoveries in the same vein—the alpha, beta, and gamma radiation emitted by such radioactive elements as radium suggested that secret rays were everywhere, just waiting to be found.

René-Prosper Blondlot, a prominent experimental physicist at France's University of Nancy, was one of many scientists who jumped on the radiation bandwagon. In 1903 Blondlot was exploring one of the unresolved questions about x-rays: whether they were streams of high-energy particles or a type of electromagnetic wave, like light. (Modern scientists know that, like all forms of radiation, x-rays can behave as both.) The orientation of electromagnetic waves would be altered, or polarized, as the waves passed through a transparent prism; but x-rays seemed not to be affected. In Blondlot's view, however, this did not mean x-rays were not wave energy; he believed that they were preoriented by the x-ray source, a cathode-ray tube. Blondlot's 1903 experiment was intended to prove this.

The conventional experimental setup to measure the intensity of x-rays linked the emitting tube to an electrical coil and to two wires ending in pointed ends. These points opposed one another across a gap, like fangs. As the cathode-ray tube discharged its electrical current, a spark flew across the gap between these points; if x-rays were present,

Physicist Robert Wood *(right)* debunked n-rays in 1904, about five years before this photograph was taken.

the spark was boosted and could leap gaps of increasing breadth as power was increased. This permitted scientists to measure the intensity of the x-ray emission by measuring the length of the spark.

Blondlot's tack was to use changes in the spark's brightness rather than its length to determine whether the x-rays were being polarized—a trickier procedure, since it involved using either the often unreliable eye or photographic plates to assess differences. And here he discovered a peculiar effect. With the gap between points aligned with the cathode rays, Blondlot could reduce the spark's apparent intensity by inserting a lead or glass screen between the tube and the spark gap. But when the gap was at right angles to the cathode rays, the screens had no effect. This suggested to him that, as he had suspected, the x-rays were being preoriented at the source.

With

the confidence of an experienced experimentalist, Blondlot then added a further touch: He tried deflecting the energy emitted by the cathode tube with a quartz crystal prism. Physicists had proved that x-rays could not be bent by a crystal—yet the beam was deflected, and, if Blondlot could believe his own eyes, the electric spark seemed brighter in the presence of the prism. With the same apparatus in place, he turned down the voltage of the cathode tube far enough that, according to his calculations, no x-rays would be emitted. Again, the spark seemed to brighten—*something* was still being emitted, but, because it was refracted by a quartz prism, it could not be x-rays. Abandoning scientific caution, Blondlot leapt the gap to explanation: Clearly, he hypothesized, the cathode tube was emitting another form of radiation never before observed. He named it the n-ray, after his university and town.

Blondlot's discovery stirred up a great deal of excitement among other physicists, and the excitement mounted as

he announced still more evidence of n-rays. They were, he said, produced by a household gas lamp but not by a Bunsen burner. They seemed to pour from tempered steel whenever it was deformed or strained. A simple brick could capture and store n-rays, yet the strange emissions could not even penetrate a thin sheet of water.

Such mysteries inspired other scientists to follow in Blondlot's footsteps. After running their own experiments, Nancy biophysicists declared that such ferments as vinegar and alcohol were emitters— even the human nervous system emitted n-rays. This invisible energy, moreover, increased the powers of sensory organs, including vision. Enhanced sight was a boon to the n-rayists, who by necessity worked in the dark because it made the jumping spark more visible. Incredibly, the very subject of the experiment supposedly increased the acuity of the observing eye, which might otherwise miss the subtle differences in brightness that marked the generation of n-rays. Augustin Charpentier, a professor of medical physics at Blondlot's university, declared that talking and even simply thinking stepped up the body's n-radiation so much that he could measure the difference. Human cadavers, he maintained, kept up their emissions after death.

By 1904 a score of French researchers had confirmed the existence of n-rays. But the mysterious new energy suffered in translation—German and English scien- ◊

A little more than two decades before his supposed discovery of n-rays, French physicist René-Prosper Blondlot *(left)* posed proudly in the robes of the French Academy of Sciences.

tists remained skeptical. Unable to reproduce the experimental results of Blondlot and his French colleagues, they grumbled that Blondlot's methods, especially his reliance on the naked eye to judge the brightness of a spark, were perilously subjective. German physicist Otto Lummer noted that a light source appears brighter when it is viewed with peripheral vision instead of a direct gaze because more retinal rods—the eye's dim-light receptors—come into play. Well aware of this phenomenon, astronomers used their peripheral vision when viewing faint stars.

Stung by allegations of subjectivity, Blondlot began recording the sparks on photographic plates. But this did not satisfy his severest critics, who pointed out that it would be easy to alter exposure times, consciously or unconsciously, in such a way as to produce the desired results. The French did not take kindly to foreign carping. Teutonic and Anglo-Saxon naysayers were, according to the Gallic patriots, so dulled by fog and beer that they were unable to appreciate what French science had accomplished.

But the truly devastating critic of n-rays was not a European but a young physics professor at Johns Hopkins University in Baltimore, Maryland. A skilled experimentalist who had won acclaim for his work in analyzing electromagnetic radiation, Robert Wood professed himself unhappy about "wasting an entire morning" trying to get the results that Blondlot claimed. Encouraged by other similarly frustrated colleagues, Wood booked passage to France in September 1904 to see the French physicist's laboratory for himself.

An accommodating host, Blond-lot was pleased to display his n-ray experiments. He performed, apparently to his own satisfaction, a demonstration of how a spark's brightness could be reduced simply by placing a hand between the n-ray source and the pair of electric wires. Wood, however, later wrote that he could not detect the slightest change in the spark.

A second experiment gave Wood the opportunity to play what proved to be a devastating trick. Blondlot set up an apparatus that supposedly deflected n-rays through an aluminum prism and onto a screen with a strip coated with fluorescent paint, which would glow in the presence of n-radiation. The test, which had to be run in the dark, was performed for the watching Wood. As Blondlot was preparing for another run, the American plucked the aluminum prism from the apparatus and slipped it into his pocket. Unaware of his guest's sleight of hand, Blondlot carried on with the experiment as if nothing were amiss. The absence of the supposedly critical prism, according to Wood, had no effect whatever on the results Blondlot claimed to get—even without the prism, he continued to see the luminous strip glowing with n-radiation. After about three hours of experimentation, Wood declared that he was "unable to report a single observation which appeared to indicate the existence of the rays." The French scientists, he said, must have been "in some way deluded."

Published in 1904 in *Nature,* a well-respected British journal, Robert Wood's account of his visit to Blondlot's laboratory whipped up a controversy. Hoping to settle the matter once and for all, the French journal *Revue Scientifique* proposed a foolproof test of the n-ray hypothesis. A piece of tempered steel, a material believed to be an n-ray source, would be sealed in a box; a second box would contain a piece of lead, which Blondlot's experiments had ruled out as a source. Blondlot would then test them "blind" for n-ray emissions; only after his experiments were complete would he learn the contents of the boxes.

Blondlot hesitated to pick up the challenge and finally declined to try the magazine's proposal. He labeled the experiment "simplistic," adding "the phenomena are much too delicate for that. Let each one form his personal opinion about N-rays, either from his own experiments or from those of others in whom he has confidence." By that time many scientists had already formed their personal opinions of n-rays—and they were negative.

In December of 1904, only three months after Wood's article appeared, the editors of the *Revue* published their conclusion: N-rays were not a physical phenomenon, but a psychological one, not deserving scientific credence. But the editors were careful to underscore their esteem for Blondlot and the scientists who had enthusiastically endorsed his discovery. The scientific tenor of the times, the editors rightly noted, had made people too willing to accept new discoveries in electromagnetic radiation. Unfortunately, n-rays were a trick of the eye—a delusion, as Robert Wood had so bluntly put it.

In 1909 the 60-year-old Blondlot retired from the University of Nancy but continued his study of n-rays, never conceding any error or reneging on his original claims. At his death in 1930 he was still convinced of their reality. □

The fossilized impressions of three-lobed, crablike creatures called trilobites crowd into a single slab *(right)* of rock from Canada's Burgess Shale.

Shale Game

A crucial accident took place, many paleontologists believe, midway through the Cambrian period some 530 million years ago, in shallow waters not far from the seashore. The upper portion of a gentle muddy incline slumped and began sliding downslope. Worms, shellfish, algae, sponges, mollusks, and the crablike creatures called trilobites were tumbled along by the turbulent flow; mud began to fill the spaces between their shells and soft bodies and work its way into their gills and joints and down their gullets. By the time the creatures came to a stop near the bottom of the slope, so much mud had penetrated their bodies that the sediment piling up on them did not crush them. Because their final resting place was a stagnant lower basin devoid of oxygen, the remains did not decay. The muddy tomb was slowly transformed into a smooth black shale that encased these intact, fossilized animals in exquisite detail; a carnivorous worm's gut, for instance, still held the fossilized remains of its last meal.

The buried creatures went undetected until August 31, 1909, when near the end of a summer of fossil hunting, Mr. and Mrs. Charles Doolittle Walcott split open an interesting block of shale they had just found on a ridge in the Canadian Rocky Mountains. Secretary of the Smithsonian Institution and arguably the world's leading authority on Cambrian paleontology, Walcott had been drawn repeatedly to the area by its rough beauty and, perhaps, by what he had read about earlier fossil finds there. The block's contents confirmed his instincts, for he saw immediately that he and

his wife had a great trove before them. His attention was riveted not by the ossified shells, however, but by the extant traces of soft body parts—rare treasures for a paleontologist, since they are almost never preserved as fossils.

The season was almost over, but the following summer Walcott located the outcrop from which the serendipitous block had fallen. Called the Burgess Shale, a single layer of rock some eight feet thick yielded the most spectacular assemblage of fossils ever found in North America. During five summers Walcott collected more than 60,000 specimens—a landmark in the study of life's evolution.

More than a hundred species of animals and plants are preserved in the Burgess Shale, and Walcott identified scores of previously unknown types, finding a place for each one in the taxonomic system. Taxonomy—the science of classification—groups closely related species, both living and extinct, into genera, assembles allied genera into families, and continues grouping more and more generally on up through the hierarchical system to the phylum and kingdom. The members of a phylum have the same basic body plan but may be quite different in detail—all animals with a backbone, for example, belong to the phylum Chordata. Walcott concluded that the Burgess Shale fossils were the simple forebears of more sophisticated modern animals—close enough kin that there was no need to invent new phyla; each Burgess specimen was pigeonholed in an existing phylum occupied by its presumed descendants.

Neither during Walcott's life nor for nearly four decades after his

death in 1927 did anyone take serious issue with his analysis of the Burgess Shale lode. The specimens gathered Smithsonian dust until 1966, when Harry B. Whittington of Cambridge University, the world's leading expert on fossil trilobites, took a fresh look at the old specimens and gathered some new ones from the site. Whittington and his team of naturalists soon took exception to Walcott's classification, which had obscured the significance of the entire collection. Many of the Burgess creatures, Whittington reported later, were not the usual trilobites, but bizarre oddities that should have been labeled as unique. Like nothing under the modern sun, the vanished or- ◊

ganisms had nevertheless been stuffed into established phyla.

Examining the fossil denizens of the Burgess Shale anew has lead Whittington and his team to recategorize many of them. The foot-and-a-half-long organism aptly named *Anomalocaris*, or "odd shrimp," was the largest creature Walcott discovered; but he had mistakenly divided it into three pieces. In fact, Whittington's team identified it as the largest predator of Cambrian times and placed it in a phylum all its own. The odd shrimp had swum about, propelled by a series of fins; two appendages at the front of its body made the brute the terror of trilobites—*Anomalocaris* crunched them with a ring of spiked plates housed in its mouth. Now and again this Cambrian hunter apparently lost its grip on its prey, for the shells of several Burgess trilobites bear wounds that are a good match for the plates. Another creature, *Hallucigenia*, is so bizarre that the experts are still arguing about which of its numerous appendages it walked on and which ones it waved tentacle-like overhead.

Scientists continue to weigh the numbers, but it seems likely that the Burgess Shale, where Walcott saw not one new phylum, contains well over a dozen species whose members have long since disappeared without progeny;

not one of these many body plans is manifest in a single living creature. Walcott stumbled upon a habitat that was home to a diversity of animal types far greater than exists today on the entire earth.

The question is why Walcott was blind to the richness before his very eyes. Sometimes the instruments at a scientist's disposal are not good enough, but such is not the case here. Some observers, such as Harvard University paleontologist Stephen Jay Gould, have suggested that Walcott's vision of the evolutionary process did not allow for unique dead-end animals or random disappearances caused by such minor incidents as a slumping slope. Instead, Walcott saw evolution as an order of progression—the working out in flesh and blood of God's grand plan for the gradual improvement of terrestrial life.

"From the beginning of life on earth," Walcott told audiences attending his lecture "Searching for the First Forms of Life," "there was a connection so close and intimate that, if the entire record could be obtained, a perfect chain of life from the lowest organism to the highest would

be established." In a steady ascension, he believed, various groups held pride of place for a time, only to be pushed aside—but not killed off—as a more advanced type came to the fore. The vanquished evolved into their modern avatars, keeping their phyla well-populated, but with gradually changing forms. Humans, of course, were the highest organism in this progressivist scheme, and the idea that our ancestors could have been wiped out, perhaps in a random incident as minor as the slump of a Cambrian slope, Walcott took to be absurd.

The venerable paleontologist was scarcely alone in his belief; many scientists shared his view of gradual progression from form to form. It may be that philosophy dimmed his vision. But Charles Walcott's great discovery has lost none of its luster. The Canadian government has declared the mountain outcrop that he mined a World Heritage Site, and guards patrol to prevent pilferers from erasing one of the planet's strangest paleontological histories. Walcott and, perhaps, paleontologists before and since merely missed the ancient mystery of the life forms suspended in the Burgess Shale. □

Shown in the Burgess Shale in 1912, Charles Walcott *(right)* evidently misread the fossil record there, evoking a lively but erroneous world of prehistoric swimmers, like those *(above)* painted in 1942 by Charles Knight.

Pet Rock

Sponges were Randolph Kirkpatrick's specialty, and in 1912 he took some time away from the British Museum, where he was the assistant keeper of specimens of primitive sea life, for a sponge-collecting trip. It was on Porto Santo Island off the Moroccan coast that Kirkpatrick got the first glimmer of an idea that was destined to grow into an eccentric theory explaining the composition of the Earth.

Although sponges were the focus of Kirkpatrick's expedition, he spent his spare time on Porto Santo examining volcanic rocks. The high heat they are subjected to supposedly destroys any trace of fossils, yet to Kirkpatrick's amazement the rocks at Porto Santo appeared to be stuffed with the fossilized shells of nummulites—single-celled aquatic members of the order Foraminifera that excrete a disk-shaped, chambered shell. Plentiful in ancient oceans, nummulite shells have been remarked on for thousands of years, however erroneously. Around Cairo, Egypt, their fossilized shells were so numerous that a geographer from ancient Greece thought they were lentils left behind by the slaves who built the great pyramids.

But Kirkpatrick had discerned the tiny remains in rock that should have been free of fossils. The find seemed to him so compelling that he turned away from his studies of sponges to pursue the nummulite threads he thought he saw running through nature. He named his discovery *Eozoon portosantum*, the "dawn animal of Porto Santo"—a name likely, as he well knew, to revive a controversy that had wound down almost two decades earlier. Then, a similar "dawn animal," supposedly a fossil foraminifer from Canada, had eventually been revealed as no more than a crystal formation *(pages 77-78)*.

As far as Kirkpatrick was concerned, however, the real *Eozoon* story had yet to be told. At his next stop, the island of Madeira off the coast of Portugal, Kirkpatrick encountered *Eozoon* once again. In order to embrace its broader territory, he changed the name to *Eozoon atlanticum*. The more he looked, the more he found. When he discovered what appeared to be nummulites in rock samples from the Indian and Pacific oceans, the apparently world-circling distribution inspired *Eozoon orbis-terrarum*. His next leap took Kirkpatrick into space. He checked a meteorite—more nummulites, which he decided should be called *Eozoon universum*. They seemed ubiquitous, although they were not always immediately apparent. "Sometimes I have found it necessary to examine a fragment of rock with the closest scrutiny for hours," Kirkpatrick wrote, in order to see the telltale patterns.

Finding nummulites everywhere he looked, Kirkpatrick theorized that they had been a kind of primordial building block in the days when terrestrial life was just forming in the seas. The tiny creatures, he believed, would have rained down through the depths, gradually building up a deep layer of their shells over the planet's submerged surface. Heated from the Earth's interior, the shells would have fused into other types of rocks and squeezed upward, some of them shooting into space, to return later as fossil-bearing meteorites.

The only sensible conclusion, as far as Kirkpatrick could see, was that there was but one rock in the universe: a composite of nummulites. He became completely absorbed by his theory and published at his own expense four volumes describing the formation of the Earth—the Nummulosphere, as he called it—from the little fossil disks. Their chambered spirals, in some manner that was difficult for others besides the author to grasp, expressed the very ◊

THE NUMMULOSPHERE

An Account of the ORGANIC ORIGIN of so-called IGNEOUS ROCKS and of ABYSSAL RED CLAYS

By R. KIRKPATRICK

BRITISH MUSEUM · NATURAL HISTORY

PRICE TWO SHILLINGS NET

LONDON
SOLD BY LAMLEY & CO.
1, EXHIBITION ROAD, S.W.

A meteorite in hand and a nummulite on his trident, Neptune rules a watery Earth in this cover design for the first volume of Randolph Kirkpatrick's *The Nummulosphere.*

essence of life. Not only were they everywhere—they were everything.

Kirkpatrick recognized that his views were "received with a good deal of skepticism." That understated his reception: Scientists who did not think Kirkpatrick merely foolish thought him mad. Still, he hewed to his hypothesis through his British Museum tenure, which ended in 1927, and until his death in 1950.

Yet for all his eccentricity where nummulites were concerned, Kirkpatrick had made lasting and important contributions to science. After his Porto Santo expedition, Kirkpatrick had identified enigmatic fossils, widely believed to be the remains of corals, as sponges—a view few paleontologists shared. But in the 1960s marine biologists discovered close living relatives of the supposedly extinct creatures in the Caribbean and belatedly verified Kirkpatrick's intuition. He had seen the sponges clearly; but he had never seen the nummulites at all. □

No Names, Just Initials

The Pickering brothers, mid-19th century additions to the old Boston family of that name, grew up to earn fame as astronomers, but fame of very different kinds. William, the younger and more impetuous of the two, made a far bigger splash with his daring, innovative brand of field astronomy—and was sometimes gloriously wrong. The highly respected Edward, 12 years older and more conventional than his brother, became the director of the Harvard Observatory, where, among other things, he found room under his wing for William as an assistant professor of astronomy, a position the younger Pickering did not exceed in 37 years there.

During his 42-year tenure as the observatory's director, the steady and methodical Edward amassed the world's largest collection of stellar photographs. William followed a more flamboyant career trajectory, enjoying such off-campus forays as stalking solar eclipses around the globe and establishing an observatory in Jamaica, which he directed for Harvard from 1911 until his retirement in 1924, when the Jamaica facility became his own private observatory.

William Pickering's greatest moment of glory came in March 1899, however, long before his West Indian ventures. Studying a photographic plate that showed the sky around Saturn, he noticed a faint object near the planet. It proved to be a previously unknown moon, which was named Phoebe. Pickering's discovery was a strange satellite—unlike any other moon identified at that time, Phoebe had a retrograde motion—that is, it orbited in a direction opposite to the direction of the planet's rotation.

No mean achievement, discovering Phoebe gave Pickering a taste for more celestial treasure hunting, and he got caught up in a decades-long search for more unknown planets in the Solar System. The quest made sense at the time. Slight perturbations in the orbit of Uranus, possibly caused by the gravitational sweeps of another planet, had led to the 1846 discovery of Neptune. Now, similar troubling of the orbits of both Uranus and Neptune suggested yet another sphere somewhere in the void beyond.

Pickering and another well-known astronomer, Percival Lowell *(pages 49-50)* of the famed Lowell Observatory, near Flagstaff, Arizona, were rivals in this endeavor, although they had much in common. Like Lowell, Pickering held and widely publicized his sometimes bizarre ideas about extraterrestrial life. He asserted, for instance, that the dark spots on the Moon were caused by migrating insects and believed that the crater-pocked satellite was laced with canals and sustained a rudimentary form of vegetation near active volcanic vents.

But Pickering was a much bolder predictor than his competitor. While Lowell spoke about the possibility of finding a single missing planet, which he labeled X, Pickering forecast the discovery of multiple planets—O, P, Q, R, S, T, and U. The confident Pickering even went so far as to assign specific features to planet O, including its distance from the Sun.

In 1930 Lowell Observatory's Clyde Tombaugh discovered the Solar System's ninth planet not far from the area where Pickering had

After predicting the existence of several unknown planets, William Pickering *(inset)* claimed credit for the discovery of the planet Pluto, shown at right *(center)* with its moon, Charon, in a 1990 image taken by the Hubble Space Telescope.

predicted planet O was hiding. Pickering felt thoroughly vindicated. But his peers were unwilling to give him credit because he had changed his mind so many times about the predicted planet's location. In the opinion of his critics, the most that could be said was that Pickering had made a lucky guess. His long-standing penchant for wild speculation also made more sober scientists loath to give him the benefit of the doubt. In later years, when more was known about the new planet, some scientists argued that its mass was too small to generate sufficient gravity to disturb the orbits of Uranus and Neptune. Thus, Pickering could not even have made an educated guess about its location; he had simply put planet O where he thought it ought to be.

Pickering eventually gave credit where it was due, more or less. The little planet was named Pluto, not only because it evoked the dark underworld of Greek myth, but because the first two letters of its name were Percival Lowell's initials. Not exactly true, countered Pickering—the P and L actually stood for Pickering and Lowell, roughly in their order of importance. The ploy was vintage Pickering. Until the end of his career, he could find what he wanted to find, anywhere he looked. □

Man with a Porpoise

Among the rare animals to rival humans in proportionate brain size are the ocean's great marine mammals. The sheer bulk of their nervous systems and their apparent ability to communicate complex concepts to their fellows has inspired a good deal of speculation about animal intelligence. But for a medical doctor named John C. Lilly, the mysterious potential of dolphins and whales suggested something more—perhaps a secret, superhuman intellect adapted somehow to the sea.

Lilly's single-minded interest in cetacean intelligence began in the late 1940s, when he was working as a professor at the University of Pennsylvania. On a Massachusetts holiday in 1949, he saw his first cetacean brain—the excised brain of a beached pilot whale, much larger than a human's. In subsequent travels, Lilly encountered examples of communication and complex social behavior among bottle-nosed dolphins and evidence of killer whales transmitting sonic messages through the sea. Contact by contact, his fascination came to center on the clicks, squeaks, barks, and whistles dolphins produced—a complex of sounds that could only be dolphin language.

Following this star, in 1958 the 43-year-old researcher established his own laboratory—the Communications Research Institute—at St. Thomas in the Virgin Islands. After lining up financial support from the Department of Defense, the National Science Foundation, and other government bodies, the doctor set to work in 1960 to analyze the tuneful chatter of his captive dolphins.

Soon, said Lilly, "we began to realize the dolphins wanted to communicate with us," and he undertook to translate their language, which he called "Delphinese." His laboratory sprouted complex hydrophonic and computer systems to aid in the effort. Before long, Lilly and his assistants were discerning conversation in this amplified, closely analyzed chorus from the sea.

If what they heard was Delphinese, Lilly pondered, what must such creatures be? Scientists until now had rated marine mammals with other lower warm-blooded species, but the laboratory's dolphins were clearly more than lab mice. As Lilly began to speculate about the implications of his research, he became visionary; it seemed that he had inadvertently made contact with a kind of parallel society that differed from humans only in its world-view and the fact

that it made the ocean its home. He envisioned a future marked by interspecies dialogues and mutual accommodation. The government would be called upon to provide a special "educational system" for dolphins to reinforce their links with humanity. In return, dolphins would perform services for the country, such as helping the military: "They might sneak up on an enemy submarine sitting on the bottom and shout something into the listening gear," he speculated.

Dolphins inspired others as well. In 1963 filmmaker Ivan Tors made the movie and television series *Flipper*, a watery version of *Lassie* starring a smiling, helpful, human-loving dolphin. Lilly served as a consultant to Tors, whose wife, Constance, served as a kind of consultant to Lilly, leading him into his next exploration: Experiments in which Lilly floated in a darkened wa-

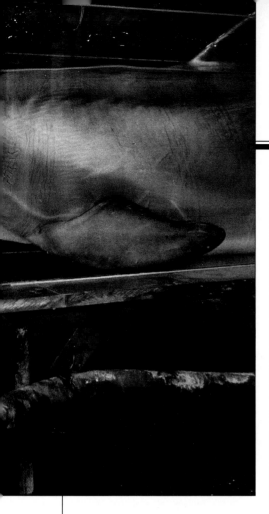

ter tank—a sensory deprivation chamber—after injecting himself with the hallucinogenic drug LSD. Not surprisingly, Lilly developed during these excursions from reality what he called "a strange intuition" that the dolphins in the lagoon nearby influenced him during his LSD trips. Once he injected his dolphins with LSD but detected no behavior that seemed to match his own under the drug's influence.

Eventually, Lilly concluded that he could no longer condone experimenting with such intelligent animals. This decision, together with legal and financial problems, brought an end to the Communications Research Institute in 1967. The last days were tragic: Just before Lilly announced the closing to his employees, five of the institute's dolphins died. Lilly was convinced that they had committed suicide.

Although the dolphins were gone, they were hardly forgotten. After nearly a decade's hiatus, Lilly and his supporters created the Human/Dolphin Foundation, a nonprofit institution that endured until 1985. Lilly has reflected on and preached the creatures' intelligence in articles, speeches, and workshops. His work was celebrated in the Robert Merle novel and 1973 movie *The Day of the Dolphin.* His visionary outlook remains intact. In five books Lilly has suggested that dolphins have a culture that they pass on orally from generation to generation. Consequently, he says, all aquariums housing dolphins should install underwater telephones to permit the inmates to communicate from tank to tank. The phone lines, he adds, should in some cases be extended to the sea so that the captive dolphins' families and friends can talk with them. At the least, the animals should be guaranteed a "limited term of service" in captivity lasting no longer than a year. Dolphins are due other rights as well, Lilly has written, including full legal parity with humans and the right to sue humans who jeopardize their welfare.

Other scientists have concluded that dolphins are indeed intelligent, resourceful mammals, with extraordinarily complex social structures and skills that are still far from fully understood. They have rejected most of Lilly's conclusions, however, on grounds of distorted scientific method and the absence of published papers on his results. Although dolphin research continues, John Lilly is almost as alone in his belief today as he was four decades earlier, one of the few who claim to have discerned the deeper texture of the subtle creatures whom he calls the humans of the sea. □

Leading Questions

Good science, according to textbook descriptions of its methods, depends upon an observing eye that is undimmed by bias. An intelligent robot might measure up to this standard 100 percent of the time, but human beings are often not so objective as they would like to believe. Even the most scrupulous scientist can, it seems, fall into the trap known as "experimenter expectancy."

In 1963 Harvard University researcher Robert Rosenthal and his colleague Kermit Fode made a systematic study of observer bias, using 12 undergraduate psychology students as unwitting experimental subjects. The students were told that each of them would be teaching five rats to run a maze. Half of them were "maze-bright" rats bred, according to the researchers, from intelligent ancestors with a knack for running a maze quickly. The researchers said that the other group was composed of "maze-dull" rats descended from ordinary, slower-witted ancestors. In reality, there was no difference whatsoever in the ancestry of the rats, none of which had any maze-running experience.

The rats were put into a maze shaped like a T. The two halves of the crosspiece, one painted white and the other gray, were interchangeable—but the food reward ◊

The movement of flatworms *(above)* in response to light tested the effect of expectation on experimental results.

The rat sniffing the air at left is from a laboratory strain that was used in Harvard University's observer-bias study, which found that rats labeled "maze bright" seemed smarter.

Water Wonderland

awaiting the successful maze runner was always in the gray arm. Presumably a brainy rat would master the trick faster and head directly to its reward. To assess the skill of the five rats, students simply timed how long it took each rat to choose the dark arm.

Rosenthal and Fode found that the animals touted as maze bright consistently received better times. The explanation was not, it seemed, consciously falsified data. A questionnaire revealed that the students who were assigned maze-bright rats found them not only smarter, but more pleasant and more likable; classmates burdened with rodent dullards were less enthusiastic about the animals. The researchers speculated that a student's good feelings might somehow be communicated to the rats and boost their performance. Although Rosenthal and Fode could not pin down the mechanism at work, they concluded that a student's bias, whether positive or negative, affected the experiment's outcome.

A second foray into experimenter expectation probably did not involve rapport between humans and animals, since the subjects were planarians, or flatworms. Lucian Cordaro and James Ison asked their University of Rochester psychology students to note the reactions of 34 planarians in a water-filled plastic trough when the worms were exposed to bright lights. Cordaro and Ison had trained all of the planarians to shrink from light by giving them an electric jolt whenever a light was shined on them. However, the teachers told the student experimenters that only some of the subjects had been light-shock trained; as a consequence of this training, they said, these subjects would show a more dramatic response to the light than their supposedly untrained mates, turning their heads away or contracting their muscles.

To test the influence of expectation, Cordaro and Ison divided the class into three groups of varying levels of expectancy, based on whether they had light-trained or untrained worms. The instructors told one group of students that all of the planarians they would observe had been trained. Another group was led to believe that they were observing a batch of untrained worms that would presumably be less responsive to light. A third group was told the specimens were a mix of trained and untrained worms. The innocuous ruse succeeded: Students led to expect the planarians to react strongly recorded 20 times more body contractions and 5 times more turned heads than did students with low expectations.

Such experiments led the researchers to conclude that a scientist's expectations can have a strong effect on the results of an experiment. Curiously, neither pair applied this finding to their own work: They, like their duped students, had begun their research into the impact of expectation expecting to find what they found. □

Personal reputation counts for a lot in science, not least when a researcher announces a startling find; the work may not be deemed worth the scholarly time of day unless a respected senior scientist takes an interest in it—the world expects more from the famous. So it was for an obscure Russian chemist named Nikolai Fedyakin, a researcher in the physics and chemistry department of the provincial Technological Institute in Kostroma, about 200 miles from Moscow. While studying how pure water behaves when it is sealed in a very narrow glass capillary tube, Fedyakin noticed that a small second column of water was slowly forming at either end of the tube. He found it strange that the original column should spontaneously split—and odder still that the water in the second column had the consistency of petroleum jelly.

As interested as the next chemist in claiming a discovery, Fedyakin described his peculiar observation in a Russian scientific journal in 1962. His paper caught the attention of prominent Moscow chemist Boris Deryagin. Like an unknown playwright asked to contribute to a Broadway show, Fedyakin was invited to participate—from Kostroma—in a more extensive investigation by the distinguished Deryagin's Moscow team, which ultimately comprised 25 researchers.

The group plunged confidently

into what was then variously known as water II, orthowater, and anomalous water. The new compound's properties were strange indeed: It was 40 percent denser than normal water, expanded 150 percent more than water did when it was heated, and had far higher boiling and lower freezing points—about 932 degrees Fahrenheit and minus 86 degrees Fahrenheit, respectively. One way of explaining these properties was that ordinary water had been contaminated with silicon that was somehow stripped from the glass capillary tubes. Deryagin had fretted over this possibility but, taking pains to avoid contamination in replications of the experiment, had finally ruled it out.

Western experts first learned of the existence

of anomalous water in 1966, when Deryagin gave a talk at a meeting of the Faraday Society in Nottingham, England. After the conference, several laboratories turned to the task of reproducing Deryagin's work. The process was not a speedy one— even for a pro such as Fedyakin, a column of ordinary water could take a month to spawn a column of anomalous water only 6/100 of an inch long. But a new form of something as critical and ubiquitous as water seemed worthy of a large investment of time. "In my opinion," declared British crystallographer John Desmond Bernal, "this is the most important physical-chemical discovery of the century." Another vote of confidence came from Ellis Lippincott, director of the Center for Materials Research at the University of Maryland. In 1969 he published a paper that identified the structure of anomalous water as that of a polymer—a long string of molecules— and renamed the mysterious substance polywater.

Over the next two years hundreds of papers appeared in scholarly journals, and the polywater contagion spread to the daily press. Both the promises and the potential perils of polywater were the stuff of copy. One article, for example, brought a sparkle to the eye of manufacturers when it raised the possibility of shaping polywater into solid forms ranging from chairs to piping. The strange substance might also qualify as a high-temperature lubricant

or a coolant for nuclear reactors.

But if polywater evoked high profits on the one hand, it raised environmental concerns on the other. Were polywater to escape from the laboratory, worried some scientists, it might act as a template for normal water molecules, which would rearrange themselves along similar lines. The oceans would turn thick and slushy—a catastrophe for living beings everywhere. Francis J. Donahoe of Wilkes University in Pennsylvania warned in a letter to the British science journal *Nature* that polywater should be treated as "the most dangerous material on earth" until proven otherwise. Seeking to soothe such worriers, chemist Deryagin said that even if one poured an entire glass of the maligned substance into the ocean, it would do no harm.

As speculation about polywater grew, so did doubts. Joel H. Hildebrand, an emeritus professor of chemistry at the University of California, Berkeley, announced that he found polywater "hard to swallow," and he was not the only one. The possibility that the substance might be better called contaminated water also acquired new momentum. The debate progressed slowly because polywater—which by now took hours, not weeks, to generate—was still extremely scarce and difficult to make. Eventually, however, chemists were able to adapt their analytical gear to probe minuscule samples and proceeded to analyze polywater's composition. One by one, they began to report contam- ◊

Moscow chemist Boris Deryagin *(above)* explored the properties of polywater— actually a silicate solution. Here, in a capillary tube at minus 41 degrees Fahrenheit, a trace of liquid polywater **(1)** has formed among segments of normal ice **(2)** and air bubbles **(3)**.

inants in the solution—not only the predicted traces of silicates but fatty substances quite possibly from the sweaty hands of experimenters. A nail was hammered into polywater's coffin when skeptical chemists added silicon to pure water—and got a product that exhibited the qualities of the suspect substance.

At first, a defensive Deryagin contended that these doubters must be guilty of sloppy laboratory work. Then, in 1973, he wrote a letter of surrender to *Nature.* It had not been a modification of water that had caused all the excitement, he said. A peculiar reaction between water vapor and the surfaces of the glass capillary tubes in which it was confined had drawn traces of silicon into the fluid. It was a disappointing finale: Hundreds of scientists had spent millions of dollars tracking Fedyakin's mirage. Some, perhaps, took comfort from the fact that science, once it got down to business, had again proved itself self-healing. For poor Fedyakin, however, it meant the end of his moment on the great stage of international science and a return to the exile of a rural lab. □

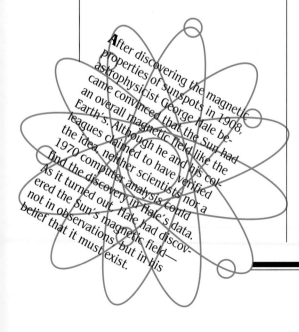

After discovering the magnetic properties of sunspots in 1908, astrophysicist George Hale became convinced that the Sun had an overall magnetic field like the Earth's. Although he and his colleagues claimed to have verified the idea, neither scientists nor a 1970 computer analysis could find the discovery in Hale's data. As it turned out, Hale had discovered the Sun's magnetic field—not in observations, but in his belief that it must exist.

New Wave

In his 1916 general theory of relativity Albert Einstein described gravity waves—a gravitational equivalent of the waves that carry the energy of light and other radiation. He held out scant hope, however, that they would ever be more than theoretical, so difficult would it be to detect them. Not that gravity waves would not be plentiful—according to Einstein, any object having mass moving through the fabric of space-time would radiate such waves, much like the wake of a speedboat crossing a bay. The waves would travel at the speed of light, but they would be weak indeed compared to their electromagnetic counterparts—the gravity waves that issue from a middle-size star, for example, would be many trillions of times weaker than the star's emissions of electromagnetic radiation. It has been said that trying to detect a gravity wave would be like standing in pounding surf and listening for a kiss blown across the ocean—a daunting analogy. Still, because gravity is evidently universal, there is a persistent scientific expectation that it exists in wave form—and that, Einstein's doubts notwithstanding, it can be detected.

More sanguine than most of his colleagues, Joseph Weber *(above),* a physicist at the University of Maryland at College Park, waded into the theoretical surf in the mid-1950s. His wife reports that when their little boy, who had a penchant for banging his head on his crib, wakened Weber in the wee hours, the scientist turned his thoughts to the design of a gravity-wave detector. He was apparently alone in such meditations—all but a handful of researchers believed that building so sensitive a device would be virtually impossible.

By 1965 Weber had a gravity-wave detector up and running in his College Park laboratory. It was a solid cylinder of aluminum—the material was chosen, according to some accounts, purely because it was relatively inexpensive—three feet in diameter and five feet long and weighing about three and a half tons. In theory, a gravity wave entering the cylinder from a direction perpendicular to its axis would deform the cylinder ever so slightly, causing strain sensors to send out a corresponding electric signal to waiting electronic processors and a needle recorder. Weber's machine was designed to pick up a movement measuring a mere $1/30$ the diameter of an atomic nucleus, about a trillionth of an inch.

If gravity waves were as weak as Einstein predicted, only the most violent of celestial events—the collision of two stars, for instance—could produce them in detectable quantities. Even then, they might be masked by local interference such as noisy trucks outside or even the vibrating footfalls of people in the building. In hopes of filtering out such noise, Weber suspended the cylinder from a steel wire and sealed the entire apparatus in a vacuum.

As another defense against false alarms, Weber set up a second identical cylinder on the opposite side of the campus. He assumed that if his gravity-wave antennas registered transient vibrations at the same instant, the energy passing through them would probably be from space, not from next door.

The results were gratifying: Within two years, the twin antennas detected a large number of simultaneous readings. But Weber was uneasy with this facile success and thought that perhaps his sensors had been too close together to rule out a local source. He moved one to the Argonne National Laboratory located near Chicago, 600 miles away from his Maryland headquarters. Connected by telephone lines to a computer, the two cylinders continued their long-distance pas de deux. In 1969 Weber reported that they vibrated almost simultaneously as often as three times a day. Most of the signals, he said, seemed to emanate from the center of the Milky Way.

Weber's news was exciting—but it was also surprising enough to raise skeptical eyebrows. An immediate question was what was going on in the Milky Way to produce gravity waves of such magnitude every day. A star's detonation as a supernova would generate detectable gravitational ripples but would not explain the frequency Weber reported: Such stellar explosions occur only perhaps three times a century in any given galaxy. Another idea was that the waves were emanating from a huge black hole—the very dense remnant of a collapsed star whose gravity is so powerful that even light cannot escape its grasp—lurking in the center of the Milky Way, where each day it gobbled up a star.

The theoretical sources offered for the reported waves drew criticism; Weber himself drew scorn. Some critics attacked his devices as crude and inadequate, while others assailed his method of analyzing data from the antennas. Nevertheless, his apparent success attracted a legion of physicists eager to get in on the action. At perhaps 10 laboratories around the world gravity-wave sensors were soon being assembled. To eliminate random atomic jigglings in the cylinders that might mask gravity waves, some went so far as to operate their devices at a temperature close to absolute zero—minus 459.67 degrees Fahrenheit. Despite such refinements, none of the gravity-wave watchers seeking to emulate Weber was able to confirm his results, and by 1975 the general enthusiasm for attempting it was on the wane.

No one knew exactly what to make of Weber's observations. It was not impossible that wishful thinking in some way had a hand in them. Ready to give him the benefit of the doubt, some scientists are convinced he was undoubtedly detecting *something*—but what it was, they are unsure. Others have wondered whether Weber had the cosmic good fortune to listen in on some extraordinary gravitational event at the right and only instant; by the time others tuned in, the event was over.

Although they could not be reproduced, the signals detected by Joseph Weber raised scientific expectations that, as Einstein had predicted, there were gravity waves out there—detectable ones. The United States government, for one, continues to take the idea seriously and funds gravity-wave research at Massachusetts Institute of Technology and California Institute of Technology. The two universities plan to construct the Laser Interferometer Gravitational-Wave Observatory. With a sensitivity that may be a thousand times greater than that of Weber's cylinders, LIGO is expected to be plucking gravity waves out of thin air before the year 2000—if they are there, and if the observatory can see them. □

Supernova 1987A, the closest in four centuries, may have produced detectable gravity waves.

Short Fuse

Among the many holy grails pursued by the world's scientists is that of controlled nuclear fusion, a tamed version of the raging thermonuclear reaction that gives the sun its light and the hydrogen bomb its destructive power. Unlike nuclear fission, which releases energy by splitting atoms of such heavy elements as uranium, fusion extracts its energy from joining atoms of light elements. Its principal raw material is the most plentiful element in the universe: hydrogen, which produces vast energy when forced to take the heavier atomic form of helium. The trouble is that the conditions needed to force atoms to fuse—the multimillion-degree temperatures and crushing pressures found in stars and, for a split second, in the crucible of an exploding thermonuclear bomb—are difficult to create and sustain. Thus, most attempts to harness fusion have involved elaborate, costly experimental machines—most, but not all. In fact, the only time nuclear fusion has seemed to be within the grasp of science, the device used was elementary: a beaker of water, an electric source, and two optimistic chemists.

For a brief moment in 1989, B. Stanley Pons of the University of Utah and Martin Fleischmann of Britain's University of Southampton thought they had achieved fusion—and much more. On March 23, Pons and Fleischmann called reporters to a press conference in Salt Lake City, where they announced that they had produced nuclear fusion in a jar, at room temperature. Their apparatus, the researchers said, was nothing more elaborate than an ordinary source of electricity attached to a palladium rod wrapped in a platinum coil and inserted into a beaker of heavy water—water in which the two hydrogen atoms are replaced by heavy hydrogen, or deuterium, atoms. The Utah chemists said that the electric current caused deuteri-um atoms to enter the palladium and fuse, creating an isotope of helium and releasing energy in the form of heat and neutron radiation—more energy than was put into the experiment.

Their announcement held out the promise of almost limitless, cheap, nonpolluting energy. The key element, deuterium, is abundant in nature—there is enough deuterium in the top 10 inches of Lake Superior, for example, to supply the entire electrical needs of the United States for 5,000 years. The fact that the fusion reaction had evidently proceeded at room temperature and pressure evoked a future powered by great fusion engines silently creating electricity from heavy water and palladium rods.

Pons and Fleischmann became instant celebrities. Their discovery was proclaimed by one scientist to be "perhaps as significant as the invention of the wheel." Another said it "may be the most important discovery since fire." The pair was pursued by reporters, television crews, and other scientists. Fax machines operated overtime distributing hastily jotted descriptions of the experiment to universities and research centers throughout the world. Not quite three weeks after the March press conference, 7,000 chemists descended on the annual meeting of the American Chemical Society in Dallas, Texas, to hear Pons describe the breakthrough. According to some accounts, the crush was such that Pons traveled under an alias; even so, he was forced to change his hotel twice.

To many scientists, however, the news from Utah seemed too good to be true. The fact that Pons and Fleischmann had sought out television cameras before going to their peers did not sit well with the scientific community. Their appearance—a futile one, as it turned out—before a Congressional committee to request $25 million for further cold-fusion research likewise annoyed their colleagues.

Although Pons and Fleischmann were forthcoming with the press, scientists found them less generous with details. When the Utah experimenters submitted their paper on cold fusion to the British journal *Nature*, it was rejected. *Nature* wanted revisions and additional detail, which the authors said they did not have time to add, and they withdrew the paper. Editor John Maddox explained tersely: Their claims were "unsupported by the evidence."

Hundreds of researchers tried to reproduce the Salt Lake City results but none quite succeeded. Some thought they saw evidence of fusion, but when they pressed for more details or a hint as to how they might improve their results, Pons and Fleischmann failed to reply. Some said the silence was imposed by the University of Utah, which wanted to patent the process. Others were less kind: There were no details to supply. Eventually, the pair withdrew their claims of finding neutrons and helium-4—the only compelling evidence that fusion might have occurred.

Now an offended scientific establishment turned upon the fusioneers. A group of theoretical physicists declared the cold fusion report to be an example of "incompetence" and "delusion," saying

they were "furious" it had ever been taken seriously. Mixing his metaphor but not his meaning, Peter Bond of the Brookhaven National Laboratory said that "the whole way this is being done is putting science in a stinking light." Nathan Lewis, a physical chemist at the California Institute of Technology, dissected the Pons and Fleischmann experiment in great detail at a meeting of the American Physical Society in May of 1989, pointing out ways it could have produced erroneous results. The main lesson, Lewis declared, was that it showed "how easy it is to fool oneself." The *New York Times* called it "one of the most bizarre episodes in science." Indeed, the cold-fusion debate of 1989 involved researchers, journalists, attorneys, and public officials in an intellectual brawl that flared as brightly as the Sun until, like a dying star, it faded from view.

As it became clear that Pons and Fleischmann were unwilling, or unable, to share the useful data they claimed to be getting, their credibility—and visibility—also dimmed. The low point came in October 1990, when the two chemists failed to show up for a technical inquiry by the University of Utah. They were out of the country, where, according to an attorney who spoke on their behalf, their work was "going better than ever." Many guessed that it was not. In May of 1991, physicist Frank Close published a critical book on cold fusion, declaring flatly that Pons and Fleischmann had based their announcement on "invented" data. Cold fusion, once hailed as the greatest find since fire, was restored to its former status as a fascinating will-o'-the-wisp, still waiting to be discovered. □

Earth Day

Most of the 3,500 residents of New Madrid, Missouri, began Monday, December 3, 1990, just as they had other mornings. But this Monday was different. Many of the schools were closed. Strangers crowded the streets downtown. Some familiar faces were missing; a number of folks had left over the weekend, planning not to return until midweek or later. And there was unusual activity around Hap's Tavern, where an all-day party was getting under way. Its theme: Shake, Rattle, and Roll—not on the dance floor, but under it. New Madrid braced for its earthquake, predicted to be one of the century's worst. The strangers in town were news reporters—some from as far away as Prague, Czechoslovakia—there to witness the demise of the little town in Missouri.

The man responsible for New Madrid's strange Monday was 72-year-old Iben Browning, a business consultant with a doctorate in biology and a checkered career in climate studies. His main line of business was a newsletter of economic forecasts based on long-term weather patterns. But Browning's interests ranged far and wide. He held numerous patents. At one time he had promoted the use of whales as nuclear weapon carriers and developed a theory that periods of climatic warming produced religious messiahs, while cooling periods spawned reformers.

Browning had pronounced New Madrid's death sentence in August. Noting the celestial approach of an unusually close alignment of the Earth, Moon, and Sun, he—along with a handful of other self-styled seers—assumed that this would ◊

so focus the tug of solar and lunar gravity that Earth would be swept by monstrous ocean tides, and rifts, or faults, in the crust would be torn asunder, causing terrible earthquakes. He had surveyed the planet for geologic faults that might be crucially affected and decided that the odds were about even that the New Madrid area would be the site of a catastrophic earthquake within 48 hours of December 3.

Browning's choice of New Madrid was inspired in part by events of the past. Although the San Francisco quake of 1906 is better known, one of the most powerful temblors in North American history was the New Madrid earthquake of December 16, 1811. Estimated at 8.0 or higher on the Richter earthquake magnitude scale, the convulsions caused waterfalls to appear and islands to sink in the Mississippi River, which temporarily reversed its course. The cataclysm was caused by movement along a fault that was buried deep beneath the surface, running 120 miles from eastern Arkansas north through New Madrid to Cairo, Illinois.

Geologists generally agreed that the area was ripe for another major quake—perhaps in the next half-century or so. Beyond that, the current state of earthquake prediction did not permit them to go. But Browning's forecast, especially as amplified by the media, was taken seriously by the public—with some reason. The year before, a strong tremor had shaken the Loma Prieta area of northern California, killing more than 60 residents. Some newspapers and news shows reported that Browning had successfully forecast it in a speech to farm and construction equipment manufacturers in San Francisco just a few days before. Furthermore, Browning was given a vote of confidence by David Stewart, a Southeast Missouri State University seismologist who directed an earthquake information center close by New Madrid. Finally, there had been a disturbing omen: In September 1990, Missouri was shaken by mild tremors.

Experts remained skeptical, however. A transcript of the Loma Prieta "prediction" revealed only a vague reference to earthquakes and volcanoes somewhere in the world. Stewart, it was learned, had unsuccessfully predicted a major quake in 1974 in Wilmington, North Carolina—even enlisting the aid of a psychic to confirm his view. And the seismology establishment insisted that precise prediction was impossible. The public was not interested; instead, it fastened upon yet another speech by Browning to a convention of home builders near St. Louis, 150 miles north of New Madrid, where he repeated his dire prediction.

But when the fateful day arrived one week later, there was no quake—not even a jiggle. New Madrid's citizens were naturally relieved—and not a little enriched by the experience. Hap's Tavern and other establishments did a land-office business; the local museum sold thousands of earthquake T-shirts, and the Wal-Mart store just out of town sold dozens of flashlights and other earthquake memorabilia. By Monday, December 10, New Madrid was back to normal.

Iben Browning declined to talk to reporters about his failed prediction. Perhaps he was preoccupied by another, more personal forecast. That same month, the self-styled seismic prophet said that he expected to be dead in "a matter of months." He died of a heart attack on July 18, 1991. □

IN THE SERVICE OF BELIEF

Commonly imagined as the detached denizens of ivory towers and objective seekers after truth, scientists nevertheless may view the world through a filter of belief. No more immune than other humans to poisonous opinions or misplaced zeal, scholars can do great mischief precisely because they are supposed to shed bias when they enter their laboratories.

Sometimes the researcher's aim is merely to reconcile observation with some article of faith—the stories written in the Bible, perhaps, with those that are geologically inscribed in layers of rock. Comfortable with their own motives, anthropologists and psychologists may dig complacently for proof of what their prejudices have already whispered to them—that, for example, gender and race identify who is superior and who is second-rate. Ideologues of any era may try to tailor the universe to fit the dictates of a church or state and cruelly extinguish all dissent.

Rarely, the ideological enlistment of science glitters with evil, as it did in the cauldron of hatred forged by Nazi Germany. No general served Adolf Hitler better than his death-camp men and women of science. Their bizarre theories and experimentation explored every human attribute the Führer wished—and did something more besides: They demonstrated for all time the ease with which science can be converted to an ugly cause.

Plea Bargain

Rarely has science been bent to accommodate dogma more famously than in the case of Italian scholar Galileo Galilei versus the 17th-century Inquisition of the Roman Catholic church. Honored today for his trailblazing discoveries in astronomy, mathematics, and physics, Galileo has also become something of a hero in the struggle for intellectual freedom. To many, he is the man who courageously resisted until, his noble spirit finally broken by the weight of orthodoxy, he recanted his thoroughly documented belief that the Earth revolved around the Sun. But, because he was handled with extraordinary gentleness by an ecclesiastical tribunal known for its cruel punishment of heresy, some historians suggest that this proud, contentious, obstinate man may not have been quite the martyr he has seemed—in modern parlance, Galileo may have copped a plea.

Early in his career, Galileo had, like most learned men of the day, accepted the traditional conception of the cosmos devised in antiquity by the Greek astronomer Ptolemy *(pages 21-23)*. According to this view, Earth sat immobile at the center of the universe, circled by the Sun and everything else visible in the sky. But in 1543 a compelling alternative scheme was revealed by a Polish canon, Nicolaus Copernicus, that challenged the Ptolemaic model. Copernicus proposed that the Earth and the other planets all orbited the Sun.

In 1609 Galileo began taking observations with the newly invented telescope, which he was the first to use for astronomy. He became increasingly convinced that the Copernican model of the universe was correct and publicly supported the idea. His advocacy drew the wrath of philosophers, who believed that Copernicanism contradicted the principles of Aristotle and of theologians, who feared that the theory would subvert the authority of the Bible. This latter issue—how Scripture should be interpreted and by whom—had vexed religious authorities since Martin Luther's day, and the desire to limit biblical debate by private individuals was quickly becoming one of the Church's highest priorities.

Never one to shy away from a dispute, Galileo responded energetically to his critics. But he was hobbled in his argument: Although he could infer from his observations that the Earth moved around the Sun, he could not prove it. Instead, he countered theological objections to Copernicanism by declaring that, where Scripture contradicted the evidence of science, it should be interpreted figuratively, not literally.

Determined to defuse the explosive issues of biblical interpretation that the Copernicus controversy raised, the Vatican summoned a commission to evaluate the theory, and in 1616 the panel concluded that Copernicanism was indeed heretical. Still, the Church moved softly on the matter. Such models of the universe were merely ways of

White bearded but defiant, Galileo Galilei stands heroically before the Inquisition in a romantic 1847 oil painting by French artist Robert Fleury. In fact, the broken 17th-century scholar recanted his belief and signed a formal abjuration *(inset)*.

explaining observed phenomena and might be discussed hypothetically, as a "mathematical supposition"; but the theory could not be held or defended. Cardinal Robert Bellarmine, the foremost theologian of the day, evidently warned Galileo to keep clear of Copernicanism—the strength and form of his warning would become a centerpiece in the scientist's ordeal 17 years later.

For almost a decade afterward, Galileo followed Bellarmine's friendly advice and remained silent about Copernicanism. Then, in 1624, Galileo sought permission from Pope Paul's successor—Maffeo Barberini, who became Urban VIII—to write about the topic. Barberini, who had opposed the 1616 decree that rendered Copernicanism a heresy, had been a great admirer of Galileo and continued to shower praise and privilege upon the scientist after ascending to the papal throne. Galileo, said the pope, could write about the design of the universe, provided he kept clear of theology and treated the systems as hypotheses, not facts. To adopt one or the other of the theories as physical reality, he told Galileo, was to constrain God to a certain configuration of universe, when, by definition, the deity could make the world in any way or shape he wished. Yet, perhaps sensing the need to keep some rein on his friend, Urban also declined to revoke the 1616 heresy decree. Eight years later, in February 1632, Galileo published his *Dialogue Concerning the Two Chief Systems of the World, Ptolemaic and Copernican*—and lit the fuse of controversy.

In the *Dialogue,* three characters debated the theories of the cosmos, but Galileo stacked the deck in favor of Copernicanism: Its advocate was a brilliant scholar with answers for every objection; in contrast, Simplicio, the spokesman for the Ptolemaic view, was depicted as an amiable dimwit. Worse, Galileo ended the discussion by having Simplicio piously argue that even if a hypothesis seemed correct, it might not be true—an omnipotent God could work in a way incomprehensible to mere human minds. Galileo had put one of Urban's favorite rejoinders into the mouth of a clown.

When the Vatican learned how one-sidedly Galileo had treated the "hypothesis" of Copernicanism—and as Galileo's Jesuit enemies insisted, how cruelly the writer had caricatured the pope—a furious Urban ordered a special commission to look into the matter. His investigators conveniently discovered in the Vatican files a memorandum—now thought by some historians to have been a fake planted to discredit Galileo—in which Cardinal Bellarmine's 1616 warning was recorded not as a gentle word of caution, but a direct order not to teach or discuss Copernicanism "in any way whatsoever, verbally or in writing." Since Bellarmine had died 11 years earlier, there was no one to support Galileo's claim that he had never received such a definitive prohibition. To the pope, however, the letter suggested that Galileo had tricked him to obtain permission to write the *Dialogue*—and had ridiculed him besides.

Ordered to report to Rome, the 68-year-old Galileo delayed as long as he could, claiming ill health and a fear of the plague that had broken out in Italy. Finally, after being advised that he could come of his own volition or be brought to Rome in chains, Galileo set out from Florence on January 20, 1633. In the Holy City, he was housed in comfortable lodgings rather than in prison for the duration of the trial—a unique concession to his prestige and age. Nevertheless, the prospect of being punished for heresy would have terrified him.

A panel of cardinals interrogated Galileo, who was charged with having taught Copernicanism as a fact rather than as a hypothesis and with disobeying the order that had been found in the Vatican's files. As the hearings unfolded, witnesses offered Galileo's own terms of derision for non-Copernicans as proof of his heresy.

At first, the defendant disingenuously claimed that his *Dialogue* had intended to demonstrate "that the arguments of Copernicus are weak and not conclusive." But, after further verbal persuasion, Galileo reported that he had now reread his work and had to admit "that in several places" it might have seemed to favor Copernicus. "If I had now to set forth the same reasonings," he went on, "without doubt I should so weaken them" that no reader could make the mistake of thinking he had ever accepted Copernicanism. "My error, then, has been—and I confess it—one of vainglorious ambition and of pure ignorance and inadvertence."

Six weeks later Galileo declared that since the warning of 1616, he had come to hold "as most true and indisputable the opinion of Ptolemy, that is to say, the stability of the Earth." No one believed him. His skeptical interrogators forced him to repeat this recantation several times and finally threatened him with torture if he did not acknowledge having once been a Copernican. With what must have been his last courage, Galileo stuck with ▷

DIALOGO
DI
GALILEO GALILEI LINCEO
MATEMATICO SOPRAORDINARIO
DELLO STVDIO DI PISA.
E Filosofo, e Matematico primario del
SERENISSIMO
GR.DVCA DI TOSCANA.
Doue ne i congressi di quattro giornate si discorre
sopra i due
MASSIMI SISTEMI DEL MONDO
TOLEMAICO, E COPERNICANO;
Proponendo indeterminatamente le ragioni Filosofiche, e Naturali
tanto per l'una, quanto per l'altra parte.

CON PRI   VILEGI.

IN FIORENZA, Per Gio:Batista Landini MDCXXXII.
CON LICENZA DE' SVPERIORI.

In the frontispiece to Galileo's contro-versial *Dialogue Concerning the Two Chief Systems of the World,* ancient philosophers Aristotle *(left)* and Ptolemy *(middle)* converse with their modern challenger, the astronomer Nicolaus Copernicus *(right).*

his lie: "I am here in your hands—do with me what you please."

Incredibly, his pro-Copernican writings were not trotted out to contradict the aging scientist. The trial was brought swiftly to a close and a verdict handed down. Despite Galileo's recantation, the cardinals found him guilty of "vehement suspicion of heresy," a grave offense in the eyes of the Church. Legend holds that when he heard the verdict, Galileo stubbornly thundered, referring to the Earth, "But it still moves!" But those who were present reported no such heroic outburst, perhaps because the defendant knew he was being treated leniently—and perhaps because his nerve was gone. At the conclusion of the trial, according to one contemporary account, he was "more dead than alive."

As punishment, Galileo was forced to sign a formal abjuration, sentenced to house arrest "during the pleasure of the Holy Office," and ordered to recite a number of penitential psalms—a chore that he was allowed to delegate to a daughter who was a nun. Confined to his home, Galileo made good use of the final nine years of his life, writing *Two New Sciences,* a work that laid the foundations of physics and engineering and, ironically, helped later generations verify that the planets did indeed circle the Sun.

Since Galileo's death in 1642

many of his views—both scientific and theological—have come to be accepted. Even his opinion that Scripture should be considered to be figurative if it conflicts with the lessons taught by science was endorsed by Pope Leo XIII in 1893. Almost 90 years later, the Vatican exonerated the martyred scientist: In 1979 Pope John Paul II acknowledged that Galileo had suffered "certain undue interventions" by the Church.

But why, historians have asked, had Galileo suffered so little? One scholar believes that the aging scientist's real heresy had been much more serious than dabbling in Copernicanism. According to Italian writer Pietro Redondi, Galileo's trial may have been a substitute for a more serious Inquisitional ordeal. While examining Vatican archives, Redondi came across an anonymous letter, dated 1624, that accused Galileo of implicitly denying the doctrine of transubstantiation—the belief that bread and wine are transformed into Christ's body and blood in the sacrament of Communion. According to the letter, Galileo had stated in a book published in 1623 that matter is composed of immutable atoms. The implication: Bread and wine remained bread and wine despite consecration. In Redondi's view, which some historians dispute, Galileo was brought to trial for Copernicanism in order to spare him from being charged with the greater—and probably fatal—heresy. If Redondi is correct, Galileo was not ruined, but rescued, by the pope his *Dialogue* had ridiculed. □

Saving Grace

Philip Henry Gosse, called by some "the finest descriptive naturalist of his day," was 19th-century Britain's preeminent popularizer of natural phenomena. He had gone on expeditions, had written numerous books about birds, botany, and marine life, and was a highly regarded lecturer. He was also a deeply devout member of the fundamentalist Plymouth Brethren, an extreme branch of Calvinism. A keen observer of the natural world, Gosse could read the eternities written in the Earth's geological record. But he also accepted the biblical dogma that Creation had occurred in a single six-day instant, not by developing over vast reaches of time.

For anyone else, reconciling the two would have been a simple matter of discarding the geological message. But Gosse was too good at his work to follow that easy road. Instead, in 1857, he published a work intended to save geology and Creation from one another. Certain that his simple—and to his mind obvious—ideas would be acclaimed for rescuing Christian doctrine from the assaults of science, and vice versa, the artless naturalist was mortified when his thesis met instead with universal derision.

Gosse entitled his book *Omphalos: An Attempt to Untie the Geological Knot.* Classical Greek for "navel," *omphalos* was an allusion to the age-old question of whether Adam, who was never connected to a mother by an umbilical cord, would have had a bellybutton. In Gosse's view, the answer was an emphatic yes. Moreover, the pious theorist added, Adam possessed in full development all of the features common to adult human beings, such as hair, fingernails, and teeth, even though he was presumed never to have undergone the developing phases of childhood.

The analogy, Gosse insisted, was obvious: Just as the freshly created Adam showed misleading signs of a past that he had never experienced, so the Earth exhibited similar false indications—geological strata and fossils, for example—of a nonexistent prehistory. Instead of developing over the course of eons, as geology suggested, Earth's innumerable layers of rock had come into being at once during the six days of Creation described in the Bible. The fossils found in those rocks, Gosse asserted, were not the petrified imprints of actual plants and animals—they were merely patterns placed there by the Almighty to spin the illusion that there had been a past. In Gosse's view, all of geology was thus a divinely written fiction describing a past that had never been. Geology *seemed* true; Creation *was* true.

Likening nature to a circle in which an egg gives way to a chicken, which is in turn supplanted by another egg, Gosse theorized that there was really no beginning and no end to the unfolding of time. But now and then, he said, God stepped into the circle. The Creation of the Earth had been just such an intercession, in which God formed the entire circle of nature in one instantaneous effort, false past and all.

To reconcile science and Scripture further, Gosse postulated the existence of two different kinds of time: The first kind, which he called diachronic, was that of the biblical Creation and other genuine events since; the other kind of time, an ideal form that he referred to as prochronic, contained the illusory but nonetheless informative events revealed by geology.

The naturalist knew that his theory would encounter scoffers, and he tried to head them off. "It may be objected," he wrote, "that, to assume the world to have been created with fossil skeletons in its crust—skeletons of animals that never really existed—is to charge the Creator with forming objects whose sole purpose was to deceive us. The reply is obvious. Were the concentric timber rings of a created tree formed merely to deceive? Were the growth lines of a created shell intended to deceive? Was the navel of the created Man intended to deceive him into the persuasion that he had a parent?" Gosse's answer: These prochronic touches had been necessary to make the finished product what it was supposed to be—an adult Adam would have been incomplete without a navel. A confident Gosse challenged all comers: "Who will dare to say that such a suggestion is a self-evident absurdity?"

Who would not? As the naturalist's son, literary critic Edmund Gosse, later recalled, "Atheists and Christians alike looked at it and laughed, and threw it away." Novelist Charles Kingsley, an influential clergyman from whom Gosse had expected congratulations, responded to *Omphalos* with the comment that he could not "give up the painful and slow conclusion of five and twenty years' study of geology, and believe that God has written on the rocks one enormous and superfluous lie for all mankind."

It had been a devastating year for Philip Gosse. A few months before the publication of *Omphalos* his beloved wife, Emily, had died. Now, Edmund Gosse wrote years afterward, "as the post began to bring ◊

in private letters, few and chilly, and public reviews, many and scornful, my Father looked in vain for the approval of the churches, and in vain for the acquiescence of the scientific societies, and in vain for the gratitude of those 'thousands of thinking persons,' which he had rashly assured himself of receiving." The senior Gosse found it all incomprehensible. "He could not recover from amazement," wrote Edmund, "at having offended everybody by an enterprise which had been undertaken in the cause of universal reconciliation."

Some of Gosse's best work was still ahead of him. Before he died in 1888, aged 78, he wrote a definitive natural history of British sea anemones and a number of popular nature volumes. But the failure of *Omphalos* had scarred him terribly. "I fancy, he began, in his depression, to be angry with God," wrote Edmund. "I think he considered the failure of his attempt at the reconciliation of science with religion to have been intended by God as a punishment for something he had done or left undone." □

Not even subatomic particles escaped hard-liners in the late Stalinist era. The notion that a particle could also be a wave was dismissed as "infamous bourgeois ideology," for example, while the uncertainty principle—which precludes knowing both the speed and the position of a particle—flew in the face of Marxist determinism. But official naysaying did little to retard Soviet scientists, who used the forbidden notions to build their first atomic bomb in 1949.

Skull Chap

Samuel Morton's collection of skulls was one of the wonders of the anthropological world, a veritable United Nations of yellowing bones that poured into his Philadelphia laboratory from all quarters of the globe. A physician and anatomy professor, Morton had been inspired to become a cranium collector in 1830 when he wanted to lecture his students on the characteristics of skulls in different races and discovered that he could not find a specimen to illustrate each of the five major races. He began gathering skulls, evidently without any motive beyond building a comprehensive collection. Then, as his specimens multiplied, he began to believe that his legion of skulls held clues to racial traits. Gradually, the prodigious mass of statistics that Morton wrung from his "American Golgotha," as the contents of his cabinets came to be called, bolstered the prevailing notion of Caucasian supremacy with a reassuring dose of science.

Upon his election to the post of corresponding secretary of Philadelphia's prestigious Academy of Natural Sciences in 1831, Morton *(opposite)* immediately tapped into the organization's worldwide network of interested colleagues. He drafted naval officers, archaeologists, colonial surgeons, professors at foreign universities, missionaries, and globe-trotting travelers to send him skulls. They complied in a most gratifying manner, often adding fascinating biographical tidbits about the skull's original owner. Thus Morton's pen pal Dr. Doornik of Batavia (now Jakarta, Indonesia) supplied the intelligence that collection item number 434 was a Dutchman of noble family who had been an army captain in the Far Eastern colony, where he died when he was not yet 30. "He was handsome," Morton noted in his catalog, "not deficient in talent, and of an amiable disposition, but devoted to conviviality and dissipation, which finally destroyed him."

A skull believed to be the remains of an ancient Phoenician came to Morton by way of a French archaeologist, and an Egyptian dig yielded skulls of quarrymen who had supplied stone for the pyramids at Giza. An American mariner named E. K.

Kane did not scruple to raid an Eskimo grave in the Greenland village of Etah on Morton's behalf. From the Sandwich Islands came the crania of two sacrificial victims whose facial bones had been removed, according to custom. In a historical aside, Morton noted that England's great seafarer Captain James Cook had been similarly modified by Pacific islanders upon his death in 1779. The skull of a Chinese pirate and a female skull that had been a trophy of Borneo headhunters also became part of the Philadelphia collection.

Perhaps Morton's most spine-tingling prize was the skull of Alexander Pearce. Convicted of stealing six pairs of shoes in Ireland, Pearce had been transported to Australia to serve seven years. He escaped and, while on the run, acquired a taste for human flesh—his favorite cut was the arm. Pearce was hanged in 1823 for his crimes and, following the court's order, "disjointed." A physician named Crockett had rescued and tidied up the cannibal's severed head and, after a time, had given his souvenir to William Cobb Hurry, Esq., of Cal-

cutta, who forwarded it to Morton.

These far-flung collaborators were so efficient, and Morton was himself so energetic, that by 1839 the professor had published *Crania Americana*, a catalog of his collection. As its title suggests, its principal focus was North and South American Indians, but Morton felt confident enough of his data to summarize the characteristic traits of five races and to rank them. Not surprisingly, Caucasians stood at the head of the class—Morton claimed for them the "highest intellectual endowments," backing up the compliment with a typical cranial capacity of 87 cubic inches. At a slightly lower level were the Mongolians, whose capacity was 83 cubic inches—sufficient, in Morton's terms, for them to be "ingenious, imitative, and highly susceptible of cultivation." The Malay race, which included all Polynesians, he called "active and ingenious" but "predaceous," noting that their cranial capacity was a mere 81 cubic inches. Still, they edged out the Indians of the Western Hemisphere by one cubic inch; from Peru to Canada, Morton reported, these people were "averse to cultivation, and slow in acquiring knowledge." Africans, with only 78 cubic inches of brain space, Morton gave the bottom rung, noting that they were in general "joyous, flexible, and indolent," but included tribes that represented "the lowest grade of humanity."

The anatomist's characterizations in *Crania Americana* and in the books that he published subsequently in 1844 and in 1849 conveniently squared with prevailing belief, which Morton reinforced with voluminous tables and

statistics. Later, critics would point out that—perhaps without meaning to denigrate all races but his own—Samuel Morton had steered his research straight toward a desired outcome. Moreover, when he realized that his results were diverging from that outcome, he did what he could to bring them back on course. Measurements were a particular problem.

The standard method of reckoning the cranial capacity of a skull was to plug all of its openings and fill it with water or small particles; the contents were then decanted into a calibrated vessel, which showed the volume of material needed to fill the skull. But these apparently straightforward steps were fraught with ambiguity. Plugging skull after skull in a completely uniform fashion was an impossible task, and there was no criterion for when a skull should be considered full. The material used to fill the skull also affected the result.

For years Morton used white pepper seed as filler, reasoning that its tiny and relatively uniform grains would settle evenly into a skull. As he discovered himself, however, his assumption was erroneous, for the same skull could seem to grow or shrink as much as four cubic inches when it was measured a second and third time with white pepper seed. Morton abandoned the substance for lead shot sometime before 1844. This cut the margin of error to about one cubic inch.

The research had other serious shortcomings that could not be blasted away with lead shot. For one thing, Morton used radically different numbers of skulls from different racial categories in the same study. In one instance, he cited figures from 338 Indian heads, com- ◊

pared to only 23 European specimens. Morton also excluded skulls that would have skewed the statistics he was seeking. For example, he classified Hindus as Caucasians but diligently ignored most of his Hindu specimens for the simple reason that they were so small—including them would have reduced the cranial capacity of Caucasians to an embarrassingly low level. However, he threw the unusually small heads of Incan Peruvians into the statistical pot when he was assessing Indians, effectively putting New World natives in their place. Morton also failed to make any allowance for the correlation—readily apparent in his own data—between stature and brain size. And when it was useful to do so, Morton baldly fiddled with his mathematics. If the measurement of a Caucasian skull included a fraction, for example, Professor Morton rounded the figure up; but if the specimen was from what he considered an inferior group, he rounded down.

When Morton died in 1851, his Philadelphia collection held 1,035 skulls. Donors bought the crania from his estate and gave them to the Philadelphia Academy of Natural Sciences, where other researchers obsessed with skulls could take advantage of the grinning display housed in oak-paneled cabinets. Not until the early 20th century was the notion that brain size is the be-all and end-all of human superiority consigned to the graveyard of self-serving science. The once-important skull collection likewise faded from public view. Today, the yellowed head bones reside where no one can see them, in a closed University of Pennsylvania storeroom that is lined with dangerously disintegrating asbestos. □

Sterile Argument

In the post-Civil War years, the prospects of getting a university education brightened for women. Vassar, Bryn Mawr, and other colleges devoted solely to the education of females were founded, some land-grant public universities began admitting women, and feminine fists grew bold enough to knock at the doors of such male-only bastions as Harvard University. Looking back on this groundbreaking period, M. Carey Thomas, Bryn Mawr's first president, recalled in 1908, "We did not know when we began whether women's health could stand the strain of education. We were haunted in those early days, by the clanging chains of that gloomy little specter, Dr. Edward H. Clarke's *Sex in Education.*"

Allegedly examining the fitness of women for education "solely from the standpoint of physiology," this alarming tract was penned in 1873 by an ear specialist. Perhaps it was the crisis looming at Harvard that prompted Clarke *(opposite)*, a member of the university's Board of Overseers and a one-time professor at its medical school, to become a sudden authority on the reproductive systems of young ladies. According to Clarke, the rigors of higher education, combined with other baleful influences such as doughnuts, corsets, and the "omission of clothing where it is needed," would assuredly enfeeble females. They would be tortured by menstrual difficulties, he wrote, along with chronic and acute ovaritis, hysteria, neuralgia, a malpositioned uterus, and other maladies over which the doctor drew a veil of modesty.

Lest he be suspected of bias, Clarke subtitled his book "A Fair Chance for the Girls" and assured his readers, "Man is not superior to woman, nor woman to man. The relation of the sexes is one of equality, not of better and worse, or of higher and lower." He based his dire predictions on a persistent notion that, contrary to what was then well known to anatomists, the female reproductive system was virtually nonexistent until the onset of puberty, when the organs purportedly experienced a uniquely intense and swift burst of development each month, during menstruation. Intoned Clarke, "No such extraordinary task, calling for such rapid expenditures of force, building up such a delicate and extensive mechanism within the organism,— a house within a house, an engine within an engine,—is imposed upon the male physique at the same epoch."

Misapplying the concept of the conservation of energy to physiology, Clarke claimed that the mental energy demanded by intense intellectual labor would diminish the amount of physical energy that was available to fuel the process of sexual maturation. "If the schoolmaster overworks the brains of his pupils, he diverts force to the brain that is needed elsewhere," Clarke warns in his book, adding that, once lost, developmental ground could never be recovered.

As evidence of his ominous appraisal, Clarke cited the examples of several women who had "graduated from school or college excellent scholars, but with undeveloped ovaries. Later they married, and were sterile." Another young lady, he reported, suffered through two years of college with "pale cheeks

and a variety of aches," rhythmical and uncontrollable twitching, and dreadful menstrual difficulties. Her worried parents took her on a year-long European tour, which restored her to fine health. She returned to school and graduated a top scholar—but an invalid. A second trip abroad was not so successful, and a plague of reproductive ailments, the ear specialist said, brought her to his office. He diagnosed the problem of another young patient, a Vassar student who he said had entered the college at the age of 14, as "an arrest of the development of the reproductive apparatus." That is, she had no breasts, and "the milliner had supplied the organs Nature should have grown."

Only by tailoring educational methods to the presumed peculiarities of female physiology could the dangers claimed to attend an overworked brain be avoided. It was imperative, in Clarke's opinion, that the sexes be educated separately. Moreover, women should be excused from their studies during their menstrual periods to allow the reproductive system to develop normally. The cost of accommodating women properly would, Clarke calculated, be so high that it was unreasonable to expect even well-endowed institutions such as Harvard to foot the bill.

Aghast at the menace that was looming over young American womanhood, the reading public anxiously snapped up Clarke's opus—a bookseller in the university town of Ann Arbor, Michigan, reportedly sold 200 copies in a single day. *Sex in Education* went through 17 editions within a few years of its publication.

Clarke's version of the pernicious "separate but equal" fallacy drew fire from critics questioning his facts and even his integrity. Vassar's resident physician said that, contrary to Clarke's claims about a patient from the college, Vassar had never enrolled a student as young as 14. But such rejoinders were mostly lost in a chorus of approval, and Clarke's critics failed to break up his influential following. The renowned psychologist Stanley Hall, president of Clark University, enthusiastically endorsed efforts to protect young women from mental overstrain in order to safeguard the functions "essential for the full transmission of life," and in England authorities warned women that seeking a degree was "one of the most dangerous occupations of life." Clarke's specious thesis—that "gloomy little specter"—retained its influence for decades, preserving the Victorian myth of female frailty and an archaic social order far beyond their time. □

The Fallen

Approximately one baby in a thousand is born with Down syndrome, first identified in 1866 by John Langdown Down, a British physician at London Hospital and superintendent of the Royal Earlswood Institution for the Feeble-Minded in Surrey. The disorder caused varying degrees of mental retardation and a shortened life span, and as Down noted, marked the victim with certain distinctive physical traits: a flat, broad face with slanting eyes; scanty, straight, and brownish hair; a small nose; and wrinkles across the forehead. The affliction was accompanied by a sallow, yellowish coloring and a vertical skin fold, or epicanthus, at the inner corner of the eye. Perceptive enough to know that it was a single affliction, but unable to intuit its source, Down decided the disorder must be what it seemed: something racial.

The syndrome, he declared, was a type of idiocy that represented a retrogression among Caucasian babies to the less advanced Mongol racial type. He called such patients "Mongol idiots," an unfortunate—and misleading—label that persisted well into the 20th century.

Down was a monogenist—that is, he believed, as most scientists do today, that human beings were a single species, of which the races were variations. The opposing position, called polygeny, held that each race was a distinct species with a unique origin, a scheme tailor-made for racial separation and qualitative ranking. Down's observations merely reinforced his views. Besides Mongol idiots, he observed among patients of European descent what he called "specimens of white negroes"—people whose white skin ▷

was coupled with facial features and hair that he classified as Ethiopian. Still other inmates were, in his eyes, strikingly similar to American Indians or to the "Malay variety" of the human race. Such ethnic anomalies, according to Down, represented a degeneration or regression to a relatively early stage of human evolution; as to possible causes, he hazarded only that tuberculosis in the parent might foster Mongol characteristics in the child.

In fact, Down's interest in questions of race and evolution was secondary; his aim had been to classify mental defects to make diagnosis easier for other physicians. His son Reginald, who was also a physician, pursued the Mongolian connection further, his curiosity piqued by the traits seen in Mongol idiots that are not characteristically Asian. He agreed with his father that such cases involved a reversion to an earlier type. But the type, he suggested in 1906, was not that of an inferior race—it was prehuman. Not long thereafter, British physician and armchair anthropologist Francis G. Crookshank appropriated the Downs' strange racial legacy, professing his indebtedness to the senior Dr. Down for his ethnic classifications.

Bent on quantifying the ideas of racial inferiority that Down's work had suggested, Crookshank gathered anecdotes and snippets of information about hair, ear lobes or the lack thereof, hand gestures, and palm prints in different ethnic groups. He was especially fussy about the details of a group's favorite posture of repose; how a sitting or squatting person arranged his limbs was, Crookshank asserted, rich in psychic data. He used his survey to argue in favor of polygeny in his 1924 book, *The Mongol in Our Midst.*

An ancient stock predating both humans and apes, he argued, had produced three branches. From one orangutans and Mongols had evolved, gorillas and Negroes from the second, and chimpanzees and Semites, or whites, from the third. Each branch, Crookshank claimed, was associated with a particular type of idiocy—Mongol, Ethiopic, and among Semites, dementia praecox, later renamed schizophrenia.

To explain the appearance of Mongol and Ethiopic disorders in English asylums such as Down's, Crookshank turned to the very ancient common stock from which, he believed, apes and humans sprang. "We can take our stand at Charing Cross," he wrote, "and can see these three Faces of Mankind borne by native Londoners: we can visit our public asylums and see them in degraded form: and we can, at the Zoo and the Natural History Museum, see them caricatured by the noisy, mischievous and lascivious chimpanzee, the dignified, philosophic and self-sufficient orang, and the slow, cunning, and brutal gorilla."

After identifying Down syndrome, 19th-century British physician John Langdon Down *(left)* mistakenly concluded that patients with the defect had Asian traits and dubbed them "Mongol idiots," an error that was compounded by Francis Crookshank *(above)* in *The Mongol in Our Midst.*

The Mongol in Our Midst enjoyed considerable popularity during the 1920s, despite critics who called Crookshank's tract trash. Determined to sever the spurious link between race and mental defects, British physician Lionel Penrose studied the blood types of his so-called Mongol patients and found nothing out of the ordinary about them—the distribution of the types was very similar to that of the non-Mongols he tested.

Thanks to champions such as Penrose, the discredited label "Mongolian idiot" was replaced, albeit slowly, by a different name, Down syndrome. Far from being an affliction limited to whites—as Down, perhaps unwittingly, had implied and Crookshank had argued emphatically—the syndrome has been discovered in every racial group. But its cause remained a mystery until 1959, when French researcher Jerome Lejeune demonstrated that the disorder had nothing to do with race but was genetic. In unafflicted humans, each cell contains 24 pairs of chromosomes, the threadlike structures that carry the body's genes. But in victims of Down syndrome, Lejeune discovered, a third number 21 chromosome occurs. The flaw, called trisomy-21, is the result of abnormal chromosomal division, which can occur in either the sperm or the egg.

Researchers have also turned up a curious echo of Crookshank's scurrilous science. Among chimpanzees, there are individuals with a cluster of traits very like the panhuman Down syndrome. Although the disorder does not, as Down believed, transport its victim from race to lesser race, trisomy-21 evidently travels up and down the evolutionary ladder. □

Insiders

As Cyrus R. Teed (right) modestly recounted years later, that fateful night of experimentation in autumn of 1869 had gone very well indeed. First, as he worked alone in his upstate New York "electro-alchemical" laboratory, the 30-year-old researcher had discovered what had eluded others for millennia. "I had succeeded," Cyrus Teed wrote, "in transforming matter of one kind to its equivalent energy, and in reducing this energy, through polaric influence, to matter of another kind." Teed did not describe the process that he employed but merely expressed his satisfaction at being "the humble instrument for the exploiture of so magnitudinous a result." He had found, he reported, the elusive "philosopher's stone," a material capable of transmuting base metals into silver and gold and extending human life. But, as Teed recalled later, that signal discovery was as nothing compared to what followed.

In his elation, Teed experienced "a peculiar buzzing tension at the forehead," then felt as if he were vibrating on a "gently oscillating ocean of magnetic and spiritual ecstasy." Enveloped in such delightful sensations, he heard a woman's voice calling to him. Then, in an aura of purple and gold light, a figure appeared—the "Divine Motherhood," according to Teed's memoir. Speaking in a gentle voice, she informed him that he had been chosen to redeem humanity: Teed was the new messiah.

In the lingering afterglow of what he called his illumination, Teed elaborated the evening's insights both spiritually and scientifically to create what he ultimately called cellular cosmogony—a universe composed of cells, all contained in a single womblike supercell. "Form is a fundamental property of existence," he reasoned, "therefore, that which has no form has no existence. Limitation is a property of form. The universe has existence; therefore it has form, hence it has limitation." Following that logic, Teed reduced the cosmos from a limitless expanse dotted with stars and galaxies to a compact hollow sphere with a diameter of about 8,000 miles and an outside circumference of about 25,000 miles—the approximate dimensions of the Earth. But, contrary to conventional cosmology, he declared, the Earth was not a globe revolving around the Sun; instead, it was the concave inner surface of an Earth-size sphere. The seemingly infinite heavens were, in fact, completely contained inside the hollow orb.

Cellular cosmogony taught that virtually nothing was as it seemed to be or as conventional science claimed. Centrifugal force, not gravity, pinned humans to their concave world. The Moon and the planets were reflections of energy from various points on or within the sphere's shell. All light and heat in the universe was generated by an invisible but extremely powerful electromagnetic battery, and the Sun was no more than a reflection of its output. Standard geology fared no better than cosmology. According to ◊

Teed, the shell of the universe contained multiple layers, some of them metallic and some mineral. The "outermost rind" was pure gold. Beyond that lay the void—space with nothing in it.

Convinced that the multitudes had been bamboozled by the "gigantic fallacy and farce of the benighted Copernicus," Teed believed that once people fully understood the scientific implications of his restructured universe they would heed the hollow Earth's spiritual call. "To know of the Earth's concavity and its relation to universal form," he wrote, "is to know God; while to believe in the Earth's convexity is to deny him and all his works. All that is opposed to Koreshanity is Antichrist." Koreshanity, the name Teed gave his movement, came from *Koresh,* the Old Testament rendering of Cyrus.

But Koresh, as the compact, stern-faced messiah styled himself, was not very successful in attracting followers to his banner. For one thing, his was only one of many religious splinter groups following a charismatic leader across New York State. Teed did better in Chicago, where, in 1886, he displayed his very real oratorical powers at a conference of the National Association of Mental Science and was elected its president. He decided to move

there and soon gathered a fiercely loyal flock. One of them, Ulysses Grant Morrow, aided Teed in a new and critical undertaking: to prove scientifically that Earth's surface was concave.

In Teed's cosmology the horizon actually curved upward, rising higher and higher in the distance; a downward-curving horizon, he asserted, was simply an optical illusion. By surveying this upward curve, the pair believed, they could demonstrate the physical reality of the Koreshan model. In 1896 Teed and Morrow began taking sightings along the long, arrow-straight Old Illinois Drainage Canal to gather evidence that the Earth's surface was concave, and not convex. Their results were evidently encouraging, but inconclusive.

The following year they moved their Koreshan Geodetic Expedition to the Gulf Coast town of Naples, Florida, not far from the movement's southern outpost at Estero. To take measurements along the

wide, virtually flat beach, Morrow devised a "rectilineator." Essentially a giant spirit level, the contraption comprised several 12-foot-long T-square sections made of mahogany, steel, and brass. The purpose of the massive instrument was to establish a straight horizontal line above the ground; if Teed's theory was correct, the distance between a projection of that "air-line" and the Earth's upward-curving surface should shrink until eventually the two intersected.

Day after day the Koreshans walked the ponderous rectilineator down the beach in increments of 12 feet and marked out the line with poles. After five weeks and some two and a half miles, they reached an inlet and, for the sake of practicality, abandoned the rectilineator and continued constructing the line with sighting poles and a telescope—much as conventional surveyors measure elevations on a convex Earth. After further labors they saw—or so they claimed—their

Continents and oceans lie on the inner surface of this opened model of Cyrus Teed's hollow Earth, with the stars and the Sun inside.

line, now four and one-eighth miles long, intersect the upward curve of the Earth out in the Gulf waters. The Koreshans were certain that they had demonstrated beyond a shadow of a doubt that the surface was concave.

With considerable justice, detractors could have argued that there was ample room for error, given the equipment and the technique used, not to mention how ardently the Koreshans hoped for the very outcome they claimed. Although not denying the Koreshans' good intentions, one critic has cited the "malleable, obliging nature of the universe, which reflects every image projected upon it and gives every experiment a tendency to gratify the experimenter."

Such remarks would have cut no ice with Teed, who was so confident of his science that he offered $100,000 to anyone who could prove him wrong. There were no takers—not, perhaps, because the rest of the world had been won over to the enclosed spherical universe, but because refuting it may be mathematically impossible. According to specialists in inversion geometry—the mathematics of turning three-dimensional figures inside out—the interior of a sphere is theoretically no different from the outside, and any mathematical argument for the Earth's convexity could be inverted to argue with equal force for concavity.

Estero, Teed hoped, would become the New Jerusalem of Koreshanity, and he made it his headquarters. He envisioned an army of believers 10 million strong strolling a model city of broad boulevards. At its peak around the turn of the century, the largely female membership was perhaps 250—disappointingly

small, but sufficient to run several businesses, including a sawmill, a printing plant, and a steam laundry. Life there proceeded, for some, in contented celibacy and focused on cellular cosmogony, picnics, literature, music, and crafts. The community's motto: We live inside.

Relations between the industrious, self-confident Koreshans and the resident citrus farmers of the region were frequently strained but deteriorated drastically after the communards turned against local political bosses and created their own party—for which they voted as one. On an afternoon in October 1906, one of their candidates was attacked by a pugnacious local in Fort Myers. Teed tried to calm the man, who turned on the patriarch, striking him several times in the face. Without knowing it, the angry man had destroyed both messiah and movement.

Teed entered a slow decline and died two years later. His followers held a vigil over his body, expecting a resurrection. After several days a health official ordered a burial, and Teed's body was laid to rest in a large cement vault. Thirteen years later a hurricane swept the tomb and its contents out to sea.

By then, however, the Koreshan community had begun to be swept away as well. Splintered by factionalism, the group's numbers steadily declined. The last communard—Hedwig Michel, a German hollow-Earther who had joined in 1940—died in 1982 at the age of 90. Cyrus Teed's cosmological colony has been a Florida state park and historic site since 1976. Today, the nearly deserted New Jerusalem is enclosed by rings of gleaming towers rising from the complex, convex world outside. □

Deborah's Destiny

An obscure 18th-century American known today only by the pseudonym of Martin Kallikak earned sudden notoriety in 1912, and for decades afterward his surname was a household word, coined by psychologist Henry H. Goddard from the Greek *kalós,* meaning "good," and *kakós,* meaning "bad." The dead man's dubious claim to fame, which Goddard explored in *The Kallikak Family: A Study in the Heredity of Feeble-Mindedness,* was the two sets of descendants he was said to have sired with two different women. The kalós brood, if Goddard had his facts right, was composed of respectable citizens, while the kakós side was a sordid lot of petty criminals, drunkards, prostitutes, and mental defectives.

Goddard, then director of research at the Vineland, New Jersey, Training School for Feeble-minded Girls and Boys, believed that mental retardation was a grave social problem. He attributed much of the nation's crime and other social ills to adults whose scores on intelligence tests put them on a par with children 8 to 12 years old. He called such people morons, after the Greek term for "dull" or "foolish."

But Goddard's views were heavily seasoned by his belief in eugenics, a reform movement based on the premise that human society could be improved by applying scientific knowledge methodically—specifically, by identifying and weeding out inferior genetic stock. In the opinion of eugenicists, human nature was genetically determined; the most extreme practitioners believed that the impact of environ- ◊

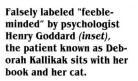

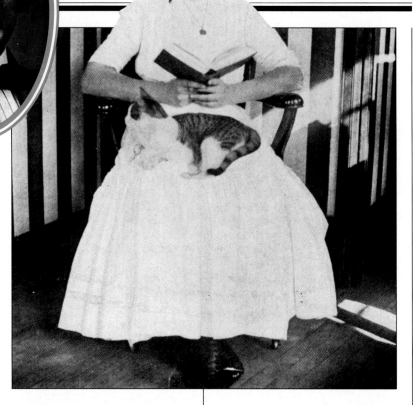

ment on an individual's character, behavior, and intelligence was, for all practical purposes, nonexistent. But even moderate eugenicists condemned attempts to improve the lot of the poor—whose genes were automatically suspect—as a waste of time and effort.

Already recognized as a pioneer on intelligence testing, Goddard had undertaken a study to determine, in a supposedly objective manner, the cause of mental deficiency. From the outset he strongly suspected that heredity was to blame—and indeed, his findings would fit the eugenicist mold. Goddard's starting point was a 22-year-old woman to whom he gave the pseudonym "Deborah." Placed in Goddard's Vineland training school when she was 8 years old by a mother who was unable or unwilling to care for her, Deborah had learned to read and write and was skilled in such diverse areas as needlework, dressmaking, music, and carpentry. Nevertheless, Goddard concluded from her intelligence test score that she was feeble-minded, possessing the mentality of a 9-year-old child. But the researcher also saw her as the tip of a family tree that would yield a rich harvest of what he deemed social misfits.

His fieldworker, a former teacher named Elizabeth Kite, took on the task of scouring southern New Jersey for Deborah's relatives and traced the young woman's lineage to a casual liaison of the Revolutionary War era. The pseudonymous Martin Kallikak was one of the principals; as to the other party, Goddard made one of his many post-

mortem assessments and declared her mentally defective and genetically inferior. As Kite could not supply even a name for Kallikak's hapless partner, Goddard habitually referred to her as "the nameless feeble-minded girl."

Although Kite had scant training in genetics, psychology, or other areas relevant to the project, she did not let such deficiencies hinder her gathering what Goddard was quick to endorse as fact. And Kite herself was also a quick study. On one visit to impoverished relatives of Deborah's, for example, she met a young boy who had become deaf as a consequence of scarlet fever. She made short work of diagnosing him: "A glance sufficed to establish his mentality, which was low." Kite also performed an instantaneous analysis of the boy's siblings, noting that

they "stood about with drooping jaws and the unmistakable look of the feeble-minded."

On the basis of such conjecture, Goddard entered the entire line of parents and offspring in the bad-blood Kallikak column. In all, 480 descendants of Martin and his genetically tainted paramour were supposedly identified. "One hundred and forty-three of these," Goddard reported, "we have conclusive proof, were or are feeble-minded, while only forty-six have been found normal. The rest are unknown or doubtful." Among these *kakós* Kallikaks, Goddard alleged, were 33 "sexually immoral persons, mostly prostitutes," 24 "confirmed alcoholics," 8 brothel keepers, and 36 illegitimate children.

In contrast to this squalid legacy were the descendants of the original

Martin Kallikak's marriage to another woman who was a Quaker, Goddard said, "of good family." This coupling supposedly propagated down through 496 individuals in whom Goddard could find "nothing but good representative citizenship." He exaggerated, but only slightly, confessing to the presence among the 496 of "three men who were somewhat degenerate." But, he immediately added, "they were not defective." Altogether, the charts tracing the Kallikaks ran to 16 pages in Goddard's book.

As far as Goddard was concerned, the inferior genetic endowment carried by the nameless feeble-minded girl constituted the only significant variable in his study. "Clearly," he concluded, "it was not environment that has made that good family." He held out absolutely no hope for improving the kakós Kallikaks of this world: "No amount of education or good environment can change a feeble-minded individual into a normal one, any more than it can change a red-haired stock into a black-haired stock."

Goddard apparently had no doubts about the scientific soundness of his work—the Kallikak family was, as far as he was concerned, a researcher's dream. "The biologist could hardly plan and carry out a more rigid experiment," he wrote,

"or one from which the conclusions would follow more inevitably." According to his critics, however, the conclusions were a little *too* inevitable—Goddard was so committed to a hereditarian point of view that he was incapable of assessing the Kallikaks objectively. To load the dice in favor of his preconceptions, Goddard had gone so far as to retouch the photographs of the kakós Kallikaks appearing in his book to make them look worse than poverty and deprivation already had.

It appears that Goddard gravely underestimated Deborah Kallikak's mental abilities, and a psychologist who has gone through the study with a fine-tooth comb believes that today she would be classified as learning disabled. Sadly, she remained institutionalized until her death at the age of 89. She was reportedly a pretty and charming woman, and visitors meeting her did not come away with the impression that she was "feeble-minded," as Goddard had claimed. Perhaps Goddard had confused a sweet disposition with low intelligence, for Deborah Kallikak bore him no ill will. Of her numerous Persian cats, her favorite was Henry. "He is named for a dear, wonderful friend who wrote a book," she once explained. "It's the book what made me famous." □

Hitler's Copernicus

In 1925 an ominous ultimatum was mailed to scientists throughout Germany and Austria. "The time has come for you to choose—whether to be with us or against us," it warned. "While Hitler is cleaning up politics, Hans Hörbiger will sweep out of the way the bogus sciences. The doctrine of eternal ice will be a sign of the regeneration of the German people. Beware! Come over to our side before it is too late."

The author of this peremptory missive was Hans Hörbiger, a 65-year-old Viennese engineer whom Adolf Hitler had praised as "the Copernicus of the twentieth century." Energized by this imprimatur, Hörbiger's singular and thoroughly absurd theory of the nature of the universe had spread through Nazi ranks like wildfire. Called Welteislehre, or "World Ice Doctrine," it ultimately attracted millions of fanatic adherents across Europe, not a few of them in England.

With the help of lunar cartographer Philip Fauth *(page 55)*, Hörbiger had first aired his icy notions in a 1913 book titled *Glacial Cosmogony.* There had been little fanfare at the time, but the publication of the second edition in 1925 was another affair. With the rise of Nazism, Welteislehre's time had come, and its chilling blast swept the bastions of orthodoxy.

Hörbiger had seen the germ of his theory years earlier, in 1894. Observing the Moon through a telescope, he had been seized by the notion that lunar mountains were made of ice. Hörbiger went on to elaborate a cosmogony in which ice covered most celestial bodies, al- ◊

Glowing at left in a photograph taken from *Apollo 10*, Earth's moon is covered in rock and dust—not the ice insisted upon by Hans Hörbiger *(below)*.

though not the Sun and the Earth. The so-called stars of the Milky Way were ice blocks, he theorized, and a fine frozen powder drifted through space. Spared the global glaciers that covered the other planets—ice 250 miles deep on Mars, according to Hörbiger—Earth was the seat of an endless cosmic struggle between fire and ice.

The new Copernicus rejected the orthodox belief that the planets moved in elliptical orbits, maintaining instead that they proceeded in spirals toward the Sun. As they traveled ever inward, small planets were gravitationally captured by large ones and became satellites— the Earth had purportedly captured and lost at least six moons before the current one, which Hörbiger estimated had been acquired only 14,000 years ago. Drawn closer and closer to Earth, each of the earlier satellites had eventually caused massive upheavals. Mountains fell and new ranges appeared, the landscape was riven by earthquakes, and great floods—among them the one that Noah rode out on his Old Testament ark—drowned the planet. The final catastrophe was a rain of ice and rock from the disintegrating moon—the onset, in the Hörbigeran scheme, of yet another geologic age.

Between catastrophes, Hörbiger believed, Earth had enjoyed periods of calm lasting a hundred thousand years or more. During these interludes, civilizations ruled by a race of wise and benevolent giants sprang up all over the

Earth; Hörbiger attributed their 15-foot stature to a weakening of gravity caused by the succession of moons. But the giants were not alone—they had their subjects, humans of ordinary dimensions.

Predictably, Hörbiger asserted that the Germanic people were the descendants and spiritual heirs of the vanished giants and were destined to rule the world; non-Aryans, who were the descendants of the ancient underclass, would be reduced to their proper status as subjects. As evidence of this he offered his belief that the last of the giant kings had lived in the chilly elevations of the Andes and the lost continent called Atlantis, in climates not unlike a German winter. As a Welteislehre, or WEL, pamphlet stridently proclaimed, "Our Nordic ancestors grew strong in ice and snow; belief in the World Ice is consequently the natural heritage of Nordic man." So, it seemed, was national socialism, since Hörbiger's version of history accorded so well with the Nazi doctrine of racial superiority.

Mainstream scientists overwhelmingly dismissed Hörbiger as a crackpot, and he returned their contempt with interest. Fulminating against skeptics, he thundered, "You

put your trust in equations but not in me! How long will it be before you understand that mathematics are nothing but lies and are completely useless?" All scientific evidence that contradicted the ice doctrine Hörbiger angrily denounced as fakery by his personal enemies in the scientific establishment.

Treating WEL as a political cause, Hans Hörbiger's followers opened recruiting offices, attended lectures to heckle orthodox astronomers, and released a torrent of publications that included the monthly magazine *The Key to World Events*. The zealous ice mongers hoped to have belief in WEL declared compulsory in Germany, and indeed, its association with Nazism was very intimate. Nevertheless, the dogma never became official; the German Propaganda Ministry let people off the official hook by declaring that "one can be a good National Socialist without believing in the WEL."

Even without that endorsement, the cosmic ice theory weathered every adversity: Hörbiger's death in 1931, the cataclysm of World War II, and Germany's defeat. Diminished but not dead, Welteislehre still had perhaps a million faithful adherents in the mid-1950s, most but by no means all of them German—an ominous demonstration of an ugly faith's resilience. □

Kinvolk

After going on two scientific expeditions to Tibet as an aide, in 1937 German zoologist Ernst Schäfer was eager for a third trip to the remote country, but this time he wanted to organize and head the expedition himself. When Heinrich Himmler, the head of Nazi Germany's dread SS organization, learned of the zoologist's plans, his interest was piqued for a peculiar reason. The SS leader fantasized that there might be, in Tibet's mountain fastnesses, Asian descendants of the ancient Aryans, a supposedly superior race of proto-Germans whom the Nazis proclaimed as the forebears of modern Germans.

Heinrich Himmler extended an offer of support to Schäfer through an SS agency called the Studiengesellschaft für Geistesurgeschichte Deutsches Ahnenerbe—the "Society for Research into the Spiritual Roots of Germany's Ancestral Heritage," or Ahnenerbe for short. An avid amateur archaeologist and historian, Himmler had recently launched Ahnenerbe and given it the official task of exploring "the geographical extent, spirit, achievement, and heritage of the Indo-Germans of Northern race." In other words, by sifting the past the society was to furnish the proof that Nazism was the ideological descendant of an ancient and heroic Teutonic culture—and superior to all other ideologies.

Given the Nazi fixation on things racial, however, Ahnenerbe was much more than a simple anthropological foray: It quickly became a bizarre counterpart to other nations' academies of sciences. Ahnenerbe established some 50 divisions that embraced subjects as varied as folk medicine, German musicology, runes, nuclear physics, occult sciences, forests and trees in Aryan thought, animal geography, and speleology. Many German scientists scorned the organization, which they rightly considered a hotbed of Nazi pseudoscience. But others, including numerous notable experts, were less fastidious, suppressing any distaste they might feel in order to pursue a favorite project—within the agency that constituted the Nazi science establishment.

Despite the prestige of its members, however, Ahnenerbe soon proved itself an institute of thugs. Ahnenerbe experts played a major role in looting the treasures of conquered European countries, identifying scientific collections—sometimes the entire contents of museums—for shipment back to ◊

the Fatherland. Ahnenerbe doctors busied themselves with various unspeakable cruelties in Nazi concentration camps. But much of the scientific business of Ahnenerbe continued to be shaped by the whims of the very powerful.

During a critical stage of the war, for example, Heinrich Himmler found time to suggest a new line of meteorological inquiry to the Ahnenerbe chief of staff Wolfram Sievers. "In future weather researches," said Himmler, "I request you to take note of the following: The roots, or onions, of the meadow saffron are located at depths that vary from year to year. The deeper they are, the more severe the winter will be; the nearer they are to the surface, the milder the winter. This fact was called to my attention by the Führer."

Ernst Schäfer had no trouble following such whims and felt no doctrinal conflict with Ahnenerbe; he had joined the SS when he was a university student in Göttingen. Still, his interest in Tibet was mainly scientific, and he planned to investigate such subjects as its population, geography, climate, plant life, and animal population while he looked for Himmler's lost Aryans. A wrangle with bossy Ahnenerbe officials over plans for the expedition lost him the society's financial support but not its official sponsorship. Schäfer was able to raise the necessary funds himself, and he left for Tibet in 1938.

A year later, Schäfer was back in Germany laden with specimens and data. Keeping Himmler's obsession in mind, his scientists had performed exhaustive blood tests and body measurements on Tibetans, but these efforts did little to fulfill the SS chief's wish for evidence of

Asian Aryans. Expedition anthropologist Bruno Beger, a Nazi, faulted the mission as a whole for its failure to display a "spirit of national socialist unity." Despite Beger's carping, the Tibetan probe earned its leader praise from Ahnenerbe and favorable notice throughout Germany. Among other things, Schäfer brought back wild grasses with the potential to increase yields when bred with cultivated grains—a matter of importance, with possible food shortages looming.

In 1940 the zoologist accepted a permanent position in Ahnenerbe and went on to become head of research for Central Asia. His wartime assignments, however, were anything but scientific. He first took part in a short-lived scheme to arm and lead Tibetans in battle against the Anglo-Indian army, but it foundered during the planning stage due to squabbles among Nazi leaders. Another dud of a scheme was an expedition modeled after his 1938 foray to Tibet, this one to the Caucasus in the southern USSR to explore whether the Jewish presence there warranted a visit by "Death Commandos." With Himmler's blessing he had lined up 150 men and scores of trucks when Nazi military reverses on the eastern front put a stop to the operation.

Although Schäfer ran Ahnenerbe's largest research division, he somehow missed the postwar trials of key Nazi figures. Ahnenerbe director Sievers was hanged by the Allies as a war criminal, and Heinrich Himmler took a fatal dose of cyanide after being captured by the British in May 1945. But Ernst Schäfer lived on into the 1990s. Of his experience with the Nazis, he has only said, "I was their tool"— and a very good tool at that. □

Doctor Death

Dressed in the grayish green uniform of the SS and holding a polished cane in his white-gloved hand, the handsome Dr. Josef Mengele cut an impeccable figure on the railroad platform at the Auschwitz concentration camp in southern Poland. Given to whistling operatic airs as he surveyed the incoming flood of new victims, the doctor decided who would become slave laborers, who would go to their deaths, and who would be spared in the name of German science. Those marked for death usually died within hours. The men, women, and children Mengele saved for science, however, became living guinea pigs in a nightmarish perversion of experimental medicine—one that earned Josef Mengele the sobriquet Angel of Death and made him forever the personification of science gone mad.

In preparation for his role at Auschwitz, Mengele had been thoroughly steeped in Nazi theory at the University of Frankfurt's Institute for Hereditary Biology and Racial Hygiene. Trained as a medical doctor and anthropologist, he had eagerly joined the ranks of fanatics bent on improving the biological quality of the German people. In 1933 Germany had passed a law "for the prevention of genetically diseased offspring," which sanctioned the sterilization of people with such disorders as hereditary blindness, manic depression, or epilepsy. From that it was an easy leap to the murder of the incurably insane and from there, to the extermination of entire races deemed inferior to the Nazis' Aryan ideal.

When Mengele volunteered for the post of senior physician at Auschwitz in 1943, the 32-year-old medic had in mind continuing the research into racial biology that he had begun at Frankfurt. From an experimental standpoint, the situation was ideal: There would be no shortage of subjects, and the subjects would be unable to resist. Although Mengele was nominally responsible for the health of inmates, his medical duties were undemanding—it would have been absurd to try to cure patients already marked for death. Thus when an outbreak of typhus swept the camp, Mengele ordered more than a thousand prisoners suspected of being infected to the gas chamber.

But Mengele had not come to Auschwitz to heal—he was there to explore the secrets of heredity. This interest caused him to search the crowds of new arrivals for hunchbacks, dwarfs, and others with obviously inherited characteristics and for his perfect guinea pigs: sets of twins.

Multiple births had long provided living laboratories for studies of heredity. The genetic instructions of identical twins—created when a single fertilized egg divides into two viable embryos—are carbon copies of each other. Fraternal twins, who arise from two fertilized eggs but are born together, have similar, but not identical, genetic material. It had

become common practice to use such pairs, often taking one as a control and the other as the experimental subject, in conventional heredity studies—tests that Mengele hoped to extend at Auschwitz.

The children Mengele selected for experimentation were housed in special barracks, where, perversely, he showed his captives little kindnesses, often bringing them beautiful clothes, ribbons, and such scarce treats as chocolate. Pairs of twins were transferred to a camp hospital as Mengele required them. In an exhaustive examination that could last for hours, their every external feature was carefully measured and recorded, with particular attention to any differences between the two children.

Then came Mengele's experiments, if his cruel, pseudoscientific whims can be called that. Both children might be injected with typhus

germs or have a body part amputated, so that Mengele could see how their reactions differed. On another day he might inflict wounds and introduce germs or inject one pair of twins with blood extracted from another, unrelated pair. Children who survived their ordeals were returned to their barracks. In one case, a witness reported, young twins were brought back fetid with gangrene after having been sewn together back to back.

Countless children died as a direct result of what Mengele did to them, and those who did not were often gassed, shot, or killed by injection. Sometimes, survivors reported, his curiosity would be piqued, and he would kill children just to autopsy them. In a postwar affidavit, an inmate physician who worked for Mengele testified that on a single evening his superior had administered lethal injections of chloroform directly into the hearts of seven pairs of Gypsy twins. Dissection was the last step in the comparisons Mengele made between twins, noting any differences in their organs and general physical development.

Mengele had a further obsession with one inherited trait in particular: eye color. The Nordic ideal demanded blue or gray eyes, and the doctor evidently wanted to find a technique for changing undesirable brown or black eye pigmentation to a more Aryan hue. To this end, he injected dyes into ▷

Josef Mengele looms menacingly from a train in a 1939 snapshot, taken four years before his terrible work at Auschwitz began.

Hyg.-bakt. Unters.-Stelle
der Waffen-SS, Südost   29.JUN.1944

Auschwitz OS., am 29.Juni 1944.

Anliegend wird übersandt:

Material: Kopf einer Leiche (12-jähriges Kind)
zu untersuchen auf   entnommen am
                  Histologische Schnitte
Name, Vorname:

Dienstgrad, Einheit: siehe Anlage
Klinische Diagnose :

Anschrift der einsendenden Dienststelle: H.-Krankenbau
Zigeunerlager Auschwitz II, B II e
Bemerkungen :

                     Der l.Lagerarzt
                     K.L. Auschwitz II

                     SS-Hauptsturmführer
                     (Stempel, Unterschrift)

A chilling scrap of extant documentation from Josef Mengele's experiments at Auschwitz, this signed laboratory form requests tissue samples from the head of a dead 12-year-old Gypsy child.

Formula Racers

When anthropologist Hans F. K. Günther was appointed professor of *Rassenkunde*—racial science—at the University of Jena in 1930, the faculty members who raised a noisy protest were already doomed to be swept aside or drowned by Germany's rising tide of racist ideology. At universities across the land, the science of anthropology—the study of human origins, cultures, and biology—was being transformed into a quest for proofs of Aryan, or Nordic, racial superiority.

Günther owed his new post to the good offices of the Nazi government of the state of Thuringia, which had evidently been attracted by his efforts to demonstrate the physical and cultural superiority of the Nordic race. Happily for Günther and his colleagues, their science meshed nicely with the racial ideas expressed by Adolf Hitler in his 1925 autobiography, *Mein Kampf*. The Aryan race "absolutely and alone was the founder of higher humanity, and therefore constitutes the original type of what we understand by the term 'human being,' " the future Führer had written. "If he is eliminated, deep darkness will again descend upon the earth, perhaps in only a few thousand years, human civilization will disappear and the world will revert to desert."

The obsession with Nordic superiority was nothing new when *Mein Kampf* was written—it had flickered ominously in Germany since the mid-19th century. Early in the 1920s the contagion had spread to anthropologists, who drew on genetic principles used in animal breeding to identify supposedly

the eyes of dozens of victims, some of whom went blind as a consequence—if they were not killed immediately afterward. One witness reported later that in a part of the Gypsy compound at Auschwitz he had seen a table spread with samples of eyes. "They each had a number and a letter," he recalled. "The eyes were very pale yellow to bright blue, green, and violet." Years later, a woman could not forget the horror she felt upon seeing eye specimens "pinned up like butterflies" on Mengele's laboratory wall: "I thought I was dead and already living in hell."

The Auschwitz doctor's research pleased his superiors, who praised his methodical work and devotion to Nazi ideals. Colleagues outside Auschwitz were kept informed of his experiments, which evidently were not considered to be very far from the prevailing mainstream. In fact, while at Auschwitz he remained a kind of remote assistant to Otmar von Verschuer, his friend and mentor at the Kaiser Wilhelm Institute of Anthropology, Human Genetics, and Eugenics. Mengele's busy pathology laboratory, where he performed his dissections, had been built with institute grant money.

But the career of Josef Mengele was as short as it was cruel. By the end of 1944 the Soviet Army threatened Auschwitz, and Mengele was forced to conclude his research. In less than two years, an estimated 3,000 twins had passed through his hands, along with an unknown number of other experimental victims; the doctor's shining baton had waved 200,000 to 400,000—estimates vary—into the Auschwitz death line. Evading Allied occupation troops for several years after the war, Mengele eventually fled to South America, where he reportedly lived under a series of assumed names. Hints and rumors finally led authorities to a Brazilian grave whose contents were identified as Mengele's remains by forensic examiners in 1985. He had drowned while swimming in 1979, his family claimed, but the death had been kept secret. Not everyone believed that the skeleton was Mengele's, however.

Ironically, it was hereditary science—although not the kind that he had pursued to such monstrous extremes—that gave Mengele away. In 1992 his son voluntarily submitted to a genetic test that showed a link between his DNA and the DNA of the bones unearthed in Brazil, proving the two were genetically related. The match should have been conclusive evidence that Mengele had finally left forever. But for some, including a surviving handful of his Auschwitz twins, it may not have been enough. The Angel of Death has become immortal, so great was the evil that he did. □

In a 1933 demonstration, German anthropologist Robert Burgen-Villengen measures a dummy's head with his patented plastometer, which was used by scientists of the day in attempts to quantify minute cranial differences between racial types.

"pure" breeds of humans and to give racial inequality a rational, scientific basis. One of the point men in this movement, Günther defined a race as a group of people with a unique combination of physical features and spiritual characteristics; such a group bred true, he said, reproducing only its own kind. Groups who did not meet the racial criteria, on the other hand, were not races at all, but the ignoble and degenerate product of miscegenation.

Rassenkunde anthropologists let almost no detail of physique pass unassessed and unrecorded and published tables identifying standard colors of skin, eyes, and hair that they linked to different racial groups. They also assigned psychological features to the races. Europe's native population, according to Günther's scheme, was divided among five races: Nordic, Alpine, Mediterranean, Balkan, and East Baltic. Jews, Günther proclaimed, were a mixture of two non-European races, the African and the Oriental.

Fair skin, blond hair, and blue or gray eyes were deemed markers of the Nordic type. Tall, slender, and graceful, the Nordic paradigm represented the ideal of beauty and possessed superior athletic ability. On the psychic side, Günther attributed to Nordic males unusual will power, cool deliberative judgment, truthfulness, and "an inclination to knightly justice." Because of the race's remarkable creative and intellectual powers, he preached, Nordic representation was disproportionately high among the leaders of Western countries; and, conversely, Günther took note of "the relatively low number of famous men and women without noticeable Nordic strain."

Aryan superiority manifested itself in many other ways, according to Günther, who evidently let no detail escape him. He found Nordics were inherently cleaner than members of other races, a quality he linked to their pioneering such hygienic innovations as soap and the hairbrush. Proof of the greater virtue of Nordic women was ubiquitous—detectable, to the sharp-eyed Günther, even on streetcars. He observed that Nordic females sat primly with their knees together, while women of other races allowed their legs to drift apart.

Even for Professor Günther, however, it was easier to define a race than it was to discover its pure exemplars. Of the German population, or *Volk*, Günther determined that only about seven percent could be considered "pure Nordic." Other European races made up even smaller proportions of the Volk; the great majority was a mix of two or more races. To Nazi purists Günther offered the consolation that half the blood flowing in German veins was probably Nordic—a comfortingly rich mixture.

The blending of races was of great concern to Rassenkunde ideologues. The attributes of the Nordic race, Günther warned, could easily be diluted and ultimately lost if ◊

Germans took no preventive action. Men, Rassenkunde said, must avoid the traps laid by "diabolically alluring" females of inferior races and choose virtuous Nordic mates. Once a proper mate had been secured, the professor advised, Germans must vigorously pursue "a victorious birth rate."

Günther had summarized his theories in a 1922 volume entitled *A Short Ethnology of the German People.* A mixture of science, anecdote, and mysticism, the book was a remarkable success, selling some 275,000 copies in a country that was wracked by economic depression. Thereafter, as the Nazi star had continued to rise, so had Günther's. Hitler himself attended Günther's inaugural lecture at Jena, and in 1935 the anthropologist won a prestigious new post in racial science at the University of Berlin.

Other racial scientists enjoyed success under the Nazis, filling newly established positions in Rassenkunde at most of the major universities and assuming powerful positions in the many party and government agencies concerned with matters of racial purity. Their services were not always in the realm of theory; one prominent anthropologist served as a judge in a court that decided who should be sterilized under a law "for the prevention of genetically diseased offspring." Like his fellows, Günther practiced what he preached. He was one of several anthropologists who helped the Gestapo organize the secret sterilization of racially mixed children born in the Rhineland following its post-World War I occupation by French African troops.

Academic opponents of the racial scientists got short shrift—and sometimes much worse—for displays of integrity. University of Göttingen anthropologist Karl Saller, for example, argued against Nordic superiority and asserted that race was not, as Rassenkunde specialists declared, determined solely by heredity. The university dismissed him, and his works vanished from German bookstores. Friedrich Merkenschlager, a botanist who launched a comprehensive attack on Günther's work, was imprisoned in the Dachau concentration camp.

Such instances of resistance to Rassenkunde were exceptions, and the disapproval voiced abroad did little to dampen German enthusiasm for ideologically skewed an-

thropology. In 1938 Theodor Mollison, director of the Anthropological Institute in Munich, vigorously defended his colleagues against foreign critics. Declaring "absurd" the allegation that German scientific thought was not free, he wrote to American anthropologist Franz Boas, "I assure you that we German scientists know very well the things for which we may thank Adolf Hitler, not the least of which is the cleansing of our people from foreign racial elements, whose manner of thinking is not our own. With the exception of those few individuals with ties to Jewish or Masonic groups, we scientists support wholeheartedly the salute, 'Heil Hitler.' " At the time, his was the voice of German reason.

Professor Günther was suspended from teaching in 1945. But, until his death in 1968, he continued to write about racial science just as though Hitler, a world war, and the Nazi concentration camps had never happened. □

Aryan Physics

Like all science in Hitler's Germany, physics quickly acquired the ideological cast of Nazi doctrine and its obsession with national origins and race. For renowned experimentalist Philipp Lenard, however, there was something especially compelling in what he ultimately championed as "Aryan physics."

Born in the Austro-Hungarian Empire in 1862, Lenard was educated at the German universities of Heidelberg and Berlin and stayed on in Germany to do research and teach. Despite the man's considerable abilities, Lenard's character was flawed by a tendency toward envy, resentment, and bitterness. He chafed under what he considered his slow climb up the career ladder and complained that his work was not receiving the recognition it deserved—indeed, there may not have been enough recognition in the world to satisfy his needs.

In 1905 the 43-year-old Lenard had received the Nobel Prize for his experiments with cathode rays. Even that honor was not enough to assuage the feeling that he was not receiving sufficient credit for his work. He took the opportunity of his Nobel lecture to denounce an English colleague who had supposedly snatched some glory due him. Lenard claimed that he had shared the results of some of his experiments with the man—who had repaid him, said Lenard, by publishing the data as his own.

The Nobel was not the only milestone in Lenard's career that year. Albert Einstein published his theory of special relativity in 1905, changing physics fundamentally.

Abstruse theories laden with difficult mathematical concepts began to intrude upon the traditional physical and experimental preoccupations of physicists. By inclination and training, Lenard favored the less esoteric strata of experimental work, and he believed that theoreticians scorned mere experimenters as inferiors. Lenard's animosity and bitterness deepened in 1914, when Einstein received an appointment to Berlin's prestigious Prussian Academy of Sciences—a position that Lenard had coveted. He took Einstein's appointment as he did everything: as a deliberate personal slap.

Bitter in good times, Lenard was doubly so following World War I, when the German economy collapsed under the pressures of wartime debt and postwar reparations. Seeing his investments made worthless by inflation, Lenard, like many of his compatriots, blamed Jewish influence on the government. ◊

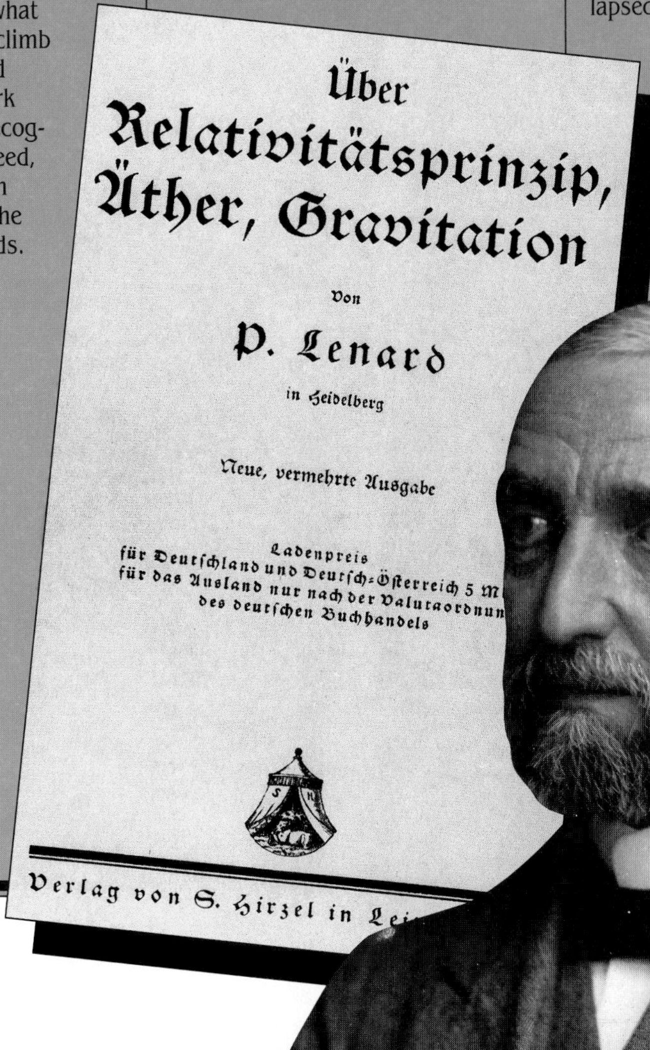

Viciously anti-Semitic, Austrian scientist Philipp Lenard (right) lashed out in the 1920 pamphlet shown here against the theory of relativity, in part because it was propounded by Jewish physicist Albert Einstein.

Über
Relativitätsprinzip,
Äther, Gravitation

von

P. Lenard

in Heidelberg

Neue, vermehrte Ausgabe

Ladenpreis
für Deutschland und Deutsch-Österreich 5 M
für das Ausland nur nach der Valutaordnun
des deutschen Buchhandels

Verlag von S. Hirzel in Lei

In 1922 Lenard touched off a riot among leftist students and workers when he refused to close his laboratory during a mandatory day of mourning for Germany's assassinated foreign minister, Walter Rathenau, who was a Jew. This mean-spirited action made Lenard into a hero to anti-Semitic right-wingers throughout Germany.

For the brooding Lenard, the fact that Einstein was Jewish became transcendentally important; the growing scientific eminence of the rival became more than Lenard could bear. Einstein personified all that Lenard abhorred both in science and, increasingly, in political life. Not only had Einstein donned the mantle of the foremost theoretician in physics—he was a socialist, a pacifist, and an internationalist as well, anathema to Lenard's passionate nationalism.

When Einstein received the 1921 Nobel Prize for physics, Lenard lodged a protest with the committee, then went public with his opposition. Becoming rabidly explicit in his denunciations, he labeled Einstein's theory of relativity as "a Jewish fraud."

Among Adolf Hitler's first and most fervent supporters, Lenard began to enjoy the backing of the state for his anti-Einstein crusade when the Nazis came to power in 1933. Warning his compatriots against what he called the "mathematically botched-up theories of Einstein," Lenard declared, "We must recognize that it is unworthy of a German to be the intellectual follower of a Jew. Natural science, properly so called, is of completely Aryan origin. Heil Hitler!"

The fullest expression of Lenard's doctrines came in 1936, when he published the first of four volumes titled *German Physics*. Proclaiming that "in reality, science, like everything else mankind creates, is conditioned by race and blood," he castigated "Jewish physics" as "a phantom and a phenomenon of degeneration of fundamental German physics." Stripped of its racist rhetoric, however, Lenard's German physics was simply the science of an earlier day, a rehash of the 19th-century teachings he had learned half a century earlier.

Not all German scientists were so quick to discard the new physics, however. Understanding the value of Einstein's theories, they set about making them ideologically palatable simply by rewriting history. A scientific conference held in 1942 reported that "Aryan scientists"—their number included one Frenchman—"had created the foundations of the theory of relativity." Albert Einstein's role, they declared, had been secondary, since he had "merely followed up the already existing ideas." But by then, German science had been thoroughly sterilized by its infusion of Nazi dogma. Einstein and many other notable physical theorists had long since fled the country, leaving Aryan physics in the hands of such ideologues as Lenard, who had managed to rid Germany of its finest scientific talent.

Lenard lived to see his adoptive homeland defeated once again and, perhaps, to gnash his teeth over the atomic bombs that brought World War II to an end in Japan in 1945—bombs that were largely the creation of men and women he had helped drive from Europe. He died in 1947, aged 85, his cup of bitterness kept full to the last by the manifest success of the "Jewish physics" he had vilified. □

Dead Heads

Psychologist Lewis Terman of Stanford University spread the gospel of IQ, or intelligence quotient—a term coined by German psychologist William Stern—with missionary fervor. He also developed the Stanford-Binet test, named for Stanford University and French psychologist Alfred Binet *(pages 83-84)*—the first intelligence-measuring examination to be widely used in the United States. But Terman's conviction that intelligence could be measured as reliably as temperature or weight was too strong for him to keep within his own time. A skilled evaluator, he believed, should also be able to gauge precisely the innate mental ability of the dead. Boldly putting his methods to the test, Terman organized a postmortem IQ exam of famous men and women from the past.

Fascinated by the intellectually gifted, Terman took the view that their mental endowments were innate, inherited intact and little changed by training and environment. Given its purely hereditary source, Terman reasoned, the distinction between geniuses and dullards should be apparent early in childhood. Accordingly, he focused his historical endeavor upon that stage of life.

Terman first tried out his retrospective method in 1917 on the late British eugenics pioneer Francis Galton—a fitting choice, since Galton had been a notable collector of anthropological statistics. Delving into Francis Galton's biography, Terman gleaned details of his subject's youthful activities. Precocious achievements such as learning Latin at the age of four were taken as evidence of high intelligence, as were

"early maturity of moral attitude or judgment" and other less tangible factors. When Terman was satisfied that he had enough biographical data, he pronounced "the IQ that would most reasonably account for the recorded facts." Young Galton was awarded the whopping quotient of 200—the maximum allowed on the Stanford-Binet scale.

Inexplicably, Terman now felt that his highly subjective procedure was scientifically shipshape and took on a graduate student, Catharine Morris Cox, as his research assistant. For a database they used a list of the 1,000 most eminent figures in history compiled by one James McKeen Cattell, who had handled the Herculean task with simplicity: He had measured the space devoted to each in biographical dictionaries. From this compilation, Cox picked 301 persons for whom adequate information could be found, especially for their youthful achievements. Mostly natives of Europe, Great Britain, or the United States, all of Cox's picks had lived between 1450 and 1850.

Cox, Terman, and three associates shared the task of pulling together biographical data on these several hundred achievers and reckoned their intelligence quotients. Instances of precocity earned a subject extra points—but where such evidence was absent or could not be obtained, points were subtracted. Applying what they called their "exact science," each of the quintet calculated two IQ values for each subject, one for the age of 17 and the other for the age of 26; an average figure was then derived from the different calculations. However, two team members doled out IQs that differed markedly from those measured by the other three; one was overly generous with high scores, while the other tended in the opposite direction. In some, this might have prompted second

thoughts about how exact the science was. But Cox was too confident to be bothered by the deviation and simply tossed out the IQs the pair had provided, on the grounds that their contradictory numbers would have canceled each other out anyway.

Not surprisingly, the study began to indicate exactly what belief had led the psychologists to expect: High IQs had gone hand in hand with high achievement, as defined by Terman, Cox, and their collaborators. Still, Cox was not satisfied with the average IQs the team had calculated. They were concentrated in the 135 to 145 range—too low, she thought, given the abilities of her subjects. Once again, she hit upon a simple solution. With a fine disregard for scientific method, she added 20 points to each average, boosting them to 155 to 165. With that adjustment, the scores fell closer to her expectations.

Achievers in similar fields tended to wind up at the same level. As a group, military men did the worst, with several scoring only slightly above 100, the average score of common humanity. With IQs ranging between 120 and 130, such notables as Abraham Lincoln, Simon Bolívar, and George Washington fared somewhat better, but they still ranked below the "near genius" level of 140. Leonardo da Vinci, Sir Isaac Newton, Beethoven, and Napoleon also fell short of that point—until Cox corrected their IQs with her 20-point bonus. Philosophers and scientists received the highest scores, and British economist John Stuart Mill wound up at the top of the class, tying Francis Galton at 200.

Compared to that group, musicians and painters, even remark- ◊

Among the posthumous IQs assigned by psychologist Lewis Terman (left) and his research team, the highest were those of British eugenics pioneer Sir Francis Galton, shown at top in a silhouette made when he was 12, and 18th-century economist John Stuart Mill (above). Both men were rated at 200—the maximum possible score.

ably precocious ones, had been shortchanged by heredity. Cox offhandedly dismissed Wolfgang Amadeus Mozart, perhaps music's greatest prodigy, with the comment that he was "probably above the average level of his social group." Even so, Mozart could be thankful for his IQ range of 150 to 160. Dutch painter Rembrandt van Rijn, despite the brilliance of his art, posted a lackluster 110 to 120.

Class, it seemed to the IQ raters, must also play some part in fostering intellectual ability, and they duly awarded additional points to the children of the wealthy and well connected. Those from humbler families received lower scores. Because his father had repaired pots and pans for a living, 17th-century English poet John Bunyan, author of *Pilgrim's Progress*, had to make due with a paltry 100 points, despite the permanence of his work. But in one case, at least, they were caught on a dilemma.

Commonly thought to have sprung from plain stock, William Shakespeare promised to destroy the precision of their study. On the one hand, a high score for the world's greatest dramatist would have called into question the assumption that heredity conveyed more benefits in good families than in poor ones. A low score, on the other hand, would have been equally indefensible in view of the overwhelming evidence of Shakespeare's genius. Their solution suggests that Terman, Cox, and the others may have experienced a failure of faith. When *The Early Mental Traits of Three Hundred Geniuses* appeared in 1926, the second volume of Terman's definitive *Genetic Studies of Genius*, the problematic Bard was nowhere to be seen. □

Chaff

At the 1948 meeting of the Lenin All-Union Academy of Agricultural Sciences, Trofim Denisovich Lysenko celebrated victory in a decades-long academic struggle. To a crowd of delegates who had stood and cheered for Soviet dictator Joseph Stalin, Lysenko offered further proof that the doctrines of Marxism were mirrored in genetics and biology. The Communist Party's Central Committee, he proudly announced, had formally approved his biological theories—ideas that, while ridiculed by the international scientific community, were now dogma. Dissenting scientists risked being branded as decadent reactionaries in the service of bourgeois capitalism. In Stalin's purge-ridden Soviet Union, such critics were rare.

Lysenko's triumph merely consolidated the enormous influence that the biologist had wielded for years. Parting company with foreign scientists, Lysenko had spurned as thoroughly bourgeois the theory that new traits arise because of random genetic mutation—the hereditary mechanism that propels natu-

ral selection. Such a haphazard process was too slow and uncertain to meet the deterministic needs of Marxism. Denying the very existence of genes, Lysenko had claimed that traits acquired by individual members of a species could be passed on to their offspring—and create a virtual new species in the space of only a single generation. Stabilized in the offspring, the new traits would then be passed on to future generations. Lysenko's politicized

In 1962 controversial agronomist Trofim Lysenko *(left, with cap)* displays his wheat specimens at Lenin Hills experimental farm to Soviet premier Nikita Khrushchev. Two years later, both Khrushchev and Lysenko fell from power.

biology promised a grand revolution in Soviet agriculture—a shortcut to improved species of grains and vegetables that would be available virtually on demand.

A perfect instance of the scientist as politician, Lysenko had been born in 1898 to a Ukrainian peasant family and had come of age during the turmoil of World War I and the Russian Revolution. He had trained as an agronomist while working at experimental stations in the early 1920s, as the new Communist regime was still consolidating its hold in rural areas.

Lysenko first won a name for himself in 1929 through experiments in what was called vernalization. Russians depended heavily on winter wheat, a high-yield variety that was typically sown in the fall, then sprouted quickly once the weather warmed and could be harvested in spring. Winter wheat carried the risk that the famed Russian winter would kill the seeds in the ground. But in dry years, wheat planted in spring took its chances with the Ukraine's scant summer rainfall. Vernalization was an effort to train wheat seeds to germinate more or less on demand, permitting farmers to plant and harvest at optimum times during the year.

Lysenko seemed to have solved the problem. He had planted a winter wheat in the spring, after conditioning the seeds in snowbanks for a short period; the crop matured swiftly and was harvested in late summer. Transferred to the Institute of Selection and Genetics in Odessa, Lysenko continued his experiments in a special vernalization laboratory established there.

In 1935 Lysenko began longer-term experiments with a type of winter wheat called *kooperatorka*—and obtained an astonishing new result. As before, the conditioned wheat seed germinated swiftly when planted in the spring. But this time, when Lysenko planted seeds that were taken from that crop, the resulting wheat plants retained some of their parent's accelerated growth properties. In just three generations, he reported, he had effectively reset the germination clock of the kooperatorka seed. Lysenko's findings defied all the laws of Mendelian genetics, suggesting that the parent had passed acquired new traits along to its progeny.

There was a major experimental catch, however: Lysenko had obtained his results using a single plant and its descendants (a second parent plant had died). In the view of Western scientists and some of his colleagues at home, his sample was ridiculously small. Nevertheless, the notion of a shortened growth period in a country with a ◊

brief growing season was so attractive that the statistical inconvenience was overlooked. Several established biologists expressed interest in Lysenko's work, and political authorities perked up their ears. Confronted by food shortages, party managers were quick to seize on vernalization, which, according to Lysenko, could be adapted to potatoes, beans, and other crops.

But obstacles remained. "The Party and the government have set our plant-breeding science the task of creating new varieties of plants at the shortest date," he wrote. "Nevertheless, the science of plant breeding continues to lag behind and there is no guarantee that this socialist task will be carried out within the appointed time." The stumbling block: "bourgeois science," which he urged his colleagues to replace with his own "materialist principles of development, which actually reflect the dialectics of heredity." In short, superior new plant species could be produced by applying the same principles used to create a new Marxist society.

Lysenko's political jargon was music to the ears of apparatchiks, but not to his fellow scientists. Prominent geneticists noted that the central element in Lysenko's theory, the inheritance of acquired traits, had never been demonstrated experimentally by anyone, anywhere. As dedicated as Lysenko to building socialism, these critics called for more attention to improving plant species through proven methods of hybridization. For some it was a fatal mistake.

Stalin himself had thrown his support behind Lysenko, and dissent—even experimental evidence at odds with Lysenko's ideas—carried the threat of dismissal and exile. Nikolai Vavilov, the most distinguished Soviet geneticist, was removed from his post as president of the Academy of Agricultural Sciences in 1935 and later died in a Siberian prison camp. His two successors were arrested in purges. Lysenko himself assumed the presidency in 1938.

Some muted criticism of Lysenko's views persisted, but the 1948 meeting of the Academy of Agricultural Sciences seemed to cement his position. Hundreds of geneticists soon lost their jobs; their laboratories were disbanded and academic curricula were reorganized. Elections to the USSR Academy of Sciences packed the biology division with Lysenko's allies.

But events soon conspired to undermine Lysenko. Word got around, for example, that a massive reforestation project governed by his principles was a gigantic flop. Almost 300,000 acres of seedlings were planted in a region rendered extremely inhospitable by its chronic dryness and sweeping winds. Nevertheless, Lysenko believed that if trees of the same species were planted in clusters, they would thrive. Although he admitted that there was competition among species, he denied its existence within a species: Even in the plant kingdom, individuals benefited by subordinating their own needs to the welfare of the group as a whole and aiding the group in its struggles against competing species. Unfortunately, individual trees needed water and food more than they needed political theory, and the resulting extensive losses of seedlings left Lysenko vulnerable.

Then, in 1953, the study of genetics took a giant step forward with the discovery of the double-helix structure of the DNA molecule, which was already believed to carry hereditary instructions. The breakthrough renewed the interest in bourgeois genetics among prominent Soviet biologists and among physicists, chemists, and mathematicians as well. That same year, Stalin died, leaving Lysenko without a powerful friend at court.

In 1956 Lysenko was forced to resign as president of the Academy of Agricultural Sciences, but his hegemony over Soviet biology was not over. Ever the politician, he cultivated Nikita Khrushchev, another son of Ukrainian peasants, who became premier in 1957. Lysenko's renewed clout lasted until his new protector was ousted in 1964. Now Lysenko's scientific detractors pounced. A commission established to investigate the agronomist's experimental farm determined that Lysenko's research methods were flawed and his agricultural practices either ineffective or actually harmful. He was stripped of his powerful positions in scientific organizations but permitted to retain control of his farm, where he worked until his death in 1976.

But Lysenko's influence lived on. In the former Soviet Union, an entire generation of biologists and politicians who owed careers to their allegiance to Lysenko's aberrant theories continued to hold high positions in the vast agricultural bureaucracy and still justified their science in political terms. For example, books dealing with DNA and molecular biology adopted modern genetics, once a reviled capitalist creation, as a biological expression of dialectical materialism. Even dead wrong, Lysenko had cast a long shadow. □

Cometary Commentary

The publication of Immanuel Velikovsky's *Worlds in Collision* in 1950 was greeted by a tumult in keeping with its catastrophic contents. Outraged scientists denounced it and threatened to boycott the Macmillan Company, which fired the editor who had bought the manuscript and sold the rights to the book to another publisher. The work rapidly became a bestseller and in the next quarter-century went through more than 70 printings.

The controversy occasioned by *Worlds in Collision* stemmed from the author's breathtaking claim that in ancient times an erratically wandering comet caused massive upheavals on Earth that corresponded to events described in the Bible and other ancient writings and folklore. But Velikovsky's comet was unlike any others. Astronomers believe that comets formed on the fringes of the Solar System as it coalesced about 4.5 billion years ago and are rather small projectiles of ice and dust, which flake away to create the familiar tail. The comet that was proposed by Velikovsky, however, was a comparative newcomer, somehow ripped from the flank of Jupiter, with the size and mass of a planet.

Around 1500 BC, Velikovsky wrote, this hurtling Jovian fragment made its first close approach to the planet Earth. The disturbances its passage created were noted worldwide, Velikovsky claimed, in Mayan manuscripts, the chronicles of Chinese emperor Yahou, the Finnish epic *Kalevala*, and numerous other records. The Earth's surface was wracked by great storms and tremors so violent that mountains collapsed, the seas boiled, and a rain of meteorites and petroleum fell from the sky.

These were not just catastrophic events, however—Velikovsky's planet-size comet was triggering the miraculous events recorded in the Old Testament's Book of Exodus. The waters of the Red Sea on Egypt's eastern shore parted, allowing the Israelites who were held captive there to escape and begin their long trek to the Promised Land. The manna that sustained them during their 40 years of wandering in the desert showered down from the celestial intruder, which then sped away from Earth and finally disappeared.

But its work had barely begun. Fifty-two years later, according to Velikovsky, the comet returned to wreak terrestrial havoc once again—and to serve some theological ends as well. In his view, a comet-generated earthquake, not trumpets and shouts, shook down the ancient walls of Jericho, and the comet's slowing of the Earth's rotation made the Sun seem to stand still in the sky after Joshua's great victory over the powerful Amorites.

In the eighth century BC, Velikovsky believed, the rogue comet ricocheted off Mars, which veered toward Earth, making an approach so close that the two atmospheres mingled, causing the conflagrations foretold by the Old Testament prophet Amos. For sixty years Mars menaced the Earth, then somehow returned to its accustomed orbit around the Sun. As for the caroming comet, it became the second planet from the Sun—Venus.

Whatever the merits of his proposed cosmic calamities, Velikovsky was no stranger to terrestrial upheavals on the grand scale. Born in Vitebsk, Byelorussia, in 1895, he had trained as a physician and a psychoanalyst before immigrating to the United States in 1939. He had endured the First World War and Russia's revolution early in the century and lived through the rise of Hitler. Throughout, Velikovsky had evidently preserved a strong Jewish orthodoxy, seeing the Bible as a literal history—whose miracles he believed science could explain.

The transplanted Russian was far from the first to attempt harmonizing biblical accounts with natural events or using comets to force nature into a biblical mold. That honor is often accorded to English mathematician William Whiston, who in 1696 published a book correlating biblical catastrophes with cometary wanderings.

Whiston was acclaimed by his peers. Velikovsky, his latter-day kindred spirit, garnered wealth and a kind of fame but little support from scientists. Most of them decried his lack of credentials in such fields as physics, paleontology, and astronomy, which his histories had turned upside down. Unperturbed by such allegations and aggressively contemptuous of his critics, Velikovsky deplored the "collective scotoma," or blind spot, that made conventionally trained scientists reject works such as his. "The scholars who have taught and written and published not only have a vested interest in orthodox theories," he wrote, "but they are for the most part psychologically incapable of relearning." His opponents exhibited, he said, a kind of psychological repression of new ideas; he wanted them to listen.

Not until he was 78 did Velikovsky have his hearing. In 1974 the ◊

prestigious American Association for the Advancement of Science organized a symposium on his theories, which had lost little of their fundamentalist appeal over the years. In his presentation, Velikovsky cited predictions of his that had come true: the discovery of lunar magnetism, radio signals from the planet Jupiter, a hot surface on Venus. He pointed out that he must have been onto something or the establishment would not have felt so threatened by his revelations and portrayed himself as a victim of entrenched orthodoxy.

But in a series of opposing papers, scientists ripped apart his theses: His predictions had been general, not specific, and they had been more often wrong than right. One astronomer demonstrated that it would take an expenditure of energy equaling the Sun's entire annual output to propel an object the size of Venus out of Jupiter's gravitational grasp and dismissed the cometary near misses proposed by Velikovsky as impossibly improbable. The orderly dynamics of the Solar System could not be achieved in only a few centuries, said another—the orbits of Venus and Mars must have been established very early in the Solar System's life. Ancient astronomical records presented by yet another scholar showed that the planet Venus had been observed before the year 1900 BC—400 years earlier than the first pass of Velikovsky's comet—and there was evidence that observations of Venus might have been made as early as 3000 BC. He took Velikovsky to task for making a muddle of ancient texts when he combed them for parallels to amazing events that are described in the Bible. Among them, they mounted an unanswerable barrage of facts to counter his "reconstruction" of cosmic events.

At the end of the daylong debate, according to the journal *Science,* both sides claimed victory. Neither the scorn nor the well-marshaled facts of the scientific establishment were able to demobilize the self-taught savant's troop of fol-

lowers or dent his own belief. Velikovsky died in 1979, aged 84, but his wondrously wrongheaded ideas have acquired a life of their own. *Worlds in Collision,* the work with which he opened the argument, continues to be sold, offering an illusion of congruence between science and belief. □

In a 19th-century etching by Gustave Doré *(top),* the Sun stands still after Joshua's biblical victory over the Amorites at Gibeon. According to Immanuel Velikovsky *(above),* Earth's rotation was actually interrupted by a giant comet.

130

This Side Up

"Earth flat," a recent newsletter from the Flat Earth Society of Covenant Peoples Church asserts telegraphically. "Entire Bible tells you one way is UP, one way is DOWN, right?" All scientists, particularly those who purvey the notion of a spherical Earth, are, according to Society leaders Charles and Marjory Johnson, "witch doctors, sorcerers, tellers of tales." The Lancaster, California, couple charge them with ignoring proof that the Earth is flat—such proofs, for example, as the fact that, in her native Australia, Marjory walked upright. "Australia," her husband concurs, "is not down under the world!"

The position adopted by the Johnsons has a venerable history stretching back 2,500 years and more. The core of the argument is a discrepancy between observations of the world's globularity, as flat-Earthers call it, and religious dogma. Many fathers of the early Christian church concluded from various biblical passages that the Earth could not be round. In the Book of Daniel, for instance, a tree is said to grow out of the center of the Earth. The prophet says that "the height thereof reached unto heaven: the sight thereof was even to the end of all Earth." Such visibility, it has been argued, would be possible only on a flat Earth; if the Earth were round, its curvature would block the view of the tree from most points on the globe.

Such faith was given a modern, supposedly scientific foundation by a British fanatic named Samuel Birley Rowbotham in the mid-1800s. Not content to cite the Bible, he performed what he fancied were valid experiments to back up religious tradition. In a typical endeavor, Rowbotham took sightings through a telescope fixed in the stern of a boat traveling a straight six-mile stretch of Cambridgeshire's Old Bedford Level Canal between two parallel bridges—the Old Bedford Bridge at one end and the Welney Bridge at the other. Throughout the entire distance, he claimed, no part of Old Bedford Bridge was lost from view, whereas if the Earth were round, the structure's lowest seven feet or so would have slipped below the horizon.

That it did not was less the result of the planet's flatness than Rowbotham's predisposed eye. Nevertheless, his pseudoscience made the Old Bedford Level Canal hallowed ground for flat-Earthers and won over a band of followers who bravely withstood "word-blows"—by which they meant criticism—and reminded one another "that many have been burnt to death for up- ◊

This badly blurred photograph of the Old Bedford Level Canal in England, a prime site for flat-Earth experimentation, was taken in 1904 by believer Lady Blount, who offered it as proof of the "Earth's unglobularity."

holding the truth." The followers called themselves Zetetics, after their leader's 1849 pamphlet *Zetetic Astronomy: A Description of Several Experiments which Prove that the Surface of the Sea is a Perfect Plane and that the Earth is Not a Globe!* The name harked back to the Greek verb *zeteo*, "to inquire after."

Rowbotham, the chief Zetetic, could make results follow dogma outside the laboratory, too. He was adept at sidestepping the snares laid for him by orthodox scientists in print and from the audience at his lectures. When pressed too closely on a point, the flat-Earther would politely tell the interrogator that the queries had taken up enough time, then call on someone else in the audience. Indeed, Rowbotham was so polite and reasonable that one cane-wielding adversary reportedly had to be restrained from attacking him.

One avid Rowbotham fan was biblical fundamentalist John Hampden. He was so certain the Earth was flat that in 1870 he offered £500 to anyone who could prove otherwise. Strapped for cash and eager to partake of what looked like fairly easy pickings, famed naturalist and evolutionist Alfred Russel Wallace *(pages 45-46)* quickly took up the gauntlet. On March 5, the two adversaries met to settle the matter at Rowbotham's former haunt, the Old Bedford Level Canal. Also present were two referees. Wallace chose one, a local surgeon and astronomer, while the other was a flat-Earther picked by Hampden. Wallace placed a marker reaching 13 feet 4 inches above the water's surface at the three-

mile point, midway between the Welney Bridge and the Old Bedford Bridge. He hung a banner at the same height above the water from each bridge. When the center marker was viewed from the corresponding elevation on either bridge, he explained, the curvature of the Earth would make the banner on the other bridge appear to be about 5 feet lower. If the Earth were perfectly flat, the marker would align perfectly with both banners.

Sure enough, a look through a telescope mounted 13 feet 4 inches above the canal's surface on the Welney Bridge showed that the center marker was indeed below the horizontal line of the cross hairs, and the banner on the Old Bedford Bridge six miles away was even lower. Wallace pointed out, correctly, that this meant the Earth sloped down and away from the viewer. Hampden, however, irrationally insisted that they were merely seeing the effect of perspective and that the results proved that the Earth was flat. Not surprisingly, the ref-

erees disagreed about the import of the experiment, and a third party had to be called in to adjudicate. When he awarded the money to Wallace, Hampden claimed a gross injustice had occurred. Rowbotham had little sympathy for Hampden and chided him for putting himself

Flat Earth Society president Charles Johnson displays his map of a flat world, centered on the North Pole and rimmed by antarctic ice.

In an experiment devised by Alfred Russel Wallace, a marker *(black disk on rod)* was placed halfway between two bridges six miles apart on the Old Bedford Level Canal. On each bridge a colored banner *(red)* was placed at the same height above the water as the halfway marker. The marker and banner were then viewed from each bridge through a surveyor's telescope, also set up at the same height above the water.

On a flat Earth, the telescope would have shown the marker disk, the banner, and the telescope's horizontal cross hair aligned *(below, left)*. But the Earth is round, and, as Wallace had predicted, the telescope showed the cross hair above the marker disk, and the disk above the bridge banner *(below, right)*—evidence of a curved planet.

at the mercy of a crafty scientist.

For the rest of his life the aggrieved Hampden hounded Wallace, demanding the return of his £500 and calling him a liar and an "infernal thief" in scathing letters variously addressed to newspapers and to the naturalist or to his wife. More than once Hampden's unrelenting attacks on Wallace landed the flat-Earther in jail, and he never succeeded in retrieving a single farthing. In one sense, however, Wallace had lost the wager. The fruitless libel suits he had brought against Hampden and the emotional trauma caused by years of persecution added up to considerably more than the £500 he had won.

Perhaps worse, the Bedford Level Canal test had not budged the flat-Earthers from their position. If anything, the movement was nourished by the long dispute. From 1900 to 1904, for example, wealthy Lady Elizabeth Anne Mould Blount published *Earth*, a journal dedicated to the cause. In one impassioned article she described returning to the Old Bedford Level Canal and making photographs that afforded "undeniable proof of the Earth's unglobularity." Those and other proofs continue to suffice for such surviving flat-Earthers as Marjory and Charles Johnson. Although they live near Edwards Air Force Base, the primary landing site for NASA's space shuttles, these leaders of today's Flat Earth Society are not swayed by space photographs and other data that verify the roundness of the Earth. Indeed, they label the entire space program a "carnie con-game" intended by a duplicitous government to spin an illusion of roundness. They dismiss such events as Neil Armstrong's walk on the Moon in 1969 as well-staged drama. While they admit that the abundance of round-Earth images makes their mission more difficult, the Johnsons, like the Zetetics before them, are confident that they—perhaps only they—know which way is up. □

ACKNOWLEDGMENTS

The editors wish to thank these individuals and institutions for their valuable assistance:

Josef Ackermann, Göttingen, Germany; Diane Barounis, National Down Syndrome Congress, Park Ridge, Illinois; Hanno Beck, Bonn; Jo Bigelow, Koreshan Unity Foundation, Estero, Florida; Charles Burns, Archivio Segreto, Città del Vaticano, Rome; Laurel Bybell, U.S. Geological Survey, Reston, Virginia; Ellen Caldwell, National Down Syndrome Society, New York; R. A. Gilbert, Bristol, England; Stephen Jay Gould, Museum of Comparative Zoology, Harvard University, Cambridge, Massachusetts; Bernard Greenberg, Department of Biological Sciences, University of Illinois at Chicago, Chicago; Mott Greene, University of Puget Sound, Tacoma, Washington; Heinz Höhne, Grosshansdorf, Germany; Robert F. Howard, National Solar Observatory, Tucson, Arizona; Istituto Archeologico Germanico, Rome; Toge Johans-

son, East Berne, New York; Charles Johnson, Lancaster, California; Michael Kelly, Abiah Library, Wichita State University, Kansas; Gerhard Klare, Astronomische Gesellschaft, Heidelberg; Heidi Klein, Bildarchiv Preussischer Kulturbesitz, Berlin; Hannelore Landsberg, Museum für Naturkunde, Humboldt-Üniversitat zu Berlin, Berlin; William Lanouette, General Management Review Group, Washington, D.C.; John McCosker, California Academy of Sciences, San Francisco; H. Lewis McKinney, Lawrence, Kansas; Alan Mann, University of Pennsylvania, Philadelphia; Yvonne Mannevy, Bibliothèque Municipale, l'Aigle, France; Sybil Milton, National Holocaust Memorial, Washington, D.C.; Mara Miniati, Istituto e Musco di Storia della Scienza, Florence; Earl Mitchell, Chapel Hill, North Carolina; Janet Monge, University of Pennsylvania, Philadelphia; Gabrielle Nettekoven, Medizin-Historisches Institut, Universitätskliniken, Bonn; New Madrid Museum, New

Madrid, Missouri; William Pendergrass, Carolina Biological Supply Company, Burlington, North Carolina; Cardinal Paul Poupard, Segretariato per i non crecenti, Città del Vaticano, Rome; Helena M. Pycior, University of Wisconsin, Milwaukee; David Roddy, U.S. Geological Survey, Flagstaff, Arizona; Hans Roth, Zentralasiatisches Seminar, Universität, Bonn; Raymond Rye, Smithsonian Institution, Natural History Museum, Washington, D.C.; Robert Schadewald, Burnsville, Minnesota; Paul Spudis, Lunar and Planetary Institute, Houston, Texas; Walter W. Stewart, National Institutes of Health, Bethesda, Maryland; Hans Sues, Smithsonian Institution, Natural History Museum, Washington, D.C.; Beverly Sullivan, Washington, D.C.; Charles R. Tolbert, Department of Astronomy, University of Virginia, Charlottesville; Gerard Werktin, Koreshan Unity Foundation, New York; Don Wilhelms, San Francisco, California; Ewen A. Whitaker, Tucson, Arizona.

PICTURE CREDITS

The sources for the illustrations that appear in this book are listed below. Credits from left to right are separated by semicolons, from top to bottom by dashes.

Cover: Bildarchiv Preussischer Kulturbesitz, Berlin, background, U.S. Geological Survey, Reston, Va. **3:** Bildarchiv Preussischer Kulturbesitz, Berlin. **7:** John Shaw/Bruce Coleman, New York, background, M. Angelo/Westlight, Los Angeles. **8:** Courtesy of the National Portrait Gallery, London—the Hulton Picture Company, London. **9:** Mary Evans Picture Library, London—Ann Ronan Picture Library, Taunton, Somerset, England. **10:** Ann Ronan Picture Library, Taunton, Somerset, England. **11:** Giraudon, Paris, courtesy of Musée Condé, Chantilly. **12:** From *Time's Arrow, Time's Cycle*, by Stephen Jay Gould, Harvard University Press, Cambridge, Mass., 1987. **13:** The Natural History Museum, London—Lauros-Giraudon, Paris. **14, 15:** Bildarchiv Preussischer Kulturbesitz, Berlin; William Haxby, Lamont-Doherty Geological Observatory, Palisades, N.Y. **16:** Erik Peterson/Polfoto, Copenhagen. **17:** Roger-Viollet, Paris—Bibliothèque Centrale, M.N.H.N., Paris. **19:** Giraudon, Paris—NASA, Washington, D.C. **20:** Courtesy of the National Portrait Gallery, London—NASA, Washington, D.C. **21:** Jean-Loup Charmet, Paris. **22:** Art by Time-Life Books—courtesy of Biblioteca Marciana, Venice, copied by Mirko Toso, Venice. **23:** AP/Wide World Photos, New York. **24:** Jay Chrepta. **25:** Ann Ronan Picture Library, Taunton, Somerset, England—Scala, Florence. **26:** Courtesy of the Taylor Institute Library, Oxford, England—Evan Sheppard. **27:** Bibliothèque Nationale, Paris. **29:** Mary Evans Picture Library, London. **30:** Museum für Naturkunde, Humboldt-Universität zu Berlin; John Shaw/Bruce Coleman, New York. **31:** Universiteits Bibliotheek, Amsterdam—by permission of the British Library, London (2). **32:** Roger-Viollet, Paris—Dr. Gerhard Liebig, Universität Hohenheim, Stuttgart. **33:** Polfoto, Copenhagen, back-

ground, Jane Burton/Bruce Coleman, New York. **35:** Meteor Crater, Northern Arizona, USA Meteor Enterprises Inc., Flagstaff, Ariz., background, M. Angelo/Westlight, Los Angeles. **36, 37:** Mary Evans Picture Library, London; National Solar Observatory/Sacramento Peak, Sunspot, N. Mex.; courtesy of Miss Philothea Thompson, Woodstock, Oxford, England. **39:** Roger-Viollet, Paris—Giraudon, Paris. **40:** Picture Archives of the Austrian National Library, Vienna. **41:** Amherst College Library/Special Collections and Archives, Amherst, Mass. **42:** Ullstein-Sigmund Freud Copyrights Ltd. **43:** Kobal Collection/Superstock, Inc., New York—art by Time-Life Books. **44:** The Hulton Picture Company, London. **45:** Courtesy of the National Portrait Gallery, London. **47:** Ullstein Bilderdienst, Berlin. **48:** Bildarchiv Preussischer Kulturbesitz, aus *Generelle Morphologie der Organismen*, 1866, Staatsbibliothek, Berlin. **49:** U.S. Geological Survey, Flagstaff, Ariz., insets, from *Mars and Its Canals*, by Percival Lowell, The Macmillan Company, New York, 1906, copied by Larry Sherer (3)—Lowell Observatory, Flagstaff, Ariz. **50:** Picture Archives of the Austrian National Library, Vienna. **51:** IBM Corporation, Research Division, Almaden Research Center, San Jose, Calif.—Deutsches Museum, Munich (2). **52, 53:** Library of Congress LC 36600, inset, U.S. Naval Observatory, Washington, D.C.; Mary Evans Picture Library, London. **54:** AIP/Niels Bohr Library, William G. Meyers Collection, New York—the Rutherford Museum, McGill University, Montreal, Quebec. **55:** Pfälzische Landesbibliothek, Speyer, Germany, Foto Erwin Böhm, Mainz, Germany (6)—Deutsches Museum, Munich. **56:** Claude Lacroix—Leo Szilard Papers (neg. CN4/M32/51), Mandeville Department of Special Collections, University of California, San Diego Library, inset, painting by Oswald Birley, by kind permission of the President and Council of the Royal Society, London. **57:** Robert McCoy, the Museum of Questionable Medical Devices, Minneapolis, the National Food and Drug Administration,

and the St. Louis Science Center. **58:** The Bettmann Archive, New York. **59:** Julie Yarp, George Washington University Medical Center Biomedical Communications, Washington, D.C. **60:** National Library of Medicine, Bethesda, Md. **61:** From the Personal Archive of Alexandra Dmitrievna Ulianskaya, insets, NASA, Washington, D.C. (2). **62, 63:** Photo from G. K. Gilbert Collection, U.S. Geological Survey Photographic Library, Denver; Meteor Crater, Northern Arizona, U.S.A., Meteor Enterprises, Inc., Flagstaff, Ariz.; Smithsonian Institution, Washington, D.C. **64:** NASA, Lyndon B. Johnson Space Center, Houston—NASA, Washington, D.C. **65:** American Meteorite Laboratory, Denver—Patrick Moore, Selsey, Sussex, England. **66:** Courtesy of Western Mail and Echo Ltd., Cardiff, Wales. **67:** U.S. Naval Observatory, Washington, D.C. **69:** Charles R. Knight, © 1942 National Geographic Society, background, H. D. Thoreau/Westlight, Los Angeles. **70:** Hansen Planetarium, Salt Lake City, Utah—by kind permission of the President and Council of the Royal Society, London. **72:** Mary Evans Picture Library, London; courtesy of the Fogg Art Museum, Harvard University, Cambridge, Mass., gift of Paul J. Sachs. **74:** Mary Evans Picture Library, London. **75:** By kind permission of the President and Council of the Royal Society, London. **76:** NASA/Jet Propulsion Laboratory, Pasadena, Calif. **77:** I.C.C. McGill University, Montreal, Quebec; H. J. Hoffmann, University of Montreal, Quebec. **79:** U.S. Geological Survey, Reston, Va. **80:** By kind permission of the President and Council of the Royal Society, London—the Natural History Museum, London. **81:** Case Western Reserve University Archives, Cleveland, Ohio. **83:** Roger-Viollet, Paris. **84:** Jean-Loup Charmet, Paris. **85:** Ferdinand Hamburger, Jr., Archives of the Johns Hopkins University, Baltimore, Md.—Jean-Loup Charmet, Paris. **87:** Smithsonian Institution OPPS#90-16680, Washington, D.C. **88:** Charles R. Knight, © 1942 National Geographic Society; Smithsonian Institution OPPS#84-16281, Washington, D.C. **89, 90:** The Natural History Museum, London. **91:** AP/Wide World Photos, New York—NASA/ESA. **92, 93:** Flip Schulke/Black Star, New York; Renée Comet. **94, 95:** Charles River Laboratories, Wilmington, Mass.—AP/Wide World Photos, New York—Unilever Research Port Sunlight Laboratory, Bebington, Wirral, England/Nature Volume 222, April 12, 1969. **96:** AP/Wide World Photos, New York. **97:** © Anglo-Australian Telescope Board, photograph by David Malin, 1987. **98:** Timothy A. Murphy. **100:** Renée Comet. **101:** Bildarchiv Preussischer Kulterbesitz, Berlin, background, M. Angelo/Westlight, Los Angeles. **102:** The Bettmann Archive, New York—Archivio Segreto, Città del Vaticano, Rome. **104:** Smithsonian Institution OPPS#76-15337 and OPPS#76-14440, Washington, D.C. **105:** Illustration from *Omphalos: An Attempt to Untie the Geological Knot,* by Philip H. Gosse, published by John Van Voorst, London, 1857—by courtesy of the National Portrait Gallery, London. **106:** From *Crania America: Or, a Comparative View of the Skulls of Various Aboriginal Nations,* by Samuel George Morton, M.D., J. Dobson, Philadelphia, 1839. **107:** Courtesy of the College of Physicians of Philadelphia, Philadelphia. **109:** Harvard University Archives, Cambridge, Mass. **110:** Reproduced from *Mongolism, Study Group No. 25,* published in 1967 by J. & A. Churchill, by permission of the Ciba Foundation, London; The Lancet Ltd., London. **111:** Courtesy of the Koreshan Unity Foundation, Estero, Fla. **112:** From *The Cellular Cosmogony,* by Cyrus Teed, The Guiding Light Publishing House, 1905, Estero, Fla.—The Koreshan Unity Foundation, Estero, Fla. **114:** Archives of the History of American Psychology, University of Akron, Akron, Ohio; from *The Kallikak Family,* by Henry Herbert Goddard, Ph.D., The Macmillan Company, 1912, New York. **115:** From *The Kallikak Family,* by Henry Herbert Goddard, Ph.D., The Macmillan Company, 1912, New York. **116:** NASA, Washington, D.C.—Ullstein Bilderdienst, Berlin. **117:** Ullstein Bilderdienst, Berlin. **119:** Courtesy of Time Inc. Picture Collection. **120:** Courtesy of the Simon Wiesenthal Center Archives, Los Angeles. **121:** Bildarchiv Preussischer Kulturbesitz, Berlin. **122:** Ullstein Bilderdienst, Berlin; Bildarchiv Preussischer Kulturbesitz, Berlin (2). **123:** AIP/Niels Bohr Library Photo Collection, New York; Ullstein Bilderdienst, Berlin. **125:** Mary Evans Picture Library, London—courtesy of the National Portrait Gallery, London—Stanford University Archives, Stanford, Calif., Department of Special Collections. **126, 127:** Sovfoto, New York. **130:** Gustav Dore—Fima Novek. **131:** Library of Congress LC 85176. **132, 133:** Bart Bartholomew/Black Star, New York; art by Time-Life Books, background, courtesy of Charles Johnson and Marjory Johnson of the Flat Earth Society, Lancaster, Calif.

BIBLIOGRAPHY

Books

Abbott, David (Ed.). *The Physicists.* New York: Peter Bedrick Books, 1984.

Adams, Frank Dawson. *The Birth and Development of the Geological Sciences.* New York: Dover, 1954.

Allaby, Michael, and James Lovelock. *The Great Extinction.* Garden City, N.Y.: Doubleday, 1983.

Anderson, Lorin. *Charles Bonnet and the Order of the Known.* Dordrecht, Holland: D. Reidel, 1982.

Audouze, Jean, and Guy Israël (Eds.). *The Cambridge Atlas of Astronomy.* Cambridge: Cambridge University Press, 1985.

Badash, Lawrence. "Commentary on the Paper of Erwin N. Hiebert." In *Perspectives in the History of Science and Technology,* edited by Duane H. D. Roller. Norman: University of Oklahoma Press, 1971.

Bailey, Edward. *Charles Lyell.* Garden City, N.Y.: Doubleday, 1963.

Barber, Theodore Xenophon. *Pitfalls in Human Research.* New York: Pergamon Press, 1976.

Bauer, Henry H. *Beyond Velikovsky.* Urbana: University of Illinois Press, 1984.

Beiser, Germaine. *The Story of Gravity.* New York: E. P. Dutton, 1968.

Bellamy, H. S. *Moons, Myths and Man: A Reinterpretation.* London: Faber & Faber, 1936.

Berggren, W. A., and John A. Van Couvering (Eds.). *Catastrophes and Earth History.* Princeton, N.J.: Princeton University Press, 1984.

Bevan, Edward. *The Honey Bee, Its Natural History, Physiology and Management.* London: Van Voorst, 1838.

Beyerchen, Alan D. *Scientists under Hitler: Politics and the Physics Community in the Third Reich.* New Haven: Yale University Press, 1977.

Binet, Alfred:

L'Année Psychologique. Paris: Schleicher Frères,
1900.

L'Année Psychologique. Paris: Masson et Cie,
1905.

L'Année Psychologique. Paris: Masson et Cie,
1908.

Biot, Jean-Baptiste. *Account of a Journey Made in the Orne Department, in Order to Verify the Reality of a Meteorite Seen at L'Aigle, 6th of the Month of Floreal in the year XI.* Paris: Baudouin, 1803.

Blum, Jeffrey M. *Pseudoscience and Mental Ability.* New York: Monthly Review Press, 1978.

Bonar, James. *Malthus and His Work.* New York: Macmillan, 1924.

Bowlby, John. *Charles Darwin: A New Life.* New York: W. W. Norton, 1991.

Bramwell, J. Milne. *Hypnotism.* New York: Institute for Research in Hypnosis, Julian Press, 1956.

Broad, William, and Nicholas Wade. *Betrayers of the Truth.* New York: Simon & Schuster, 1982.

Burchfield, Joe D. *Lord Kelvin and the Age of the Earth.* New York: Science History, 1975.

Burke, John G. *Cosmic Debris.* Berkeley: University of California Press, 1986.

Burkhardt, Richard W., Jr. *The Spirit of System.* Cambridge: Harvard University Press, 1977.

Burnet, Thomas. *The Sacred Theory of the Earth.* Carbondale: Southern Illinois University Press, 1965.

Butler, Charles. *The Feminine Monarchie.* Oxford: Joseph Barnes, 1609.

Cajori, Florian. *A History of Physics.* New York: Dover, 1962.

Cantor, G. N., and M. J. S. Hodge (Eds.). *Conceptions of Ether.* Cambridge: Cambridge University Press, 1981.

Clarke, Edward H. *Sex in Education: Or, a Fair Chance for the Girls.* New York: Arno Press & The New York Times Press, 1972 (reprint of 1873 edition).

Cline, Barbara Lovett. *The Questioners.* New York: Thomas Y. Crowell, 1965.

Cloyd, E. L. *James Burnett: Lord Monboddo.* Oxford: Clarendon Press, 1972.

Colbert, Edwin H. *Men and Dinosaurs.* New York: E. P. Dutton, 1968.

Collier's Encyclopedia (Vol. 14). New York: Macmillan, 1982.

Corliss, William R. *Mysterious Universe: A Handbook of Astronomical Anomalies.* Glen Arm, Md.: Sourcebook Project, 1979.

Corsi, Pietro. *The Age of Lamarck* (rev. ed.). Translated by Jonathan Mandelbaum. Berkeley: University of California Press, 1988.

Cox, Catharine Morris, et al. *The Early Mental Traits of Three Hundred Geniuses* (Vol. 2 of *Genetic Studies of Genius,* edited by Lewis Terman). Stanford, Calif.: Stanford University Press, 1926.

Crick, Francis. *Life Itself.* New York: Simon & Schuster, 1981.

Crookshank, F. G. *The Mongol in Our Midst.* New York: E. P. Dutton, 1924.

Crowe, Michael J. *The Extraterrestrial Life Debate, 1750-1900.* Cambridge: Cambridge University Press, 1986.

Cuvier, G. *Recherches sur les Ossemens Fossiles.* Paris: G. Dufour et E. D'Ogagne, 1825.

Daniel, Glyn. *The Idea of Prehistory.* Baltimore: Penguin Books, 1962.

Darwin, George Howard. *Scientific Papers* (Vol. 5). Edited by F. J. M. Stratton and J. Jackson. Cambridge: Cambridge University Press, 1916.

Davies, P. C. W. *The Search for Gravity Waves.* Cambridge: Cambridge University Press, 1980.

Degler, Carl N. *In Search of Human Nature.* New York: Oxford University Press, 1991.

Desmond, Adrian:

Archetypes and Ancestors. Chicago: University of

Chicago Press, 1982.

The Hot-Blooded Dinosaurs. New York: Dial Press/James Wade, 1976.

The Hot-Blooded Dinosaurs. New York: Warner Books, 1977.

Deuel, Wallace R. *People under Hitler.* New York: Harcourt, Brace, 1942.

Dingwall, Eric J. (Ed.). *Abnormal Hypnotic Phenomena* (Vol. 4). New York: Barnes & Noble, 1968.

Down, J. Langdon H. "Observations on an Ethnic Classification of Idiots." In *Clinical Lectures and Reports, by the Medical and Surgical Staff of the London Hospital* (Vol. 3). London: John Churchill & Sons, 1866.

Draper, Jo (Ed.). *Dorset Natural History and Archaeological Society Proceedings* (Vol. 110 for 1988). Dorset: Dorset Natural History & Archaeological Society, 1989.

Eiseley, Loren. *The Immense Journey.* New York: Vintage Books, 1957.

Eloy, Nicolas. *Dictionnaire Historique de la Médécine.* Liège and Francfurt: J. F. Bassompierre, 1755.

Enciclopedia Universal Ilustrada. Madrid: Espasa-Calpe, 1968.

Encyclopedia Americana (Vol. 9). Danbury, Conn.: Grolier, 1986.

Epstein, Fritz T. "War-Time Activities of the SS-Ahnenerbe." In *On the Track of Tyranny,* edited by Max Beloff. Freeport, N.Y.: Books for Libraries Press, 1971 (reprint of 1960 edition).

Evans, Bergen. *The Natural History of Nonsense.* New York: Alfred A. Knopf, 1947.

Fauth, Philip. *The Moon in Modern Astronomy.* Translated by Joseph McCabe. London: A. Owen, 1908.

Fellows, Otis E., and Stephen F. Milliken. *Buffon.* New York: Twayne Publishers, 1972.

Field, James Alfred. *Essays on Population.* Port Washington, N.Y.: Kennikat Press, 1967 (reprint of 1931 edition).

Fisher, Clyde. *The Story of the Moon.* Garden City, N.Y.: Doubleday, Doran, 1943.

The Fishes (Life Nature Library series). Alexandria, Va.: Time-Life Books, 1980.

Fishes of Lakes, Rivers & Oceans (Wild, Wild World of Animals series). New York: Time-Life Films, 1978.

Franks, Felix. *Polywater.* Cambridge, Mass.: MIT Press, 1981.

The Galileo Affair: A Documentary History. Edited and translated by Maurice A. Finocchiaro. Berkeley: University of California Press, 1989.

Gardner, Martin:
Fads and Fallacies: In the Name of Science. New York: Dover, 1957.
The New Age. Buffalo, N.Y.: Prometheus Books, 1988.
Science: Good, Bad and Bogus. Buffalo, N.Y.: Prometheus Books, 1981.

Gillispie, Charles Coulston:
Dictionary of Scientific Biography (Vols. 1, 5, & 7). New York: Charles Scribner's Sons, 1980.
Dictionary of Scientific Biography (Vols. 11 & 13). New York: Charles Scribner's Sons, 1981.

Glass, D. V. *Introduction to Malthus.* New York: John Wiley & Sons, 1953.

Goddard, Henry Herbert. *The Kallikak Family: A Study in the Heredity of Feeble-Mindedness.* New York: Macmillan, 1912.

Godwin, Joscelyn. *Athanasius Kircher.* London: Thames & Hudson, 1979.

Gold, T.:
"Moon: The Debate about the Nature of the Moon's Surface." In *Highlights in Science,* edited by H. Messel. Sydney: Pergamon, 1987.
"Origin and Evolution of the Lunar Surface: The Major Questions Remaining." In *The Moon—A New Appraisal from Space Missions and Laboratory Analysis.* London: Royal Society, 1977.

Goldberg, Stanley. *Understanding Relativity.* Boston: Birkhäuser, 1984.

Gosse, Edmund. *The Life of Philip Henry Gosse.* London: Kegan Paul, Trench, Trubner, 1890.

Gosse, Edmund William. *Father and Son: Biographical Recollections.* New York: Charles Scribner's Sons, 1907.

Gosse, Philip Henry. *Omphalos: An Attempt to Untie the Geological Knot.* London: John Van Voorst, 1857.

Gossett, Thomas F. *Race: The History of an Idea in America.* New York: Schocken Books, 1965.

Goudsmit, Samuel A. *Alsos.* New York: Henry Schuman, 1947.

Gould, James L., and Carol Grant Gould. *The Honey Bee.* New York: Scientific American Library, 1988.

Gould, Stephen Jay:
The Flamingo's Smile. New York: W. W. Norton, 1985.
The Mismeasure of Man. New York: W. W. Norton, 1981.
Ontogeny and Phylogeny. Cambridge, Mass.: Harvard University Press, Belknap Press, 1977.
The Panda's Thumb. New York: W. W. Norton, 1980.
Time's Arrow, Time's Cycle. Cambridge, Mass.: Harvard University Press, 1987.
Wonderful Life. New York: W. W. Norton, 1989.

Graham, Loren R. *Science, Philosophy, and Human Behavior in the Soviet Union.* New York: Columbia University Press, 1987.

Grant, Edward (Ed.). *A Sourcebook in Medieval Science.* Cambridge, Mass.: Harvard University Press, 1974.

Grant, John. *A Directory of Discarded Ideas.* Sevenoaks, Kent: Ashgrove Press, 1981.

Greene, John C. *The Death of Adam.* New York: Mentor Books, 1961.

Gregg, Pauline. *A Social and Economic History of Britain, 1760-1965* (5th ed., rev. ed.). London: George G. Harrap, 1965.

Gutman, Israel (Ed.). *Encyclopedia of the Holocaust* (Vol. 4). New York: Macmillan, 1990.

Hales, William. *A New Analysis of Chronology and Geography, History and Prophecy* (Vol. 1). London: C. J. G. & F. Rivington, 1830.

Haller, John S., Jr. *Outcasts from Evolution: Scientif-*

ic Attitudes of Racial Inferiority, 1859-1900. Urbana: University of Illinois Press, 1971.

Halton, Cheryl M. *Those Amazing Eels.* Minneapolis, Minn.: Dillon Press, 1990.

Harrington, John W. *Dance of the Continents.* Los Angeles: J. P. Tarcher, 1983.

Hartmann, W. K., R. J. Phillips, and G. J. Taylor (Eds.). *Origin of the Moon.* Houston: Lunar & Planetary Institute, 1986.

Heide, Fritz. *Meteorites.* Chicago: University of Chicago Press, 1964.

Heilbroner, Robert L.:
The Worldly Philosophers. New York: Time, 1962.
The Worldly Philosophers (4th ed., rev. ed.). New York: Simon & Schuster, 1972.

Herbert, Glendon M., and I. S. K. Reeves. *Koreshan Unity Settlement, 1894-1977.* Restoration Study for Department of Natural Resources, Division of Recreation and Parks, State of Florida, 1977.

Hetherington, Norriss S. *Science and Objectivity.* Ames: Iowa State University Press, 1988.

Hiebert, Erwin N. "The Energetics Controversy and the New Thermodynamics." In *Perspectives in the History of Science and Technology.* Norman: University of Oklahoma Press, 1971.

Holmes, Frederic L. (Ed.). *Dictionary of Scientific Biography* (Vol. 18, supplement II). New York: Charles Scribner's Sons, 1990.

Hooke, Robert. *An Attempt to Prove the Motion of the Earth from Observations.* London: Royal Society, 1674.

Hoyle, Fred, and Chanrda Wickramasinghe. *Diseases from Space.* London: J. M. Dent & Sons, 1979.

Hoyt, Murray. *The World of Bees.* New York: Coward McCann, 1965.

Hoyt, William Graves:
Coon Mountain Controversies. Tucson: University of Arizona Press, 1987.
Lowell and Mars. Tucson: University of Arizona Press, 1976.

Hsü, Kenneth J. *The Great Dying.* San Diego: Harcourt Brace Jovanovich, 1986.

Huggett, Richard. *Catastrophism: Systems of Earth History.* London: Hodder & Stoughton, Edward Arnold, 1990.

Irvine, William. *Apes, Angels and Victorians.* New York: Time, 1963.

James, Patricia (Ed.). *The Travel Diaries of Thomas Robert Malthus.* Cambridge: Cambridge University Press, 1966.

Jastrow, Joseph (Ed.). *The Story of Human Error* (Essay Index Reprint series). Freeport, N.Y.: Books for Libraries, 1967.

Jeffrey, Francis, and John C. Lilly. *John Lilly, So Far.* Los Angeles: Jeremy P. Tarcher, 1990.

Joravsky, David. *Soviet Marxism and Natural Science, 1917-1932.* New York: Columbia University Press, 1961.

Kaplan, Fred. *Dickens and Mesmerism.* Princeton, N.J.: Princeton University Press, 1975.

Kaplan, Fred (Ed.). *John Elliotson on Mesmerism.* New York: Da Capo Press, 1982.

Kevlas, Daniel J.:

In the Name of Eugenics: Genetics and the Uses of Human Heredity. New York: Alfred A. Knopf, 1985.

The Physicists. New York: Alfred A. Knopf, 1978.

Keynes, John Maynard. *Essays in Biography.* Edited by Geoffrey Keynes. London: Rupert Hart-Davis, 1951.

King, W., and T. H. Rowney. *An Old Chapter of the Geological Record.* London: John Van Voorst, 1881.

Kircherus, Athanasius. *D'Onder-Aardse Weereld.* Amsterdam: Athanasius Kircherus, 1982.

Kirk, G. S., J. E. Raven, and M. Schofield. *The Presocratic Philosophers* (2nd ed.). Cambridge: Cambridge University Press, 1983.

Kirkpatrick, Randolph. *The Ocean Floor or Benthoplankton.* Part III of *The Nummulosphere.* London: Lamley, 1917.

Klotz, Irving M. *Diamond Dealers and Feather Merchants.* Boston: Birkhäuser, 1986.

Knight, David. *Ordering the World.* London: Burnett Books, 1981.

Knox, R. Buick. *James Ussher: Archbishop of Armagh.* Cardiff: University of Wales Press, 1967.

Koestler, Arthur. *The Sleepwalkers.* New York: Macmillan, 1959.

Kohn, Alexander. *False Prophets.* New York: Basil Blackwell, 1986.

Lagnado, Lucette Matalon, and Sheila Cohn Dekel. *Children of the Flames: Dr. Josef Mengele and the Untold Story of the Twins of Auschwitz.* New York: William Morrow, 1991.

Lambridis, Helle. *Empedocles.* University: University of Alabama Press, 1976.

Ley, Willy:

Dragons in Amber. New York: Viking Press, 1951.

Watchers of the Skies: An Informal History of Astronomy from Babylon to the Space Age. New York: Viking Press, 1963.

Lilly, John Cunningham:

Communication between Man and Dolphin. New York: Crown, 1978.

Lilly on Dolphins. Garden City, N.Y.: Anchor Press, Doubleday, 1975.

Man and Dolphin. Garden City, N.Y.: Doubleday, 1961.

The Mind of the Dolphin. Garden City, N.Y.: Doubleday, 1967.

Littmann, Mark. *Planets Beyond.* New York: John Wiley & Sons, 1990.

Lovell, John H. *Honey Plants of North America.* Medina, Ohio: A. I. Root, 1926.

Lowell, Percival. *Mars: As the Abode of Life.* New York: Macmillan, 1908.

McCall, G. J. H. *Meteorites and Their Origins.* New York: John Wiley & Sons, 1973.

Magill, Frank N. (Ed.). *The Great Scientists* (Vol. 9). Danbury, Conn.: Grolier Educational, 1989.

Malthus, T. R. *Principles of Political Economy.* London: William Pickering, 1836.

Malthus, Thomas R. *An Essay on the Principle of Population.* Homewood, Ill.: Richard D. Irwin, 1963.

Massey, Harrie. *The New Age in Physics.* New York: Basic Books, 1966.

Mazzolini, Renato G., and Shirley A. Roe. *Science against the Unbelievers: The Correspondence of Bonnet and Needham, 1760-1780.* Oxford: Voltaire Foundation at the Taylor Institution, 1986.

Medvedev, Zhores A. *The Rise and Fall of T. D. Lysenko.* Translated by I. Michael Lerner. New York: Columbia University Press, 1969.

Meigs, J. Aitken. *Catalogue of Human Crania.* Philadelphia: J. B. Lippincott, 1857.

Merrill, George P. *The First One Hundred Years of American Geology.* New York: Hafner Publishing, 1964.

Michell, John:

Eccentric Lives and Peculiar Notions. London: Thames & Hudson, 1984.

Eccentric Lives and Peculiar Notions. San Diego: Harcourt Brace Jovanovich, 1984.

Miller, Russ, and the Editors of Time-Life Books. *Continents in Collision* (Planet Earth series). Alexandria, Va.: Time-Life Books, 1983.

Minton, Henry L. *Lewis M. Terman: Pioneer in Psychological Testing.* New York: New York University Press, 1988.

Mintz, Leigh W. *Historical Geology* (2nd ed.). Columbus, Ohio: Charles E. Merrill, 1977.

Moore, Patrick. *Patrick Moore's Armchair Astronomy.* Wellingborough: Patrick Stephens, 1984.

Moore, Patrick, and Peter J. Cattermole. *The Craters of the Moon.* London: Lutterworth Press, 1967.

Moriarty, Christopher. *Eels: A Natural and Unnatural History.* New York: Universe Books, 1978.

Morley, Margaret Warner. *The Honey-Makers.* Chicago: A. C. McClurg, 1899.

Morton, Samuel George. *Crania Americana: Or, a Comparative View of the Skulls of Various Aboriginal Nations, North and South America.* Philadelphia: J. Dobson, London: Simpkin, Marshall, 1839.

Mosse, George L. *Nazi Culture: Intellectual, Cultural and Social Life in the Third Reich.* Translated by Salvator Attanasio, et al. New York: Grosset & Dunlap, 1966.

Nardo, Don. *Gravity: The Universal Force.* San Diego, Calif.: Lucent Books, 1990.

Narlikar, Jayant V. *The Lighter Side of Gravity.* San Francisco: W. H. Freeman, 1982.

The Near Planets (Voyage Through the Universe series). Alexandria, Va.: Time-Life Books, 1989.

Needham, Joseph. *A History of Embryology* (2nd ed.). Revised with the assistance of Arthur Hughes. Cambridge: Cambridge University Press, 1959.

New Encyclopædia Britannica (Vol. 1). Chicago: Encyclopædia Britannica, 1984.

Nicolson, Iain. *Gravity, Black Holes and the Universe.* Newton Abbot, Devon: David & Charles, 1981.

Nordenskiöld, Erik. *The History of Biology.* Translated by Leonard Bucknall Eyre. New York: Alfred A. Knopf, 1928.

Norvill, Roy. *Giants: The Vanished Race of Mighty Men.* Wellingborough, Northamptonshire: Aquarian Press, 1979.

Pauwels, Louis, and Jacques Bergier. *The Morning of the Magicians.* Translated by Rollo Myers. New York: Stein & Day, 1964.

Peacock, Alan T. "Malthus in the Twentieth Century." In *Introduction to Malthus,* edited by David Glass. New York: John Wiley & Sons, 1953.

Peat, F. David. *Cold Fusion.* Chicago: Contemporary Books, 1989.

Petersen, William. *Malthus.* Cambridge, Mass.: Harvard University Press, 1979.

Pitman, John Rogers (Ed.). *The Whole Works of the Rev. John Lightfoot, D.D.* (Vol. 2). London: J. F. Dove, 1822.

Porter, Roy:

The Making of Geology. Cambridge: Cambridge University Press, 1977.

A Social History of Madness. New York: Weidenfeld & Nicolson, 1987.

Porter, Roy (Ed.). *Man Masters Nature.* New York: George Braziller, 1988.

Posner, Gerald L., and John Ware. *Mengele: The Complete Story.* New York: McGraw-Hill, 1986.

Prescott, John H. "Clever Hans: Training the Trainers, or the Potential for Misinterpreting the Results of Dolphin Research." In *The Clever Hans Phenomenon,* edited by Thomas A. Sebeok and Robert Rosenthal. New York: New York Academy of Sciences, 1981.

Proctor, Robert. "From Anthropologie to Rassenkunde in the German Anthropological Tradition." In *Bones, Bodies, Behavior: Essays on Biological Anthropology* (Vol. 5 of *History of Anthropology,* edited by George W. Stocking, Jr.). Madison: University of Wisconsin Press, 1988.

Quest for the Past. Pleasantville, N.Y.: Reader's Digest, 1984.

Rádl, Emanuel. *The History of Biological Theories.* Translated by E. J. Hatfield. London: Oxford University Press, 1930.

Radner, Daisie, and Michael Radner. *Science and Unreason.* Belmont, Calif.: Wadsworth, 1982.

Redondi, Pietro. *Galileo Heretic.* Translated by Raymond Rosenthal. Princeton, N.J.: Princeton University Press, 1987.

Reymond, Arnold. *History of the Sciences in Greco-Roman Antiquity.* Translated by Ruth Gheury De Bray. New York: Biblo & Tannen, 1963.

Rhodes, Richard. *The Making of the Atomic Bomb.* New York: Simon & Schuster, 1986.

Roberts, Anthony. *Sowers of Thunder: Giants in Myth and History.* London: Rider, 1978.

Roe, Shirley A. *Matter, Life, and Generation.* Cambridge: Cambridge University Press, 1981.

Rosenthal, Robert. *Experimenter Effects in Behavioral Research.* New York: Irvington, 1976.

Rostand, Jean. *Error and Deception in Science.* New York: Basic Books, 1960.

Sagan, Carl. *Broca's Brain: Reflections on the Romance of Science.* New York: Ballantine Books,

1979.

Sambursky, S. *The Physical World of the Greeks.* Translated by Merton Dagut. London: Routledge & Kegan Paul, 1956.

Santillana, Giorgio De. *The Crime of Galileo.* Chicago: University of Chicago Press, 1955.

Sayers, Janet. *Biological Politics: Feminist and Anti-Feminist Perspectives.* London: Tavistock, 1982.

Schadewald, Robert. "Some Like It Flat: A Brief History of the Flat Earth Movement." In *The Fringes of Reason: A Whole Earth Catalog,* edited by Ted Schultz. New York: Harmony Books, 1989.

Schwarzbach, Martin. *Alfred Wegener: The Father of Continental Drift.* Madison, Wisc.: Science Tech, 1986.

The Scientific Papers of Sir William Herschel (Vol. 1). London: Royal Society and the Royal Astronomical Society, 1912.

Seabrook, William. *Doctor Wood.* New York: Harcourt, Brace, 1941.

Shklovskii, I. S., and Carl Sagan. *Intelligent Life in the Universe.* San Francisco: Holden-Day, 1966.

Shutts, David. *Lobotomy: Resort to the Knife.* New York: Van Nostrand Reinhold, 1982.

Sidgwick, J. B. *William Herschel: Explorer of the Heavens.* London: Faber & Faber, 1953.

Sinclair, M. "The Strange Case of Polywater." In *Ahead of Time,* edited by Harry Harrison and Theodore J. Gordon. Garden City, N.Y.: Doubleday, 1972.

Smith, Earl L. *Yankee Genius.* New York: Harper & Brothers, 1954.

Smith, J. David. *Minds Made Feeble: The Myth and Legacy of the Kallikaks.* Rockville, Md.: Aspen Systems, 1985.

Smith, Robert W., and Richard Baum. "William Lassell and the Ring of Neptune: A Case Study in Instrumental Failure." In *Journal for the History of Astronomy* (Vol. 15), edited by M. A. Hoskin. London: Science History, 1984.

Snyder, Louis L. *Encyclopedia of the Third Reich.* New York: Paragon House, 1989.

Stanton, William. *The Leopard's Spots: Scientific Attitudes toward Race in America, 1815-1859.* Chicago: University of Chicago Press, 1960.

Stephen, Leslie, and Sidney Lee (Eds.). *The Dictionary of National Biography* (Vol. 20). London: Oxford University Press, 1937-1938.

Stetson, Harlan True. *Man and the Stars.* New York: Whittlesey House, 1930.

Sullivan, Walter. *Continents in Motion.* New York: McGraw-Hill, 1974.

Swenson, Lloyd S., Jr. *The Ethereal Aether.* Austin: University of Texas Press, 1972.

Tarling, Don, and Maureen Tarling. *Continental Drift.* Garden City, N.Y.: Doubleday, 1971.

Teale, Edwin Way. *The Strange Lives of Familiar Insects.* New York: Dodd, Mead, 1964.

Teed, Cyrus R. *The Cellular Cosmogony: Or the Earth a Concave Sphere.* Philadelphia: Porcupine Press, 1975 (reprint of 1905 edition).

The Third Planet (Voyage Through the Universe series). Alexandria, Va.: Time-Life Books, 1989.

Thomson, Wyville, et al. *The Challenger Expedition.* London: Taylor & Francis, 1876.

Timbs, John. *Popular Errors.* London: Crosby Lockwood, 1880.

Van Helden, Albert. *Measuring the Universe.* Chicago: University of Chicago Press, 1985.

Velikovsky, Immanuel. *Worlds in Collision.* New York: Macmillan, 1950.

Velikovsky Reconsidered. New York: Doubleday, 1976.

Wallace, Alfred Russel:

Contributions to the Theory of Natural Selection. London: Macmillan, 1870.

My Life: A Record of Events and Opinions (Vol. 2). New York: AMS Press, 1974 (reprint of 1905 edition).

Walsh, Mary Roth. "The Quirls of a Woman's Brain." In *Women Look at Biology Looking at Women,* edited by Ruth Hubbard, Mary Sue Henifin, and Barbara Fried. Boston: G. K. Hall, 1979.

Weart, Spencer R., and Gertrud Weiss Szilard (Eds.). *Leo Szilard: His Version of the Facts* (Vol. II). Cambridge, Mass.: MIT Press, 1978.

Wegener, Alfred. *The Origin of Continents and Oceans.* New York: Dover, 1966.

West, Luther S. *The Housefly.* Ithaca, N.Y.: Comstock, 1951.

Whitcomb, John C., Jr., and Henry M. Morris. *The Genesis Flood.* Philadelphia: Presbyterian & Reformed, 1970.

White, Norval. *The Guide to the Architecture of Paris.* New York: Charles Scribner's Sons, 1991.

Whittington, Harry B. *The Burgess Shale.* New Haven: Yale University Press, 1985.

Wigglesworth, V. B. *The Principles of Insect Physiology.* London: Methuen, 1943.

Wilford, John Noble. *Mars Beckens.* New York: Alfred A. Knopf, 1990.

Will, Clifford M. *Was Einstein Right?* New York: Basic Books, 1986.

Williams, Harley. *Doctors Differ.* London: Jonathan Cape, 1946.

Williams, M. E. W. "Flamsteed's Alleged Measurement of Annual Parallax for the Pole Star." In *Journal for the History of Astronomy* (Vol. 10), edited by M. A. Hoskin. London: Science History, 1979.

Winch, Donald. *Malthus.* Oxford: Oxford University Press, 1987.

The Works of Aristotle (Vol. 2, 2nd ed.). Chicago: Encyclopædia Britannica, 1990.

Periodicals

Allen, Leland. "The Rise and Fall of Polywater." *New Scientist,* August 16, 1973.

Allen, Leland C., and Peter A. Kollman. "Theoretical Evidence against the Existence of Polywater." *Nature,* October 22, 1971.

Asimov, Isaac. "The Radiation That Wasn't." *Fantasy & Science Fiction,* March 1988.

"Aviation Declared a Failure." *Literary Digest,* October 17, 1908.

Badash, Lawrence. "How the 'Newer Alchemy' Was Received." *Scientific American,* August 2, 1966.

Ball, Robert S. "A Glimpse through the Corridors of Time." *Nature,* November 24, 1881.

Bartusiak, Marcia. "Einstein's Unfinished Symphony." *Discover,* August 1989.

Bascom, Willard D., Edward J. Brooks, and Bradford N. Worthington III. "Evidence that Polywater is a Colloidal Silicate Sol." *Nature,* December 26, 1970.

Baum, Richard, and Robert W. Smith. "Neptune's Forgotten Ring." *Sky & Telescope,* June 1989.

Bazell, Robert. "A Little Shaky." *New Republic,* December 10, 1990.

Begley, Sharon, Harry Hurt III, and Andrew Murr. "The Race for Fusion." *Newsweek,* May 8, 1989.

Bibber, William R. "New Boston, N.H., Museum Rounds Up the Weighty Facts." *Boston Herald,* September 8, 1963.

Blakeslee, Sandra. "Scientist Says Mystery of Polywater Has Been Solved: Russian's Test Samples Contained Sweat." *New York Times,* September 27, 1970.

Blount, Lady E. A. M. "The Flat Earth: Another Bedford Canal Experiment" (letter to the editor). *English Mechanic and World of Science,* September 16, 1904.

Booth, William:

"Riding Out an Earthquake Prediction." *Washington Post,* December 2, 1990.

"Scientist's Quake Prediction Prowess Appears Shaky to Experts." *Washington Post,* October 19, 1990.

Brady, Mildred Edie. "The Strange Case of Wilhelm Reich." *New Republic,* May 26, 1947.

Broad, William J.:

"Cold-Fusion Claim Is Faulted on Ethics as Well as Science." *New York Times,* March 17, 1991.

"Despite Scorn, Team in Utah Still Seeks Cold-Fusion Clues." *New York Times,* October 31, 1989.

"Fusion in a Jar: Recklessness and Brilliance." *New York Times,* May 9, 1989.

"Fusion Researchers Seek $25 Million from U.S." *New York Times,* April 26, 1989.

"Panel Rejects Fusion Claim, Urging No Federal Spending." *New York Times,* July 13, 1989.

Browne, Malcolm W. "7,000 Scientists Cheer Fusion-in-Jar Experimenter." *New York Times,* April 13, 1989.

Burton, M. "Mr. R. Kirkpatrick." *Nature,* April 29, 1950.

"By the Sweat of Their Brow." *Science News,* January 23, 1971.

Campbell, Leon. "William Henry Pickering, 1858-1938." *Publications of the Astronomical Society of the Pacific,* April 1938.

Cannon, Annie J. "Obituary of William Henry Pickering, 1858-1938." *Science,* February 25, 1938.

"Chilling Out." *Scientific American,* September 1989.

Chrepta, Jay. "Whatever Happened to Antigravity?" *Tufts Criterion,* Winter 1991.

Christian, P. A., and L. H. Berka. "Preparing Polywater and Other Anomalous Liquids." *Chemistry,* January 1971.

Cordaro, Lucian, and James R. Ison. "Psychology of the Scientist: X. Observer Bias in Classical Conditioning of the Planarian." *Psychological Reports,* December 1963.

Cramer, John G. "Cold Fusion, Pro-Fusion, and Con-Fusion." *Analog Science Fiction/Science Fact,* December 1989.

Dagani, Ron. "Fusion Donnybrook: Physicists Assail Utah Claims." *Chemical & Engineering News,* May 8, 1989.

Dickson, David. "Was Galileo Saved by Plea Bargain?" *Science,* August 8, 1986.

"Doubters and Deryagin." *Science News,* July 4, 1970.

"Doubts about Polywater." *Time,* October 19, 1970.

"Earthquake Forecaster Won't Discuss Failure." *Atlanta Journal & Constitution,* December 14, 1990.

"Eastward the Tots and Sots." *Time,* July 10, 1944.

Engel, Kenneth S. R. "Do Gravity Waves Exist?" *Science Digest,* February 1982.

Fauth, Hermann. "Philipp Fauth and the Moon." *Sky & Telescope,* November 1959.

Fee, Elizabeth. "Nineteenth-Century Craniology: The Study of the Female Skull." *Bulletin of the History of Medicine,* Fall 1979.

Fine, Howard D. "The Koreshan Unity: The Chicago Years of a Utopian Community." *Journal of the Illinois State Historical Society,* June 1975.

Fisher, Arthur. "The Tantalizing Quest for Gravity Waves." *Popular Science,* April 1981.

Fisher, Osmond. "On the Physical Cause of the Ocean Basins." *Nature,* January 1982.

Fowler, Glenn. "Iben Browning, 73; Researcher Studied Climate and Quakes." *New York Times,* July 20, 1991.

Gardner, Martin:
   "Bottled Mischief." *Science Digest,* September 1981.
   "Mathematical Games." *Scientific American,* July 1966.

Gates, David, and Jennifer Smith. "Keeping the Flat-Earth Faith." *Newsweek,* July 2, 1984.

Gillette, Robert. "Velikovsky: AAAS Forum for a Mild Collision." *Science,* March 15, 1974.

Glastris, Paul. "Quake Report." *U.S. News & World Report,* December 10, 1990.

Gliatto, Tom, and Ron Ridenhour. "New Madrid, Mo., Prays that a Dire Prediction Proves to be Faulty." *People,* December 3, 1990.

"Goodnight Moon." *People,* June 24, 1991.

Gould, Stephen Jay:
   "The Birth of the Two-Sex World." *New York Review of Books,* June 13, 1991.
   "Morton's Ranking of Races by Cranial Capacity." *Science,* May 5, 1978.
   "A Web of Tales." *Natural History,* October 1988.

"Gravitating toward Einstein." *Time,* June 20, 1969.

"Gravitational Waves Detected." *Science News,* June 21, 1969.

"Gravity Waves Found: Einstein Was Right."

Newsweek, October 24, 1983.

Hetherington, Norriss S. "Neptune's Supposed Ring." *Journal of the British Astronomical Association,* December 1979.

Heylin, Michael. "Sociology of Cold Fusion Examined." *Science News,* June 2, 1990.

"How Far to the Stars?" *Science Digest,* August 1982.

"How Flies Climb." *Popular Science Monthly,* September 1882.

Hoyt, William G. "Reflections concerning Neptune's 'Ring.' " *Sky & Telescope,* April 1978.

Hoyt, William Graves, "W. H. Pickering's Planetary Predictions and the Discovery of Pluto." *Isis,* December 1976.

Kauffman, William J., III. "Listening for the Whisper of Gravity Waves." *Science 80,* May-June 1980.

Kerr, Richard A.:
   "Earthquake—or Earthquack?" *Science,* October 26, 1990.
   "The Lessons of Dr. Browning." *Science,* August 9, 1991.

Klotz, Irving M. "The N-Ray Affair." *Scientific American,* May 1980.

Kohn, Alexander. "Errors, Fallacies, or Deception?" *Perspectives in Biology & Medicine,* Spring 1978.

Kohn, Moritz. "Karl Freiherr von Reichenbach (1788-1869)." *Chemical Education,* April 1955.

Landing, James E. "Cyrus R. Teed, Koreshanity, and Cellular Cosmogony." *Communal Societies,* Autumn 1981.

Langmuir, Irving. "Pathological Science," edited by Robert N. Hall. *Physics Today,* October 1989.

"La Solution du Probleme de l'Existence des Rayons N." *Revue Scientifique,* December 3, 1904.

Lemonick, Michael D.:
   "Fusion Fever Is on the Rise." *Time,* April 24, 1989.
   "Fusion Illusion?" *Time,* May 8, 1989.
   "Signals from Distant Disasters." *Time,* May 28, 1990.

"Les Rayons N Existent-Ils?" *Revue Scientifique,* October 29, 1904.

Le Verrier, Urbain Jean Joseph. "The Discovery of Vulcan, an Imaginary Planet Near Mercury." *Cosmos,* 1859.

Lifton, Robert Jay. "Mengele: What Made This Man?" *New York Times Magazine,* July 21, 1985.

Lilly, John C.:
   "Importance of Being in Earnest about Dialogues of Dolphins." *Life,* July 28, 1961.
   "Where is Science Taking Us?" *Saturday Review,* October 7, 1961.

Lippincott, Ellis R., et al. "Polywater." *Science,* June 27, 1969.

Lovi, George. "Rambling through January Skies." *Sky & Telescope,* January 1985.

Magyar, George. " 'Pseudo-Effects' in Experimental Physics: Some Notes for Case-Studies." *Social Studies of Science,* May 1977.

Martz, E. P., Jr. "Professor William Henry Pickering, 1858-1938: An Appreciation." *Popular Astronomy,* June-July 1938.

Michelson, Peter F., John C. Price, and Robert C. Taber. "Resonant-Mass Detectors of Gravitational Radiation." *Science,* July 10, 1987.

Miller, Dayton C. "The Ether-Drift Experiment and the Determination of the Absolute Motion of the Earth." *Reviews of Modern Physics,* July 1933.

Mitchell, M. E. "On Eozoön Canadense." *Isis,* September 1971.

Monagan, David. "Rising above It All." *Boston Globe,* September 19, 1982.

Nash, J. Madeleine. "Wake Up, East and Midwest." *Time,* October 8, 1990.

Newcomb, Simon:
   "Is the Airship Coming?" *McClure's,* September 1901.
   "The Problem of Aerial Navigation." *Nineteenth Century and After,* September 1908.

Nininger, H. H. "Do We See a Lunar Tunnel?" *Sky & Telescope,* June 1952.

Nye, Mary Jo. "N-Rays: An Episode in the History and Psychology of Science." *Historical Studies in the Physical Sciences,* 1980, Vol. 11, part 1.

Oberg, James. "Ideas in Collision." Part 1 of "The Velikovsky Affair." *Skeptical Inquirer,* Fall 1980.

O'Brien, Charles F. "Eozoön Canadense: 'The Dawn Animal of Canada.' " *Isis,* Summer 1970.

"Papal Plea Bargain, or Was Galileo Let Off Easy?" *Discover,* December 1986.

Parfit, Michael. "Are Dolphins Trying to Say Something, Or Is It all Much Ado about Nothing?" *Smithsonian,* October 1980.

Pickering, William H.:
   "Eratosthenes, No. 6." *Popular Astronomy,* August-September 1924.
   "Is the Moon a Dead Planet?" *Century Illustrated Monthly Magazine,* May 1902.
   "The Place of Origin of the Moon—the Volcanic Problem." *Journal of Geology,* January-February 1907.

Pool, Robert. "Cold Fusion: Smoke, Little Light." *Science,* November 17, 1989.

"Post of Scientist in Fusion Dispute is Uncertain." *New York Times,* March 24, 1991.

Pycior, Helena M. "George Peacock and the British Origins of Symbolical Algebra." *Historia Mathematica,* February 1981.

"The Quest for Gravity Waves." *Astronomy,* October 1987.

Raymo, Chet. "Big Quake Prediction Wasn't Completely Silly, but Don't Hold Your Breath." *Boston Globe,* December 3, 1990.

Regis, Edward, Jr. "Down with Gravity." *Omni,* March 1985.

Rehbock, Philip F. "Huxley, Haeckel, and the Oceanographers: The Case of *Bathybius Haeckelii.*" *Isis,* December 1975.

Rensberger, Boyce. "Science and Sensitivity." *Washington Post,* March 1, 1992.

Restak, Richard. "The Promise and Peril of Psychosurgery." *Saturday Review World,* September 25, 1973.

Robbins, William. "In New Madrid, Crowds for Quake

That Wasn't." *New York Times*, December 4, 1990.

Rogers, Michael. "The Follies of Science." *Newsweek*, May 8, 1989.

Rosen, George. "From Mesmerism to Hypnotism." *Ciba Symposia*, March-April 1948.

Rosenthal, Robert, and Kermit L. Fode. "Psychology of the Scientist: V. Three Experiments in Experimenter Bias." *Psychological Reports*, April 1963.

Rousseau, D. I., and S. P. S. Porto. "Polywater: Polymer or Artifact?" *Science*, March 27, 1970.

Rupke, Nicolaas A. "*Bathybius Haeckelii* and the Psychology of Scientific Discovery." *Studies in History and Philosophy of Science*, 1976, Vol. 7, no. 1.

Schadewald, Robert. "He Knew Earth Is Round, but His Proof Fell Flat." *Smithsonian*, April 1978.

Schechter, Bruce. "Searching for Gravity Waves with Interferometers." *Physics Today*, February 1986.

Schwartz, John, and Peter Annin. "Quake, Rattle and Roll." *Newsweek*, October 29, 1990.

"Scientists Tell of a 'New' Water." *New York Times*, September 12, 1969.

Shankland, R. S., et al. "New Analysis of the Interferometer Observations of Dayton C. Miller." *Reviews of Modern Physics*, April 1955.

"Sir Isaac Babson." *Newsweek*, August 23, 1948.

Smit, P. "Ernst Haeckel and His 'Generelle Morphologie': An Evaluation." *Janus*, 1968.

"Space Invaders." *Scientific American*, April 1990.

Steinhart, Peter. "Other Voices." *Audubon*, November 1980.

Stolzenburg, William. "When Life Got Hard." *Science News*, August 25, 1990.

Sullivan, Walter:
    "Researchers Cast Doubt on Finding that Water Can Be Converted to a Dense, Vaseline-Like Form." *New York Times*, April 2, 1970.
    "Startling Prospect of a New Form of Water." *New York Times*, June 28, 1970.
    "World Scientists' Parley Mystified by Polywater." *New York Times*, June 24, 1970.

Taylor, Michael E. "Important Fossils." *Science*, Jan-

uary 2, 1987.

Thompson, Dick. "Putting the Heat on Cold Fusion." *Time*, May 15, 1989.

Thomsen, Dietrick E.:
    "Analyzing Anomalous Water." *Science News*, January 3, 1970.
    "Gaining on Gravity Waves." *Science News*, July 11, 1970.

Trimble, Virginia. "Gravity Waves: A Progress Report." *Sky & Telescope*, October 1987.

"The Trouble with Gravity." *Time*, January 2, 1950.

"Unnatural Water." *Time*, December 19, 1969.

"The Uses of Diversity." *Economist*, May 25, 1991.

Valente, Judith. "Hate Winter? Here's a Scientist's Answer: Blow Up the Moon." *Wall Street Journal*, August 22, 1991.

Wallace, William A. "Galileo's Science and the Trial of 1633." *Wilson Quarterly*, Summer 1983.

"The Waves That Beat on Heaven's Shore." *Economist*, November 28, 1987.

Weber, Joseph. "The Detection of Gravitational Waves." *Scientific American*, May 1971.

Westrum, Ron. "Science and Social Intelligence about Anomalies: The Case of Meteorites." *Social Studies of Science*, November 1978.

Wilford, John Noble:
    "Fusion Furor: Science's Human Face." *New York Times*, April 24, 1989.
    "Letters to a Supporter Record Einstein's Search for Proof." *New York Times*, March 24, 1992.

Other Sources

Bell, John. Interview with Robin Tunnicliff. Kingsville, Md.: April 1, 1992.

"Cultural Looting of the 'Ahnenerbe.' " Report prepared by Monuments Fine Arts and Archives Section. Berlin, Germany: OMGUS, March 1, 1948.

"Flat Earth News." Newsletter, Issues 79-81. Lancaster, Calif.: International Flat Earth Research Society.

"The French Institute in the World Today." Exhibition

catalog. Paris: French Academy of Sciences, 1986.

"Genetic Fingerprint Proves Mengele's Death in Brazil." News release. Berlin: UPI, April 8, 1992.

Greene, Mott. Interview with Robin Tunnicliff. Tacoma, Wash.: February 26, 1992.

Habicot, Nicolas. "Gigantologie ou Discours des os d'un Géant." Pamphlet. Paris: J. Houzé, 1613.

Izarn, Joseph. "About the Stones Which Fell from the Sky or Atmospheric Lithology." Pamphlet. Paris: Delalain Fils, 1803.

Johansson, Toge. Interview with Robin Tunnicliff. Berne, N.Y.: December 1991.

Lescarbault, Edmond. Letter to Urbain-Jean-Joseph Le Verrier. Orgeres, France, December 22, 1859. Reports from the Meetings of the French Academy of Sciences, 1860.

McCosker, John. Interview with Robin Tunnicliff. San Francisco, Calif.: March 27, 1992.

Mitchell, Earl. Interview with Robin Tunnicliff. Chapel Hill, N.C.: March 4, 1992.

Rideout, George M., Jr. Brochure and letter to Time-Life Books Inc. Wellesley Hills, Mass.: Gravity Research Foundation, March 27, 1992.

Riolan, Jean. "L'Imposture Découverte des os Humains Supposés et Faussement Attribués au Roi Theutobocheus." Pamphlet. Paris: P. Ramier, 1614.

Robins, C. Richard. Interview with Robin Tunnicliff. Miami, Fla.: March 31, 1992.

Schmidt, Johannes. "The Breeding Places of the Eel." Annual Report. Washington, D.C.: Board of Regents of the Smithsonian Institution, 1925.

Shimanuki, H. Interview with Robin Tunnicliff. Beltsville, Md.: December 1991.

Sues, Hans. Interview with Robin Tunnicliff. Washington, D.C.: February 19, 1992.

"The Value of the Human Being: Medicine in Germany, 1918-1945." Exhibit catalog. Berlin: Ärztekammer Berlin, 1991.

"William Frend." Obituary. Monthly Notices of the Royal Astronomical Society. London, 1843.

INDEX

Numerals in italics indicate an illustration of the subject mentioned.

A

Abian, Alexander, 38

Acquired traits: theory of evolution, 39, 126, 128

Algebra: Frend's theory about, 37-38

Almagest (Ptolemy), 21

American Association for the Advancement of Science, 83, 130

Angel of Death. *See* Mengele, Josef

Animal magnetism, 74, 75

Annals of the Ancient and New Testaments

(Ussher), 8

Anomalous water, *94-95*, 96

Antigravity, 23, 24

Aphids: honeydew produced by, 32

Apollo 10, 20, 116

Apollo 11, 64

Archaeopteryx, 41

Aristotle, 21, 25, *32*, 102, *104*

Armstrong, Neil, 133

Aryan ideal, 116-119, 120-*122*

Atomic theory: Greek view, 50

Atoms: chain reaction, *56*, 57; proof of, 50-*51*, 53; Rutherford's experiment, 56; splitting, *56*, 57, 98

Auschwitz concentration camp, 118-120

Autosuggestion, 83

B

Babson, Roger, *23*-24

Balance theory: and Earth's rotation, 16

Barringer, Daniel, *63*

Becquerel, Antoine Henri, 54

Bedford Canal: flat-Earth test, *131*, 132, *133*

Bees: Aristotle's theories about, 32

Beethoven, Ludwig van, 125

Bell, Alexander Graham, 52

Bellarmine, Robert, 103

Bernal, John Desmond, 95

Bertholon, Pierre, 17

Bible stories, explanation of natural phenomena: age of Earth, 8, 9-10, 28, 102, 103; comets and, 129, *130*, 131; Creation, 8, *9-10*, 77, 104-105; Great

Flood, 9-10, 12, 28
Big bang theory, 66
Binet, Alfred, *83-84*, 124
Biorhythms, *43*
Biot, Jean-Baptiste, *17*, 18
Black holes, 24, 97
Blackwall, John, 30-31
Blondlot, René-Prosper, 84-*85*, 86
Bloodletting, 74
Blount, Lady Elizabeth, 133
Bolívar, Simon, 125
Boltwood, Bernard, 54
Boltzmann, Ludwig, *50-51*
Bondi, Hermann, 66
Bonnet, Charles, *26-27*
Braid, James, 75
Brain size: intelligence and, *83-84*, 106-108
Brownian motion, 51
Browning, Iben, 99-100
Buffon, Count of. *See* Leclerc, Georges-Louis
Bunyan, John, 126
Burgen-Villengen, Robert, *101*, *121*
Burgess Shale, *69*, *87-88*
Burnet, Thomas, 9-10
Burnett, James. *See* Monboddo, Lord
Butler, Charles, 32

C

Carpenter, William B., 77
Catastrophism, 12-13
Cellular cosmogony, 111-113
Chadwick, James, 56
Challis, James, 76
Charpentier, Augustin, 85
Chemistry: early approaches to, 38-39; theory of od, 40
Chladni, Ernst, 17-18
Clarke, Edward H., 108-*109*
Classification of races: intelligence and, 109-111
Close, Frank, 99
Coccoliths, 78-79, *80*
Cold-fusion experiment, *98-99*
Combustion experiments, 38
Comet Ikeya-Seki, *67*
Comets, theories about: cause of catastrophes on Earth, 129-130; creation of Earth, 10-11; Jupiter as origin of, 129, 130; origin of life on Earth, 67, 68; source of viruses and bacteria, 66-68
Concentration-camp studies of heredity, 118-120
Continental drift, *14-15*, 34
Cook, James, 107
Copernican view of world, 70, *104*
Copernicus, Nicolaus, 23, 70, 102, 103, *104*, 112
Cosmic ice theory, 55. *See also* World Ice Doctrine
Cosmology: big bang theory, 66
Cordaro, Lucian, 94
Cox, Catharine Morris, 125-126
Cranial capacity: intelligence and, *83-84*, 106-108

Craniometry, 83, *84*, *121*
Craters: lunar, *65-66*; Meteor crater (Arizona), *35*, *62-63*, 65
Creation stories, 8, *9-10*, 77, 104-105
Crookshank, Francis G., *110*, 111
Cuvier, Georges, *12-13*, 28
Cycles: theory held by Fliess, 42-43

D

Darwin, Charles, 11, 20, 28, 30, 44, *45-46*, 47, 48, 77, 78
Darwin, Erasmus, 45
Darwin, George, *20-21*
Dawes, William R., 76
Dawson, John William, 77
Deryagin, Boris, 94, *95*, 96
Descent of Man, The (Darwin), 28
Deuterium, 98
Dewitz, Hermann, *30*, 31
Dialogue concerning the Two Chief Systems of the World (Galileo), 103, *104*
Dinosaurs, 12, 13, *41*, 42, 44
DNA: discovery of, 128
Doctrine of eternal ice, 115-116
Dolphins, *92-93*
Donahoe, Francis J., 95
Down, John Langdown, 109-*110*, 111
Down syndrome, 109-111
Dürer, Albrecht: woodcut by, *72*

E

Earth: collison with asteroid, 13; flat-Earth experimentation, *131*, *132*, *133*; four-elements theory, *25*, 38, 39; geocentric theories, *21-22*, 70, 102, 103, *104*; Hörbiger's cosmic ice theory, 115-116; Moon's separation from, 20-21; orbit, *22*; rotation, 16, 20, 129-130; Teed's model of, *111-112*, 113
Earth history: age of, various explanations for, 8, 11, 12, 13, 26, 53-54; biblical story of Creation, *9-10*, 10-11, 77, 104-105; catastrophism vs. uniformitarianism, 12-13; continental drift, *14-15*
Earthquake prediction, 99-100
Edison, Thomas, 23, 52
Eels: discovery of larvae, *33-34*
Einstein, Albert, 7, 19, 24, 51, 57, 82, 96, 97, 123, 124
Elements: four-elements theory, *25*, 38, 39
Elliotson, John, 74-75
Emboîtement, 26-27
Embryologists, 26-27
Embryos, 48
Empedocles, *25*
Enlightenment, 17, 18
Epigenesists, 26, 27
"Ether," 54, 81, 82, 83
Eugenics, 113-114, 120-121; Soviet wheat experiment, *126-127*, 128
Evolution: Darwin's theory of, 44, *45-46*, 47, 48, 53-

54, 77, 78; early theories of, 11, *12-13*, 28; Haeckel's theory, *47-48*; inheritance of acquired traits, 39, 126, 128; Lamarck's theory of, 39; Monboddo's theory of, *28-29*, 30; race, intelligence and, 109-111; Walcott on, 88
Experimenter expectation, 93-94
Experiments: chemistry, 38-39; cold-fusion, *98-99*; combustion, 38; flat-Earth, *131*, *132*, *133*; observer bias and, 93-94
Extraterrestrial life: comet as origin of life on Earth, *67*, 68; Herschel's ideas of life on the Moon and Sun, 36-37; Lowell's ideas of life on Mars, *49-50*, 60-61; Pickering's ideas of life on the Moon, 90

F

Fauth, Philipp, *55*, 115
Fedyakin, Nikolai, 94, 95-96
"Feeble-minded," Goddard's study of, 113-*115*
Ferguson, James, 36
Fisher, Osmond, 21
Flamsteed, John, *70*, 71
Flat Earth Society, 131-*132*, 133
Flatworms, experiment with, *93*, 94
Flies: Blackwell's theories of, *7*, *30-31*
Fliess, Wilhelm, *42-43*
Flight: theories of, *52-53*
Fode, Kermit, 93-94
Food and Drug Administration (FDA), 58
Foraminifers, 77, 78, 89
Fossils: *Archaeopteryx*, 41; in Burgess Shale, *69*, *87-88*; Darwin's observations, 44; first evidence of dinosaurs in North America, 41; Kircher's theories about, *31*; nummulites, *89-90*; pre-Cambrian, discovery of, 77, 78
Four-elements theory of the Earth, *25*, 38, 39
Franklin, Benjamin, 74
Freeman, Walter, *59-60*
Frend, William, *37-38*
Freud, Sigmund, *42*, 43, 57
Freundlich, Erwin, 19

G

Gable, Clark, *43*
Galilei, Galileo, *102-104*
Galton, Francis, 124-*125*
Genetics: Marxist doctrine toward, 126-128. *See also* Heredity; Intelligence
Geocentric view of the world, *21-23*, 70, 102, 103, 104
Geology: catastrophism vs. uniformitarianism, 12-13; continental drift, *14-15*; early views of, 41-42; Gosse's view of, 105; 19th-century discovery of fossils, 41-42, 77, 78
George II, 36
George III, 29
Giant: skeleton attributed to, 27-28
Gilbert, Grove, *62-63*
Goddard, Henry H., 113-*114*, 115

Gold, Thomas, 24, 64, 66
Gosse, Edmund, 105-106
Gosse, Philip Henry, 104-*105*, 106
Gould, Stephen Jay, 88
Gravity: Einstein's definition of, 19; warping, 24; waves, 96-97
Gravity Research Foundation, 23-24
Great Chain of Being, 28-30
Great Flood (biblical story of), 9-10, 12, 28
Gunther, Hans F. K., 120-*122*

H

Habicot, Nicolas, *27*-28
Haeckel, Ernst, 46-47, *48*, 78, 80
Hale, George, 96
Hall, Stanley, 109
Hampden, John, 132-133
Hawking, Steven, 24
Heliocentric universe, 21, *22*, 23, 70-71, 102, 103, 104
Heredity: concentration-camp studies, 118-120; DNA and, 128; Goddard's research into intelligence and, 113-*115*; Soviet experiments with winter wheat, *126-127*, 128
Heresy: charge against Galileo, *102-104*
Herschel, John, 75
Herschel, William, *36-37*, 75
Hildebrand, Joel H., 95
Himmler, Heinrich, 117, 118
Hind, John Russell, 75-76
Hitchcock, Edward, *41-42*
Hitler, Adolf, 101, 115, 118, 120, 122, 123, 124
Holmes, Arthur, 15
Honeydew: produced by aphids, 32
Hooke, Robert, 70-71
Hörbiger, Hans, 55, 115-*116*
Howard, Edward, 18
Hoyle, Fred, *66*, 67
Hubble Space Telescope, *90*
Huxley, Thomas, 11, 45, 77, 78, *80*
Hypnotism, 74-75

I

Infrared radiation, 36
Inheritance of acquired traits, 39, 126, 128
Intelligence: brain size and, 83-*84*, 106-108; classification by race, 109-111; of dolphins, *92-93;* Goddard's research into, 113-*115*
Intelligence testing, 84, 124-126
Interferometer, *81*, 82, 83
Ison, James, 94

J

John Paul II, 104
Johnson, Charles, 131, *132*, 133
Johnson, Marjory, 131, 133
Johnson, Samuel, 30
Jupiter, 21, 22, 55, 129, 130

K

Kallikak, Deborah, 113-*114*, 115
Kallikak Family: A Study in the Heredity of Feeble-Mindedness, The (Goddard), 113-*114*, 115
Kaup, Johann, 34
Kelvin, Lord, *53*-54, 82
Kennedy, Roy, 83
Kepler, Johannes, 23
Khrushchev, Nikita, *127*, 128
King, William, 77, 78
Kingsley, Charles, 105
Kircher, Athanasius, 31
Kirkpatrick, Randolph, *89-90*
Koreshans, *112*-113

L

Lamarck, Jean-Baptiste, 38-*39*
Lancet, 74, 75
Lassell, William, 75-76
Lavoisier, Antoine-Laurent, 17, *38-39*
Leclerc, Georges-Louis, 8, 10-*11*
Lejeune, Jerome, 111
Lenard, Philipp, *123*-124
Leonardo da Vinci, 125
Leo XIII, 104
Lescarbault, Edmond, 18
Le Verrier, Urbain-Jean-Joseph, 18-*19*
Lightfoot, John, *8*
Lilly, John C., *92-93*
Lincoln, Abraham, 125
Linnean Society, 31
Lippincott, Ellis, 95
Lobotomy, 59-60
Lowell, Percival, *49-50*, 60, 90, 91
Lunar craters, *65-66*
Lunar evolution, 20-21
Luther, Martin, 23
Lyell, Charles, 12-*13*
Lysenko, Trofin Denisovich, *126*-128

M

Mach, Ernest, 50, *51*
Magnetism: mesmerism and, 74, 75; of the Sun, 96
Malthus, Daniel, 71
Malthus, Thomas Robert, 71-*72*, 73
Manhattan Project, 57
Mariner probes, *19*, 50, *61*
Mars, 21, *22*, 55; comet's effect on, 129, 130; theories of life on, 49-50, 60-61
Marxism: science and, 106, 126-128
Mathematics: in 18th century, 37
Mazuyer, Pierre, 27, 28
Memory: chemical basis of, 73
Mengele, Josef, 118-*119*, 120
Mental retardation: Goddard's research into feeble-mindedness, 113-*115*
Mercury, 18, *19*
Mesmer, Franz Anton, 74
Mesmerism, 74-75
Meteorites: Arizona crater, *35*, *62-63*, 65; lunar craters, *65-66*; theories of origin, *17*-18
Michelson, Albert A., 81, 82, 83
Mill, John Stuart, *125*
Miller, Dayton, *81*, 82-83
Mine fish, *31*
Mineral crystallization, 77-79
Monboddo, Lord, 28-*29*, 30
Monera, 48, 78, 80
Monism, 47-48
Moniz, Antonio de Egas, 59, *60*
Monogenist, 109
Moon: Hörbiger's cosmic ice theory, 55, 115-*116*; landing, *64*, 133; life on, theories of, 36-37, 90; movement of, 22; origin of, *20*-21; theories about, 39, *55*, *64*, *65-66*; weather problems on the Earth and, 38
Morley, Edward W., 81, 82
Morrison, Phillip, 24
Morrow, Ulysses Grant, 112
Morton, Samuel, 106-*107*, 108
Mozart, Wolfgang Amadeus, 126
Mundus Subterraneus (Kircher), *31*

N

Napoleon I, 12
NASA: images from spacecraft, *49*, 50, *61*, *76*, *116*
National Academy of Sciences, 83
National Institute of Sciences and Arts, 18
Natural History (Leclerc), 10
Natural selection, 44, 45, 46, 77, 126
Nature, 80, 86, 95, 96, 99
Nazi Germany, 57, 101, 117-118; doctrine of racial superiority, 115, 116, 117-124
Negative numbers, 37-38
Neptune: discovery of, 18-19, 75; rings, 75-76
Neutron: discovery of, 56
Newcomb, Simon, 52-53
New Madrid, Missouri: prediction of earthquake in, 99-100
Newton, Isaac, 9, 15, 23, 50, 125
Nininger, Harvey, 65-66
Nose: Fliess's theory about the, 43
N-rays, 85-86
Nuclear fission, *56*, 57, 98
Nuclear fusion, 98-99
Numerology, 42, 43
Nummulites, *89-90*

O

Observation: autosuggestion and, 83; observer bias, 93-94; personal bias, 101; in science, 51; scientific method, 93
Observer bias, 93-94
Od: Reichenbach's theory of, 40
Okey sisters, 74, 75
Omphalos: An Attempt to Untie the Geological Knot (Gosse), 104, *105*, 106
Orangutans, 28-30
Orgone Energy, 57-58
Orgone Energy Accumulator, *57*, 58

Origin of Species, The (Darwin), 11, 44, 46, 77
Ostwald, Wilhelm, 50, *51*
Overpopulation: Malthus on, 71-73
Ovists, *26*
Owen, Richard, *44-45*

P
Pangaea, 14-15, 34
Parthenogenesis, 26
Pasteur, Louis, 57
Peacock, George, 38
Penrose, Lionel, 111
Philosopher's stone, 111
Phlogiston, 38
Picard, Jean, 71
Pickering, Edward, 90
Pickering, William, 90-*91*
Planetary movement, *21, 22-23*
Plato, 25
Pluto: discovery of, 90-*91*
Polygeny, 109
Polywater, *94-95,* 96
Pons, Stanley, *98-99*
Principles of Geology (Lyell), 13
Psychosurgery, 59, 60
Ptolemaic universe, *21-23*
Ptolemy, 21, 22, 102, 103, *104*
Pulsars, 64

R
Race: classification by, 109-111
Racial superiority: Nazism and, 115, 116, 117-124
Radiation: x-ray experiments, 84-85
Radioactive decay, 51, 53, *54,* 56
Radioactivity: discovery of, *54*
Rats: experiment to test observer bias, 93-*94*
Rectilineator, *112*
Reich, Wilhelm, *57-58*
Reichenbach, Karl von, *40*
Relativity: Einstein's theory of, 24, 82, 96, 123
Rembrandt van Rijn, 126
Retrograde motion, 21, 22, 23
Riddle of the Universe, The (Haeckel), 48
Riolan, Jean, 28
Röntgen, Wilhelm, 84
Rosenthal, Robert, 93-94
Rowbotham, Samuel Birley, 131, 132
Rowney, Thomas H., 77, 78

Royal Academy of Sciences, 17, 18
Rutherford, Ernest, 51, 53, *54, 56*

S
Sacred Theory of the Earth, The (Burnet), 9, 10
Sargasso Sea, 34
Saturn, 75, 90
Schäfer, Ernst, *117,* 118
Schiaparelli, Giovanni, 49, 50
Schmidt, Johannes, *33,* 34
Scientific method, 93
Seafloor spreading, *15*
Sex in Education (Clarke), 108, 109
Shakespeare, William, 126
Shklovskii, Josif Shmuelovich, 60-*61*
Skulls: Morton's collection of, *106*-107. *See also* Brain size; Intelligence
Soddy, Frederick, 53, 54, 56
Solar System: geocentric view, *21*-23, 70, 102, 103, 104; heliocentric view, 21, *22,* 23, 70-71, 102, 103, 104
Soviet science, 106; winter wheat experiment, *126-127,* 128
Species, changes in. *See* Evolution
Stalin, 106, 126, 128
Stanford-Binet test, 124
Stellar parallax, 70-71
Stern, L. William, 84, 124
Sun: *36;* at center of Solar System (heliocentric view), 21, *22,* 23, 70-71, 102, 103, 104; Herschel's theory of life on, 37; magnetic field, 96; warping effect of, 19
Sunspots, 37, 68, 96
Supernovas, 64, *97*
Szilard, Leo, *56-57*

T
Teed, Cyrus R., *111-113*
Telescope: first used by Galileo, 102
Terman, Lewis, 124-*125,* 126
Theory of general relativity, 24, 96, 123
Theory of special relativity, 82
Theutobocheus, 27-28
Thomson, William. *See* Kelvin, Lord
Tombaugh, Clyde, 90
Trepanning, 59
Trilobites, 77, *87, 88*
Twins: Mengele's concentration-camp studies of, 119-120

U
Ungar, Georges, 73
Uniformitarianism, 12, 13
Universe as machine theory, 17
Uranus, *36,* 90, 91; moons, 75
Urban VIII (pope), 103
Ussher, James, *8*
Utopianism, 71

V
Velikovsky, Immanuel, 129-*130*
Venus, 49, 129, 130
Vernalization, 127
Volf, Christian Adolf, *16*
Vulcan, 18-19

W
Wakley, Thomas, 74-75
Walcott, Charles Doolittle, 78, 87, *88*
Wallace, Alfred Russel, 45-46, 132, 133
Wallich, George Charles, 78
Walpole, Horace, 30
Warping: of space, 19, 24
Washington, George, 125
Weather: Moon and, 38, 39; orgone and, 58
Weber, Joseph, 96-97
Wegener, Alfred, *14-15*
Whales: sonic communication of, 92
Whiston, William, 129
Whittington, Harry B., 87-88
Wickramasinghe, Chandra, 66, 67
Winter wheat: Soviet experiments with, *126-127,* 128
Women: myths of frailty and, 108-109
Wood, Robert, *85,* 86
World Ice Doctrine, 115-116. *See also* Cosmic ice theory
Worlds in Collision (Velikovsky), 129, *130*
World War II, 57, 116, 117, 118, 120, 122, 124. *See also* Nazi Germany
Wright, Orville, *52*
Wright brothers, 52-53

X
X-rays, 84-85

Y
Young, Thomas, 37

Time-Life Books is a division of Time Life Inc.,
a wholly owned subsidiary of
THE TIME INC. BOOK COMPANY

TIME-LIFE BOOKS

PRESIDENT: Mary N. Davis

MANAGING EDITOR: Thomas H. Flaherty
Director of Editorial Resources: Elise D. Ritter-Clough
Executive Art Director: Ellen Robling
Director of Photography and Research:
John Conrad Weiser
Editorial Board: Dale M. Brown, Janet Cave, Roberta
Conlan, Laura Foreman, Jim Hicks, Blaine Marshall,
Rita Thievon Mullin, Henry Woodhead
*Assistant Director of Editorial Resources/Training
Manager:* Norma E. Shaw

PUBLISHER: Robert H. Smith

Associate Publisher: Sandra Lafe Smith
Editorial Director: Russell B. Adams, Jr.
Marketing Director: Anne C. Everhart
Director of Production Services: Robert N. Carr
Production Manager: Prudence G. Harris
Supervisor of Quality Control: James King

Editorial Operations
Production: Celia Beattie
Library: Louise D. Forstall
Computer Composition: Deborah G. Tait (Manager),
Monika D. Thayer, Janet Barnes Syring, Lillian Daniels
Interactive Media Specialist: Patti H. Cass

**Library of Congress
Cataloging-in-Publication Data**
Science astray / by the editors of Time-Life Books.
p.   cm.   (Library of curious and unusual facts).
Includes bibliographical references.
ISBN 0-8094-7691-6
ISBN 0-8094-7692-4 (lib. bdg.)
1. Science—Miscellanea. 2. Science—Philosophy-
Miscellanea. 3. Truth—Miscellanea.
I. Time-Life Books. II. Series.
Q173.S399 1992
500—dc20   92-19180 CIP

LIBRARY OF CURIOUS AND UNUSUAL FACTS

SERIES EDITOR: Carl A. Posey
Series Administrator: Roxie France-Nuriddin
Art Director: Cynthia Richardson
Picture Editor: Sally Collins

Editorial Staff for *Science Astray*
Text Editors: Sarah Brash (principal), John Sullivan
Senior Writer: Stephanie A. Lewis
Assistant Editors/Research: Michael E. Howard,
Jennifer A. Mendelsohn, Terrell Smith
Assistant Art Director: Alan Pitts
Senior Copy Coordinator: Jarelle S. Stein
Copy Coordinator: Juli Duncan
Picture Coordinator: Jennifer Iker
Editorial Assistant: Terry Ann Paredes

Special Contributors: George Constable, Eliot Marshall, Peter Pocock, Anthony K. Pordes (text); Vilasini
Balkrishnan, Ellen C. Gross, Catherine B. Hackett,
Robin S. H. Tunnicliff (research); Louise Wile Hedberg
(index)

Correspondents: Elisabeth Kraemer-Singh (Bonn),
Christine Hinze (London), Christina Lieberman (New
York), Maria Vincenza Aloisi (Paris), Ann Natanson
(Rome). Valuable assistance was also provided by An-
gelika Lemmer (Bonn); Barbara Gevene Hertz (Copen-
hagen); Christine Alcock, (London); Trini Bandrés
(Madrid); Wibo Van de Linde (Netherlands); Elizabeth
Brown, Katheryn White (New York); Leonora Dods-
worth (Rome); Dick Berry, Mieko Ikeda (Tokyo).

The Consultants:
Stanley Goldberg is an independent scholar who has
taught at Antioch College, the University of Zambia,
and Hampshire College. He specializes in the history
of science and is currently working on a biography of
Leslie R. Groves and the Manhattan Project.

William R. Corliss is a physicist-turned-writer who
has spent the last 25 years compiling collections of
anomalies in the fields of geophysics, geology, ar-
chaeology, astronomy, biology, and psychology. He
has written about science and technology for NASA,
the National Science Foundation, and the Energy Research and Development Administration (among others). Mr. Corliss is also the author of more than 30
books on scientific mysteries, including *Mysterious
Universe, The Unfathomed Mind,* and *Handbook of
Unusual Natural Phenomena.*

Other Publications:

LOST CIVILIZATIONS
ECHOES OF GLORY
THE NEW FACE OF WAR
HOW THINGS WORK
WINGS OF WAR
CREATIVE EVERYDAY COOKING
COLLECTOR'S LIBRARY OF THE UNKNOWN
CLASSICS OF WORLD WAR II
AMERICAN COUNTRY
VOYAGE THROUGH THE UNIVERSE
THE THIRD REICH
THE TIME-LIFE GARDENER'S GUIDE
MYSTERIES OF THE UNKNOWN
TIME FRAME
FIX IT YOURSELF
FITNESS, HEALTH & NUTRITION
SUCCESSFUL PARENTING
HEALTHY HOME COOKING
UNDERSTANDING COMPUTERS
LIBRARY OF NATIONS
THE ENCHANTED WORLD
THE KODAK LIBRARY OF CREATIVE PHOTOGRAPHY
GREAT MEALS IN MINUTES
THE CIVIL WAR
PLANET EARTH
COLLECTOR'S LIBRARY OF THE CIVIL WAR
THE EPIC OF FLIGHT
THE GOOD COOK
WORLD WAR II
HOME REPAIR AND IMPROVEMENT
THE OLD WEST

*For information on and a full description of any of
the Time-Life Books series listed above, please call
1-800-621-7026 or write:*
Reader Information
Time-Life Customer Service
P.O. Box C-32068
Richmond, Virginia 23261-2068

This volume is one in a series that explores astound-
ing but surprisingly true events in history, science,
nature, and human conduct. Other books in the series include:

*Feats and Wisdom of the Ancients
Mysteries of the Human Body
Forces of Nature
Vanishings
Amazing Animals
Inventive Genius
Lost Treasure
The Mystifying Mind
A World of Luck
Hoaxes and Deceptions
Crimes and Punishments
Odd and Eccentric People
Shadows of Death
Manias and Delusions
Above and Beyond*